The USCCA Edition Of Steve Tarani's PreFense®

THE CRUCIAL ADVANTAGE

Your Step-By-Step Roadmap To Preventing Violent Attacks Before They Happen

by Steve Tarani

Send all inquiries to:
PreFense®
6929 North Hayden Rd, Suite C4-308
Scottsdale, AZ 85250

Printed in the United States of America.

Third Edition, 2016

ISBN-13: 978-0-9967874-3-7

Delta Defense, LLC
300 S. 6th Avenue
West Bend, WI 53095
www.DeltaDefense.com

Visit the author's website at:
www.PreventativeDefense.com

Disclaimer
The author and the publisher of this book are not responsible in any manner whatsoever for any injury that may result from practicing the techniques and/or following the instructions given herein. Since the physical activities described herein may be strenuous in nature for readers to engage in safely, it is essential that a physician be consulted prior to commencing any physical training.

10 9 8 7 6 5 4 3 2 1

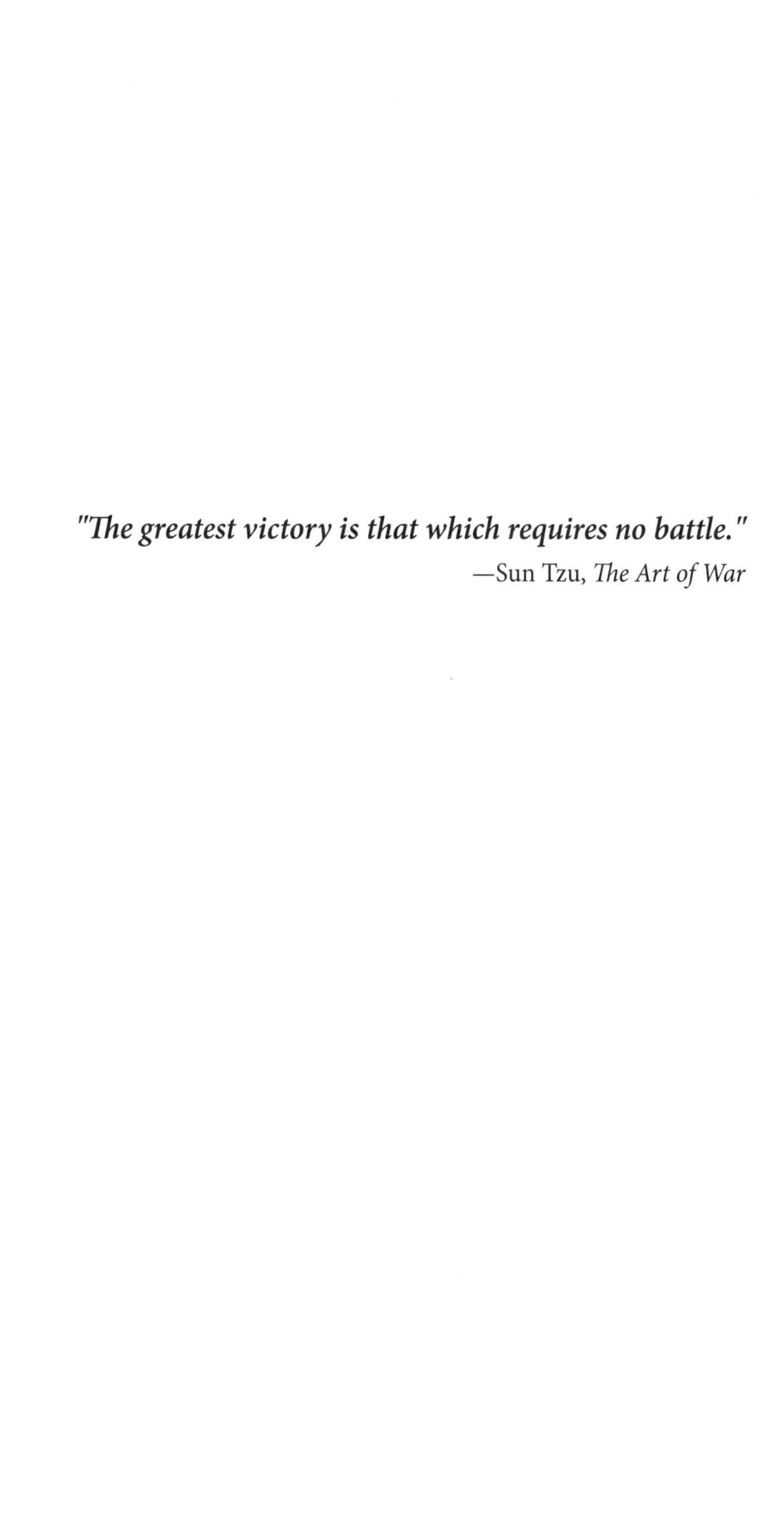

"The greatest victory is that which requires no battle."

—Sun Tzu, *The Art of War*

TABLE OF CONTENTS

Part III : PreFense Applied

ACKNOWLEDGEMENTS

To those stellar individuals who have selflessly contributed their time and support to the completion of this herculean effort, please accept this—my public acknowledgement and deepest gratitude for your generosity.

Truth be known, there is no way this manuscript would have been completed without your greatly appreciated contributions (listed in alphabetical order):

Leslie C. Andes, Mark Babyak, Diane Barton, Denise Bixler, Wayne Black, Jeff Brown, Dr. Steven P. Bucci, Amy M. Buck, Sheriff Ken P. Campbell, Julie Candice, Guy Corsey, Kavita Salvado daRocha, Doug Esposito, Paul Grybow, Rick Guilbault, Bill Hall, George Harris, Linda Harris, Patrick Henry, David Hines, Louise Horvits, Mike Hughes, Troy Lapatina, Thomas LaRochelle, Mark Lyons, Elizabeth Mansfield, Don Mihalek, Missy O'Linn, Shelly Ray, Tom Rovetuso, Pete Sandhu, Barry Shreiar, Jay Tuttle, Mike Vaiani, and Bill Wemtz.

To those of you still on the job[1] whose names cannot be listed here; yes, "no names" of course, but you know who you are and I only hope that one day I can return the solid.

Thank you my brothers and sisters for finding the time to work with me on this and in sharing your personal experiences so that others may benefit from your hard earned lessons from the field.

Thank you again for your encouragement and support to include your much appreciated "filter free" reviews, edits, critiques, opinions and recommendations—all of which were indispensable in helping me stay between the white and yellow lines of this very long and winding road.

In sincere and humble gratitude,

Steve Tarani
Author

---

1 At the time of writing, those individuals whose names must remain confidential as they are on active duty giving their all to keep us safe in our beds at night.

FOREWORD

There's a phrase we use often here at the United States Concealed Carry Association (USCCA), the company I founded more than a decade ago to provide education, training, and legal and financial protection to responsible American gun owners, that I've grown quite fond of over the years:

The best fight is the one you're not in.

To be honest, this is something Kevin Michalowski, executive editor of *Concealed Carry Magazine,* the USCCA's self-defense publication, regularly advocates in his "Editor's Shot" column and his *Into The Fray* weekly video series. So, as much as I'd like to, I can't take much credit for the incredibly solid advice.

The truth is, no one wants to be caught up in a dangerous encounter. I can't think of a single person who, given the choice, would get involved in a potentially deadly situation if he or she could somehow avoid it in the first place.

This notion of conflict avoidance is, then, a matter of life and death. After all, you can't "lose" a fight (in other words, end up injured or worse) if you're not in one.

But in order to avoid a fight, we must first acknowledge the possibility that such an attack, perhaps even an incredibly violent one, could occur—even to good people like you and me.

Listen, we both know that evil exists all around us. It's everywhere, and it does not discriminate. We know that the world can be a dangerous and unpredictable place. We know that bad things can and do happen. But the absolute biggest mistake we can make is thinking that the things we read about in the paper or the things we see on the news are outside the realm of our own world.

In fact, I've often said that the six most dangerous words on the planet are:

It will never happen to me.

Of course, we hope that bad things won't happen to us, but as my good friend Lt. Col. Dave Grossman, author of *On Killing* and *On Combat,* says, "Hope is not a strategy."

Now, I'll be the first to admit that it's often easier to give in to that false sense of security that sometimes beckons us. I've had my moments. You probably have too. But as responsible Americans, *that* is exactly when we must pay closer attention to our senses and to what is going on around us. We must train ourselves to adopt the combat mindset, to ignore the little voice in our head that tells us it's OK to let down our guard. And that means knowing, as Lt. Col. Grossman also says, "There is no safety in denial."

It also means having a plan. It means that we don't have to wait for a wake-up call—or worse—to shake us out of our comfort zones. It means preparing for the possibility—not the probability. It means adopting a mantra of readiness and survival.

No, *hope* is not a strategy...but a *plan* is.

And this is exactly where the idea of preventative defense—or "Pre-Fense®," as Steve Tarani has coined it—comes in.

The idea is revolutionary in that it just might save your life.

Throughout this book, Steve provides in-depth explanations and analysis of concepts like situational awareness, the protective mindset, and the OODA Loop, all of which come together in a step-by-step roadmap for how to identify potential threats and, in turn, use that knowledge to defeat an attack before it ever begins. There's no other way to look at it: This is *lifesaving* stuff.

The truth is that good or bad, purposefully or by mistake, the things that other people do affect us. Call them what you will—chances, circumstances, or coincidences—these things are often completely out of our control. And that can be a pretty scary feeling.

The only thing we can do is choose what *we* will do. How *we* will act. How *we* will be prepared for whatever comes our way.

We cannot control other people or their actions. What we do have control over is our own level of awareness and preparedness.

Remember: *Action beats reaction.*

Pay attention to your surroundings at all times. Trust your gut. Respond to that voice in your head or that feeling in the pit of your stomach. Take action on the information that you have available to you.

If you're walking through a dark parking structure to get to your car and you see something or someone that sets off the alarm bells in your head, use your flashlight to catch the other individual(s) off guard. Or, if the option is available to you, simply turn around and go back to a well-lit area until you can be certain there is no longer a potential threat.

If you're wrong, and you shine a flashlight in someone's face, you might get a dirty look. (You can always smile and apologize.) If you're wrong, and you head back to a place of safety, you might add a little extra time onto your evening commute. But if you're *right,* you might have just avoided a dangerous situation altogether. And if you do end up in a situation you can't avoid, well, you're already ahead of the game and can move quickly into action.

And again: *Action beats reaction.*

It's important to note that preventative defense training is not about paranoia. It's about preparation.

Follow the advice in this book by honing your conflict avoidance and situational awareness skills and you'll have a much better chance of keeping bad things from happening to you at all. And, as responsible, law-abiding citizens and just all around good people, isn't that what we hope for in the first place?

I know, I know:

Hope is not a strategy. But that's why this book is so important. It helps you bypass hope to create a real, executable plan. It gives you the upper hand over people who seek to do you or your family wrong.

Remember: *The best fight is the one you're not in.*

That's why I'm so honored to present to you *The Crucial Advantage: Your Step-By-Step Roadmap To Preventing Violent Attacks Before They Happen.*

Tim Schmidt
President and Founder
USCCA

PROLOGUE

Preventative Defense

"More powerful than any weapon—is an idea."
Anonymous

At the risk of dating myself, I remember a time when we somehow survived without the use of cell phones. In today's world of instant communications and handheld GPS, we tend to forget that people had to look at a map and make plans to go somewhere in the past. While driving, we couldn't text, email, or call the police. One particular incident in September of '89 exemplified this and ironically wound up being profoundly inspirational for me.

Stuck in peak rush hour traffic in Los Angeles, California in heavy rain on a dark night I was in a hurry and of course running late. Not one driver noticed or cared about the middle-aged woman standing alone in the rain visibly terrified and bawling her eyes out in the dark. Appearing equally as unconcerned about getting run over, I am now confident that she was inching away from her disabled car moving closer to the oncoming traffic to try and get someone's attention.

Windshield wipers on full blast, I had to swerve to avoid hitting her as she was well across the white line. Quickly pulling onto the shoulder I slammed it in park and shouted, "Excuse me Ma'am!" Approaching her on foot I found her petrified, drenched to the bone, and shaking from both cold and fear. To top it off, she didn't speak a word of English. Speaking calmly I threw my jacket around her in assurance that I was there to help and that guiding her back and away from six lanes of oncoming traffic was a very good thing.

Attempting to fix her car, I found there was not enough gas in the tank to get it started, but in the process I also noticed two empty baby seats in the back, a wedding ring on her finger and the name and address on her registration. Even with the language barrier, my using her name and pointing to her street address was enough for her to realize that I was her best option out of this predicament and she accepted a ride home.

Watching her reunite with her family that night in the downpour, having helped them avoid what might have otherwise been an unrecoverable catastrophe, it hit me that she was literally *helpless.* It got me thinking: What could she have done to *not* put herself in that situation in the first place?

Always passionate about teaching, I began working as a martial arts and defensive tactics instructor. As such, I was privy to hundreds of stories from many students about how they were mugged, raped, or otherwise assaulted by common street thugs. Teaching them what to do to *stop* the attack, I thought, "What could all of these folks have done to *not* find themselves in that situation at all?"

Later on in life, working as a part-time deputy for a rural county in northern Nevada, I was out on a call where an out-of-state felon had broken into a family's home and was holding the homeowner and his family hostage. We solved the problem, but the family was very shaken. As we started to look into what happened, we saw that they had made a number of mistakes. Why did they leave all those tools out in the backyard to assist an invader in breaking into their home? Shocked at the lack of what I considered just plain common sense, I wondered why they made it so very easy for someone to break in. This and many incidents like it drew me to the stark realization of how very little most people know about keeping themselves out of harm's way.

Many security professionals take pride in their ability to keep others safe, but for me it became a goal to teach others to keep *themselves* safe. Better to teach someone how to fish than just give them a fish, right? Maybe it was the intensity of the impact on that family and others, but something inside caused me to make a silent vow to empower others to defend themselves.

Working as a federal contractor greatly expanded my observation of this "lack of protective awareness" phenomenon, which is in fact a global trend. This was further amplified after I was recruited as a full-time employee for the CIA.

While working in certain high-threat areas I observed even "the professionals" making preventable mistakes that made me raise an eyebrow. We were asked to oversee a group of people who were clearly instructed "Do not draw attention to yourselves."

Aside from the fact that it was like herding cats, I noticed one of them wearing a New York Yankees ball cap and another one wearing an "America—love it or leave it" t-shirt. None of this would have been an issue if we were in Manhattan, but when you're moving through a high-threat anti-American region in a predominantly Muslim country it makes you a screaming target. Yet again, I thought, "What in the hell were these people thinking? Don't they know where they are? Didn't they cover all this in their environmental awareness training and pre-deployment briefings? How did these professionals get it so wrong?"

Over time and with more experience, I observed a plethora of incidents which painfully yet clearly demonstrated this "lack of protective awareness" phenomenon time and time again. Witnessing nearly a lifetime of these incidents brought me to an epiphany—a shift in perspective regarding the field of protection and personal security. Instead of spending so much time and effort planning a response to an incident, why not expend the same preparatory resources to *avoid* those situations in the first place? Wouldn't that be exponentially more effective? It really got me thinking and spurred me to take action.

To test my new theory, I volunteered my services in building programs to assist with what I called *"proactive protection"* of people in high-threat areas. I was fortunate to run this experiment in some pretty tough locations, and observing its beneficial results, I began to document the key elements of the processes and core protective concepts that really worked, as well as *why* they worked.

As I began talking with friends and acquaintances in the private sector, many of whom were working for organizations overseas, they were not only *immediately* interested, but also sincerely supportive of my work. They asked me about the successes and technical details of this new approach, which I was more than happy to share. As a result, I was invited to assist them with similar proactive protective efforts.

It was while I was working on one of these assignments that it hit me like a brick, "Wait a minute, what about everybody else living back home in the States?" My thoughts drifted back to that helpless lady in the rainstorm, and to that Nevada family who were held hostage in their own home and to my many students who had been victims of perpetual street violence. I recalled those working professionals who were still making correctable mistakes in the field, and all my family and friends, and their wives, husbands, and kids. In fact, I couldn't think of one, single person who would not benefit tremendously from such a unique and holistic approach to personal security.

Then, on April 16, 2007, tragedy struck at Virginia Tech when a gunman claimed the lives of 32 people and wounded 17 before taking his own life[1]. Having access to detailed information about the incident, I learned there were ample opportunities during which that attack could have been stopped. It was clear that nobody knew how.

Less than two years later on January 21, 2009, another attack *at the very same school* claimed the life of a young female student who was decapitated by another student wielding an edged weapon[2]. Yet again, it was an incident that could have been either avoided or greatly diminished with minimal training. It became very clear to me that somebody had to do something about this preventable violence, and that somebody was me.

All my buddies at the CIA thought I'd officially lost my marbles when I elected to follow my passion to protect others. They asked, "You're going to give up a guaranteed paycheck every two weeks and a federal pension to pursue some crazy idea about hardening untrained civilians?"

My response was "Hell yeah! Sure, not everybody cares or even thinks about their personal security, but what about those who *do?* Where can *they* go? What can *they* do to make themselves less vulnerable and less exposed to the very real threats that *we know* are out there?"

You can quit your job but you can't quit your passion, so I went full circle and began teaching personal security classes again, this time not only to military, law enforcement, and government agents—but to colleges, businesses, moms and dads, and hardworking career professionals battling rush-hour traffic to provide for their family—people like you who would take the time and effort to read this book!

My life's work, now with cell phone in hand, is geared specifically to those concerned about their protection and who want to know what they can do about it.

As a result of my epiphany, and with the intention of disseminating this unique approach to personal security utilized by SOCOM[3], I sifted through endless pages of personal notes gathered over decades of training

1. *http://www.nytimes.com.com/2007/04/16/us/16cnd-shooting.html?pagewanted=all&_r=0*

2. *http://www.huffingtonpost.com/2010/04/19/former-virginia-tech-grad_n_543350.html*

3 *Special Operations Command (SOCOM) is the unified combatant command charged with overseeing the various special operations component commands of the Army, Air Force, Navy and Marine Corps.*

and experience. It took nearly four years to collate and another three years to develop it into a streamlined threat-based learning system which I call "preventative defense" or *PreFense®*.

> *Akin to preventive medicine—a holistic approach to healthcare in preventing disease. Preventative defense or PreFense® is a holistic approach to personal security.*

Taking my new learning system and producing a writer's proof I sent it to more than a dozen of my closest associates—other professionals in the protection industry who, at the time, were working for various federal agencies—and were merciless with their red ink! Continually improving the information in this book, I will be forever grateful for their painstaking efforts. Upon review of my initial 400-page blueprint, they all agreed that this learning system is rock solid—in fact they said it was the very best they'd ever seen in the industry, but that by far my biggest hurdle would be "How are you going to reach your intended audience—readers who are not federal agents, who have no prior training or experience and who don't speak "governmentese"—remember you're not teaching military or cops here!"

It is my sincere hope that this *does* make sense and that you *would* be willing to leverage my hard work by adopting what you learn here so that neither you nor anyone close to you will ever be left facing a real world threat alone, unaware or exposed.

INTRODUCTION

The Third Option

"Panic causes tunnel vision. Calm acceptance of danger allows us to more easily assess the situation and see the options."
Simon Sinek[1]

Imagine finding yourself pinned up against a wall with a gun in your face or a knife at your throat—what would you do? Most people believe that they would simply dial 911 and wait for the cavalry to arrive. Others may decide that it's best to try and solve the problem themselves with a gun or a karate chop.

Allow me to introduce you to a *third* option—one that up until now has been available only to the privileged few—the option of handling a threat *before* it ever develops to a point where you would need to consider either of the first two options. Instead of waiting for a potential threat to develop into a physical one, why not take full advantage of limitless opportunities available to you in resolving an incident before it escalates?

Let's face it; you don't expect your home to be invaded when you're relaxing in front of your TV. You don't expect your kids to be bullied, abducted, or kidnapped when you send them off to school. You don't expect to be carjacked or physically assaulted when walking through a parking garage. You don't expect to be shot at while running errands, at work, at school, or even sitting in a movie theater. However, every day you carry out these normal activities and every day things work out just fine. As a result we are conditioned by our experiences to believe life will continue to work out just the way it always has and every day that things work out fine we reinforce our belief that this trend will continue—until the day you become one of the 32.4% of the population who will be a victim of a violent crime in their lifetime.

1 Simon O. Sinek (b. 1973) Author, motivational speaker, and military advisor on innovation and planning.

When things don't work out the way we expect, we must be prepared to handle increasingly complex threats such as active shootings, home invasions, physical assaults and the like. Protection against these threats is critical and the reality is that professional security forces (police, etc.) can do very little to stop it.

Undesired incidents are caused by unmanaged threats and it is entirely possible to handle such threats without waiting until the very last minute and then only to choose between two very limiting options. Unfortunately, as none of this is covered in our grade schools, many people consider the subject overwhelming and are consequently blindsided by its unmitigated impact.

Although it's impossible to predict exactly when or where an event may occur it is not only possible but critical to recognize and understand *how* an event will actually occur. It is this recognition and understanding that gives you the *decisive advantage* in avoiding or stopping a threat—which is the purpose of this book.

Taking Control

You control your environment or your environment controls you—it's that simple. Using *PreFense*® to identify potential threats, you can see why and how they can become actual threats and as a result be able to avoid, mitigate or successfully defeat them.

There are no rules in the threat management and protection game, and you are certainly under no obligation to follow even the guidelines presented here. However, everything in life comes with a price tag and the price for relinquishing control of your environment by disregarding your personal security can be quite costly.

Even if you were unable to initially manage a threat, by understanding how an attack works and by learning how you can directly influence attack-related behaviors you can protect yourself, your family and your assets from damage, violence, disruption or loss—and all without a karate chop or a gun.

> *By exerting control over your environment, it's possible to manage and protect against nearly all threats.*

Best Kept Secrets

The best kept secret of the professionals is to develop a consistent habit of "assessment and response" thought and action, which enables them to make sound threat management decisions.

A practical example of this is when you pull into the parking lot of a 24-hour convenience store in a sketchy neighborhood. You take a few seconds to roll up all the windows, turn off the engine, get out of the car, close and lock your car doors prior to walking into the store (good habit), as opposed to leaving your car unattended with the doors wide open, keys in the ignition, with the engine running (bad habit).

Such consistency of thought and action affords you the opportunity to adopt good habits leading to a beneficial change in lifestyle, which significantly decreases the chances of you becoming a victim.

As you might imagine, protection professionals have developed a treasure trove of information, learned by trial and error. Like most cavemen, we took those golden nuggets and hid them deep in the professional protection world—until now. Reading further will enable you to:

- Lower your personal threat profile...
- Identify and disrupt pre-attack behaviors before they convert to an attack...
- Avoid, mitigate and defend against a real world threat...
- Use your environment as an extension of your awareness...
- Leverage the one denominator common to all human predators against them...

The Why, The How, And The What

Thirty years of teaching and speaking professionally has taught me that real learning happens only when the instructor provides *why* something works, *how* it works, and *what* it is exactly. Much like an epoxy, the "why," the "how," and the "what" must be clearly presented, if not then nothing will stick.

Since it's my intention that you truly retain this valuable information and be able to use it one second after you learn it, each chapter is carefully crafted to include the "why," the "how," and the "what." To facilitate this methodology, all topics are presented in a similar format allowing you clear and easy information access:

Objectives: In This Chapter You Will Be Introduced To...

Why are you reading this? The learning objectives are clearly stated at the beginning of each chapter outlining why and what you're about to be presented.

CliffsNotes®: At A Glance

For those with little time or inclination to drill down deep into comprehensive detail, this section is designed to give you the critical elements of protection right up front.

Practical Application: *How* Do I Use This In Real Life?

This section shows you how to apply what you just learned into your busy day.

Secrets Of The Professionals: *What* The Pros Know

This section delivers the goods for those seeking to delve deeper into the clockwork and learn what seasoned protection professionals know.

This book is further divided into three parts:

> **Part I—Threat Management**—Introduces *The 90% Advantage*—a powerful threat management tool providing you the knowledge of how potential threats progress into physical threats and the principles used to avoid or prevent it from happening.
>
> **Part II—Protection**—Introduces the fundamentals of protection—the very core of *PreFense®* providing you the tools needed to raise your awareness in identifying potential threats, knowing what a predator looks for and how to stop them dead in their tracks by denying them opportunity and making them look elsewhere for victims.
>
> **Part III—Application**—Introduces *PreFense®* as applied to a wide gamut of practical scenarios ranging from handling an active shooter incident, to protecting your home, to managing your personal security when using

ground transportation, to ensuring your protection when staying at a hotel, living in a dorm, or travelling abroad.

Drawing an analogy between this book and a driving manual, Part I introduces the practical theory of driving a car and the rules of the road. Part II introduces you to the vehicle itself—what and where are the steering wheel, brakes, gas pedal and how they all work together. In Part III you then take it out for a spin, first in the parking lot, then along city streets and finally on the highway at higher speeds.

Thank you for your willingness to make a difference in your personal security and that of your family. I sincerely look forward to your gaining the decisive advantage over any potential attacker. Further, I look toward the beneficial impact on our global society when the understanding of these principles becomes so commonplace that it forces predators to look elsewhere.

Welcome to *The Crucial Advantage—Your Step-By-Step Roadmap To Preventing Violent Attacks Before They Happen!*

PART I
Threat Management

CHAPTER 1

Cycles Of Nature

"By three methods we may learn wisdom: First, by reflection, which is noblest; second by imitation, which is easiest; and third by experience, which is the bitterest..."
Confucius[1]

On Friday, June 7, 2013, a bright and sunny Southern California afternoon, I received an unexpected phone call from a buddy while I was working on this book. He informed me that an active shooter was, at that very moment, blasting his way into Santa Monica College while school was in session. Recalling that the daughter of another close friend of mine was attending the same school, I tried calling her but got no response.

Danielle had not answered the phone because she was in lockdown at the college, along with her classmates, and a gunman, the same gunman who was responsible for the deaths of five people, was just outside her classroom door[2].

Switching over to text, I asked her if she was OK. She replied that she was on lockdown at the school and that "they tried to shoot someone in my class. He ran inside, and we locked the doors." Another classmate of hers was on a bus that was also shot up by the same gunman.

"There are police with rifles outside my classroom," she texted. Even though she's a tough kid, she was scared. Keeping her mind occupied while she was hunkered down in a closet with her classmates and their biology teacher, I continued to provide her with situational updates.

Using concepts and measures you will find in the following chapters, the kids remained safely out of the line of fire until their ordeal finally

---

1 *Chinese philosopher and teacher 551-479 BCE*

2 *"Santa Monica College Shooting Leaves Five Dead Including Suspect, Several Others Wounded", 06/07/2013, Anna Almendrala & Kathleen Miles, The Huffington Post. http://www.huffingtonpost.com/2013/-6/07/santa-monica-college-shooting_n_3404689.html*

came to an end. Instructed to walk to a holding area, Danielle was then interviewed by authorities. After, she hopped on her skateboard, wove through a web of emergency-response vehicles, skirted around a puddle of dried blood, and arrived safely home.

What happened to Danielle and her classmates at school on that pleasant spring day in a quiet beach community could have been a scene out of a movie or a novel, but it wasn't. It happened in a real neighborhood with real students, a real gunman, and real people who were shot and killed with real bullets. The sobering reality of this and numerous incidents like it is that bad things can and do happen to good people.

In This Chapter You Will Be Introduced To...

...real-world examples of the bad things that happen to good people and why this is so important to understand. Conversely, you will also be introduced to one of the most equally important cycles of nature—one that is at the root cause of bad things that happen and the *very* same one that is used to prevent them from happening.

At A Glance

We watch the news and observe shootings, home invasions, physical assaults and the like. It's difficult to believe that some folks don't understand, don't care, or simply live in denial. Nonetheless, it's a fact of life that these incidents do occur.

Anytime you or your family are at home, on foot, in a car, on a train, at work, at school, at a hotel or travelling, you are exposed to any number of real-world threats. This doesn't mean that you should be walking around in a suit of armor or lock yourself in a closet—in fact, quite the opposite. Appropriately managing any threat requires the awareness to address it *without* paranoia. Part of that awareness is knowing that when it comes to preventing bad things from happening there is no "right" or "wrong," but rather what works and what doesn't. The only thing that works 100% of the time all the time are the cycles of nature.

All of nature is subject to natural cycles—such as the day/night cycle and the annual cycle of the four seasons. Human interactions are also subject to cycles. One such cycle is called the "OODA Loop," which is the key to rapid adaptation during conflict, and is therefore an essential tool to be used in defeating any adversarial attack-related behavior.

How Do I Use This In Real Life?

Colonel John Boyd was an exceptional Air Force pilot who studied and wrote extensively about the decision making cycle. Colonel Boyd proposed that every human being, knowingly or unknowing uses this cycle in the process of making a decision. It has become known in professional circles as the OODA Loop.

1. Observation—*Notice something relevant may be happening*
2. Orientation—*Choose to pay attention to it/recognize it is important*
3. Decision—*Determine a course of action based on your available options*
4. Action—*Act on your decision*

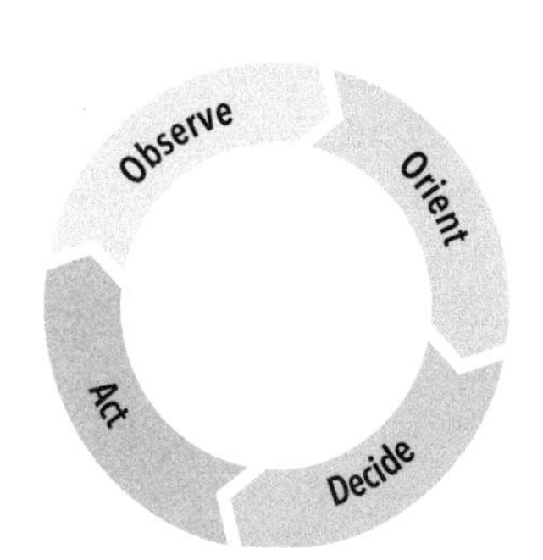

Working knowledge of the OODA Loop allows you to stay ahead of a threat by helping you make definitive and appropriate decisions quicker than your adversary.

Gary A. Klein[3] called this "recognition primed decision-making"— but the concept is the same. When it comes to violent encounters, the person who decides and acts first usually comes out on top! We will discuss this in detail later—the short version is, the more you know, the better decisions you can make in a shorter period of time.

What The Pros Know

It's impossible to solve a problem unless you know what you're up against. When it comes to finding out how to prevent bad things from happening it's critical to understand what those potential bad things are. You must first understand the common denominators and learn to recognize them quickly, so that you can start the decision making process. Step one is to get a good look at what's going on around you.

---

3 *Gary Klein is a research psychologist famous for pioneering in the field of naturalistic decision-making. His recognition primed decision (RPD) model has influenced changes in the ways the Marines and Army train their officers to make decisions.*

Whether you are a seasoned traveler, soccer mom, subway commuter or student, we all share the risk of being confronted by a threat at home, at work, school, or while traveling.

Bad Things Happen

On a Friday night in South El Monte, California, a woman was beaten in her own home by an invader using only his hands and feet. The attacker fled when the victim's husband pulled into the driveway[4].

Another evening a lady jogging in a Chicago suburb was approached by a man who tore her clothing and pulled her to the ground. He further attempted to pull her away from the sidewalk towards a vehicle but, because she fought with him, he stopped the attack. He took the woman's cell phone and then fled on foot[5].

On a school day in Philadelphia, Pennsylvania, a woman scribbled her name on a sign-in sheet and was able to walk into an elementary school classroom and have the teacher release a child without producing any identification. The woman was not a parent or guardian and abducted the child. Fortunately the little girl was eventually recovered[6,7].

While grabbing a cup of coffee and thinking about what you need to get done at work for the day, the last thing you would expect is a coworker you've known for the past 12 years to pull out a pistol and start shooting at you. But during just another day at the office a worker was told, after 12 years of service, that he no longer had a job. Pulling out a 9mm handgun, he then committed the largest workplace massacre in recent Minnesota history killing five and then taking his own life[8].

---

4 Q McCray and Leanne Suter, " South El Monte break-in suspect beat, bound woman," KABX-TVDT, December 8, 2012, http://abclocal.go.com/kabc/story?section=news/local/los_aneles&is=8913417

5 "Woman attacked while jogging in Schaumburg," Sun-Times Media Wire, July 27, 2012, http://www.suntimes.com/news/violence/14034195-505/story.html

6 Sarah Hoye, "Girl recovering after abduction by woman posing as her mom," CNN, January 17, 2013.

7 Interesting related story: Lu Ann Cahn and David Chang, "Security Lapse 2 Days After Girl Abducted?" NBC10 Philadelphia, January 17, 2013, http://www.nbcphilidelphia.com/investigations/How-Safe-Are-Philidelphia-Schools-187207771.html. NBC10's Lu Ann Cahn visited several local schools to find out how difficult it is to get in.

8 Abby Simons, Randy Furst, Matt McKinney, Paul Walsh, "Gunman lost his job, then opened fire killing 5," StarTribune, September 29, 2012, http://www.startribune.com/local/171774461.html

Traveling on a commuter train, the last thing you'd expect is to be followed and raped. But that's exactly what happened when a man followed a 52 year-old woman off the New York subway in Queens, violently threw her down a flight of stairs and then raped her[9].

A hotel guest in Huntsville, Alabama let a strange man inside his room who claimed he was sent to repair the phone. When the victim let the man inside, he revealed his true motive for knocking. "I'm not here to fix your phone. Give me everything you have." The victim complied, and the man left the room[10].

A Canadian woman in her mid-20s was found in a pool of blood in an elevator at an upscale resort in the town of Mazatlan, Mexico. Canada's official travel warning for Mexico includes Mazatlan as an area that has experienced a surge in violence related to organized crime[11].

Transforming a casual afternoon of shopping into a nightmare, gunfire rang out at a crowded mall in Columbia, Maryland, leaving two people dead and with the gunman killing himself minutes later[12].

Change What's Inside

Although you can't change what's happening out there, you can most certainly change what's going on inside. You can do many things that will cause an adversary or predator who may be considering attacking you, your family, home or property to lose interest and go target someone else.

The first step in being prepared is to understand the root of *why* bad things happen. So instead of trying to cure the symptom let's take our proverbial scalpel straight to the root cause.

Out Of The Blue

In taking the holistic approach to our own personal security, it's important to recognize that bad things don't happen out of the blue. Most folks

---

9 http://www.nbcnewyork.com/news/local/Police-Seek-Man-Violent-Queens-Rape-Rego-Par20953971.html

10 Keith Clines, "University Drive hotel guest robbed by man posing as a telephone repair man", The Huntsville Times. Published: Thursday, September 20, 2012, 8:33AM Updated: Thursday, September 20, 2012, 8:36AM http://blog.al.com/breaking/2012/09/university_drive_hotel_guest_r.html

11 http://www.huffingtonpost.ca/2012/01/22/Mexico-resort-beating-hotel-riu_n_1222299.html

12 http://www.washingtonpost.com/local/mall-in-columbia-on-lockdown-amid-reports-of-shooter/2014/01/25/4b3e8fb2-85e2-11e3-b85b-b305db87fb90_story.html

believe that all of a sudden you find yourself in some dark alley in the middle of the night with your back up against the wall and a gun in your face. Fortunately this is as absurd as saying "Yup, all of a sudden for no reason it just started raining!"

It all comes back to Mother Nature —akin to the fact that there is always a specific series of events that cause inclement weather, there is always a specific series of events that cause you to find yourself in a nasty situation.

Such specific series of events or *cycles* are at the very core of everything that occurs in nature.

We are all a part of these cycles and they include natural threats such as hurricanes and blizzards or manmade threats such as kidnappings and school shootings. One such cycle is referred to as the "OODA Loop."

The OODA Cycle

Originated by military strategist and United States Air Force fighter pilot Colonel John R. Boyd (1928-1997), the OODA Loop has been proven as a cornerstone in defeating attack-related behavior. Colonel Boyd served in the US Army Air Corps from 1945 to 1947 and subsequently served as a United States Air Force officer from July 1951 to August 1975. He was known as "Forty-second Boyd" for his ability to best any opposing pilot in aerial combat in less than 40 seconds. Col. Boyd was considered an icon by his students and a master-level instructor.

When asked about the secrets to his success in aerial combat, John responded with his "hypothesis" that all professionals "undergo a continuous cycle of interaction with their environment." This particular "cycle of interaction" adopted by the military, law enforcement and professional protection communities became, thereafter, known as the OODA Loop.

We use the OODA Loop for everything from running a business to crossing an intersection. Protection professionals have discovered that this decision making cycle is the key to rapid adaptation during a conflict and is therefore an essential tool to be used in defeating any adversarial attack-related behavior[13].

---

13 The essence of the story is that US fighter pilots, flying inferior airplanes (F-86 Sabres), nevertheless racked up a kill ratio of about 20:1 over NK and Russians in MIG-17's. Why? The US pilots' training was much better, which allowed them to make minute decisions and corrections consistently ahead of their adversaries in dogfights (getting inside their OODA Loop), eventually allowing most US pilots to get behind their opponents to bring them down.

How does this essential tool work? The OODA Loop is divided into four steps which function as a cycle:

OODA Loop and Description		***Resulting Thought***
Observe	a threat	"I see a car that might blow through that red light."
Orient	to that threat	"Yep, if I continue forward, I will be right in front of that car and will definitely get hit."
Decide	based on your orientation	"I'll wait until it passes by."
Act	action based on decision	"Don't move until that car passes."

Table 1.0 OODA Loop And Description

The OODA Loop is also how bad guys operate and knowing this gives you an advantage.

In the following example you and the bad guy are both running your own OODA Loops:

Bad Guy OODA Loop	***Your OODA Loop***
A potential threat (real bad guy) ***observes*** you getting out of your car. He ***orients*** to your position and sizes you up as a potential victim. He then ***decides*** that you are a qualified candidate for a mugging. He then ***acts*** on that decision by moving toward you. This one cycle of his entire OODA Loop maybe took about a second and a half to run.	After exiting your car you approach the ATM on foot and ***observe*** a suspicious-looking character lurking near your ATM in a dimly lit area. You then ***orient*** to this potential threat and think "Hmmmmm, why is this guy here alone and wearing a hoodie in the summer? Why did he just glance over at me? Based on your ***orientation*** you then decide that it is an unsafe risk and it's best to drive to another ATM. Lastly, you ***act*** by turning back toward your vehicle while pulling out your car.

Table 1.1 Bad Guy OODA Loop

Your actions cause the bad guy to run his next OODA Loop, in turn causing you to then run your next OODA Loop. All of which transpire in a matter of seconds.

Bad Guy OODA Loop	***Your OODA Loop***
He ***observes*** you walking away from the threat area with car keys in your hand, ***orients*** to the new set of conditions which remove you from his "qualified candidate" list. Since he's now been spotted he ***decides*** he doesn't want to risk getting caught so it's time for him to get out of there and he then ***acts*** by leaving the area.	As you're walking back toward your car, you ***observe*** that the condition of the potential threat area changes because you noticed the suspicious-looking character get into his car and drive away. You ***orient*** to the new changes in your environment as you watch him driving away into the horizon. You then ***decide*** based on your orientation to these observable changes that this is no longer a potentially threatening environment and that it is completely safe to walk back toward the ATM. You then ***act*** by going back to the ATM and completing your transaction.

Table 1.2 Bad Guy OODA Loop 2

The OODA Loop is a very powerful tool and one that you can use right now to help you prevent bad things from happening.

CHAPTER 2

The 90% Advantage

"When you have a decisive advantage, the amount of work required drops substantially and the likelihood of success goes up considerably."
Victor Cheng[1]

In This Chapter You Will Be Introduced To...

...how you can leverage the cycles of nature to your advantage in avoiding or stopping bad things from happening. As such you will be introduced to what is and how to use a threat progression, the attack cycle, and *Pre-Fense®—The 90% Advantage.*

At A Glance

Criminals, opportunists, terrorists and all sorts of miscreants are *not exempt* from the mechanics of nature. A successful attack is dependent on certain steps. These steps must be followed and in the right order. More importantly, a criminal must get every step *exactly right* to be "successful." You only have to effectively remove just one step in the cycle to stop the attack. Your knowledge of this series of events and exactly how they work can be used to effectively influence pre-attack behavior.

Not only does attack-related behavior have specific events that *must occur in a sequence*, these events can be observed. This affords you the tremendous advantage of that behavior being predictable.

A threat progression demonstrates how things can progress from a potential threat to a physical attack and just like any other cycle of nature, it follows a predictable cycle.

How Do I Use This In Real Life?

Any successful attack is comprised of specific steps in a cycle. The *physical*

1 *Stanford graduate Victor Cheng is a former McKinsey & Company management consultant, strategic planning consultant, public speaker, and author.*

attack comprises only a miniscule *10%* of that total cycle. Understanding how the entire cycle works gains you *The 90% Advantage* which gives you plenty of opportunity and options to handle any potential threat long before it progresses to a physical attack.

Instead of being relegated to reacting to a physical attack and responding with one of three bad choices—dialing 911, using a karate chop or becoming a victim, you can now use this knowledge to appropriately manage pre-attack events and behaviors. You are far less likely to need self-defense or the police to save your life.

What The Pros Know

Any threat progression begins as a potential threat and under certain circumstances a potential threat could progress into an actual threat—which in turn could progress into threatening activities culminating in a personal physical attack.

How can we leverage the cycles of nature to our advantage in preventing bad things from happening? The short answer is that things *do not happen out of the blue*—no successful activity can happen *without* following each step in a progressive series of events. Like a tripod—remove one leg and it cannot stand, break one step in the cycle and the attack never occurs!

Just Like In The Movies

If you want to succeed in "going out to dinner," there is a series of events that *must occur, in sequence* for that to happen:

1. Determine which restaurant
2. Go to that restaurant
3. Order what you want at that restaurant
4. Eat your dinner

Think of it as a short film. Everything must go *exactly right* and *in sequence* for your planned event "going out to dinner" to be successful. How could you go to "that restaurant" if you didn't know which restaurant it was? How could you possibly eat your dinner if you didn't know where you were going or what you were ordering? None of the series of events of this short film can be either *missing* or run *out of sequence* if you want the success of "going out to dinner."

The exact same concept applies to a series of events leading up to and ending with a physical threat. A minimum number of events must occur in sequence just like frames in a movie for a physical threat to happen.

Threat Progression

A threat can start out as being only *potential*—meaning that it has the capacity to develop into a bad thing happening in the future. The progression from potential threat to an actual physical attack is best illustrated by the example of a classic schoolyard bully.

Potential Threat

In any schoolyard there exists a probability that there may be a schoolyard bully present. If this is true then we have accurately described a "potential threat."

Although a potential threat, the capable bully standing in the schoolyard without motivation or opportunity poses no actual threat.

The same bully standing in a schoolyard running his OODA Loop **O**bserves his immediate environment and thinks to himself "Easy pickings here." He then **O**rients to his environment thinking "Hey, I'm the biggest, baddest kid in this entire schoolyard and I know I can take anybody here!" at which point he still remains only a potential threat. It's when he moves to the next step in his OODA Loop that things change.

Actual Threat

When the bully arrives at his **D**ecision, "Yeah, it's about time I shook this place up and scored myself some extra lunch money," he crosses that progressive line and converts from being a potential threat to an *actual threat.*

Unfortunately this internal decision-making process is not outwardly observable by anyone other than the bully until he completes his OODA Loop and **A**cts on his decision. His exhibiting observable attack-related behavior serves as confirmation of his status as an actual threat.

In summary, the threat—schoolyard bully—progressed from a potential threat to an actual threat.

Pre-Attack Behavior

Motivated by his intentions and capable of carrying out his plan the bully exhibits "pre-attack behavior" by looking around the schoolyard for a potential victim. Identifying a potential target the bully makes his final selection and verifies who he's planning to attack.

Attack Behavior

After verifying that he has in fact selected an appropriate victim, the bully plans to keep a low profile to avoid being observed by any authorities or his victim and makes further plans in accordance with his best opportunity for attack. Following his plan he approaches his chosen victim and proceeds to carry out his intentions. In this example he has moved from pre-attack behavior to attack behavior.

Table 2.0 illustrates the detailed progression of steps from a potential threat to attack behavior.

OODA Loop and Description		***Resulting Thought***
Observe	Bully takes note of his environment - the schoolyard.	Exists as a potential threat
Orient	He asseses the situation comparing himself to others.	
Decide	Based on his orientation he decides to attack	Converts to an actual threat
Act	He takes action based on his decision	Exhibits pre-attack behavior
		Exhibits attack behavior

Table 2.0 OODA Loop And Description

Just like a movie, a minimum number of events must occur *in sequence* for a physical threat to happen. Divided into four equally proportioned "threat status freeze frames," this minimum series of events, in sequence, starting from potential threat flowing to attack behavior is referred to as a "threat progression."

Potential Threat → Actual Threat → Pre-Attack Behavior → Attack Behavior

Just like watching a movie that you've seen before, you know the details of each scene and even know how it ends. You know "This is the part where the guy..." and knowing the pattern of events as they play out gains you the dual powers of being able to predict what's coming next *and* know what to do about it.

Paying attention to the detail of each individual "frame" of a threat progression and with the end goal of learning how to avoid, or stop a physical attack, let's take a closer look at the last 50% of a threat progression describing attack-related behavior.

Attack-Related Behavior

Since it's not possible to read somebody's mind, their intentions are made visible only when they take action. Although there's really not much you can actively do to stop the first 50% of a threat progression, there's plenty of opportunity to stop or avoid the threat entirely when you fully understand how to manage attack-related behavior.

All predators—human or animal that have moved from a potential threat to an actual threat and are about to move into attack-related behavior, share one thing in common: they *must* complete a specific series or cycle of events in order to be successful.

The Attack Cycle

Predators of the animal kingdom's—including lions and tigers—first step to getting dinner is to look for prey. They diligently search for the least capable, least alert and most separated from the protection of the rest of the herd—that is the *weakest,* most *unaware,* and most *exposed* who can be attacked successfully. Any two of these characteristics will garner the attention of a predator, but finding all three—*weak, unaware, and exposed,* is like hitting the 777 jackpot in Vegas!

Once they select or choose their prey they then stalk their prey to ensure that it is an appropriate selection (verify) and determine the most efficient means of attacking this animal in this particular scenario (plan).

Laying low and trying to stay out of view while stalking (verifying and planning stage) they then close in for the kill by moving to the best possible attack position preparing to pounce upon their victim. After they have maneuvered into such an advantageous offensive position and are mentally and physically prepared, they then attack their prey.

Look—Choose—Stalk—Close—Attack. In the animal kingdom this natural series of events ensures balance of the ecosystem. In the world we share, this very same predictable series of events describes how animals of the criminal sort attack their human victims—they all follow the exact same "attack cycle."

There are a total of five comprehensive steps in the attack cycle as they relate to both the animal kingdom and a human predator:

Animal Kingdom		***Human Predator***
1	***Look*** for prey	***Look*** for soft target[2]
2	***Choose*** prey	***Choose*** a specific target
3	***Stalk*** - verify that this prey is the best choice and if so then plan to move in for the kill	***Stalk*** - verify that this target is the best choice and if so then plan to close in for an attack
4	***Close*** in for the kill	***Close*** in on the target
5	***Attack*** prey	***Attack*** the target

Table 2.1 The Animal Kingdom Versus Human Predator

All bad guys ranging from schoolyard bully to purse snatcher to international terrorist follow this same cycle in planning for a successful attack.

The attack cycle is the one common denominator to all predator behavior. Let's look at an example of how this applies to our society. The schoolyard bully moving to attack-related behavior:

Schoolyard Bully		***Attack Cycle Steps***
1	***Looks*** for a soft target in the school yard.	**Look**
2	***Chooses*** what appears to him to be a soft target.	**Choose**
3	***Stalks*** his target to verify he is the soft target he appears to be and completes his plan to move in.	**Stalk**
4	***Closes*** in on his vetted target following his plan.	**Close**
5	***Attacks*** by forcing the target to give up his lunch money.	**Attack**

Table 2.2 Schoolyard Bully Attack Cycle

2 In protection parlance the term "soft target" is applied to anyone exhibiting these very same "soft target indicators" of being weak, unaware, and exposed.

Let's take a look at a well-known example of an application of the attack cycle—the suicidal attackers on Sept 11, 2001 at the World Trade Center in New York City.

Following a bit more complex variant of the attack cycle they ran the attack cycle as per Table 2.3.

The end result of the attack on the Twin Towers literally changed the course of world history. The death toll was greater than 3,000 Americans. The U.S. went to war in Iraq and Afghanistan as a result.

The impact of this particular attack cycle on the United States and the world community remains irreversible.

Suicidal Attack on the World Trade Center On September 11, 2001		***Attack Cycle Steps***
1	Looked for the best possible soft American icon to make their statement.	**Look**
2	Chose the optimal soft target—the Twin Towers in New York City.	**Choose**
3	Undertook a tremendous amount of surveillance and planning which took *five years*.	**Stalk**
4	Coordinated and fine-tuned their efforts, time on target, personnel and equipment.	**Close**
5	Brought down both towers in a successful suicide mission.	**Attack**

Table 2.3 World Trade Center Attack Cycle

Let's take a look at a more opportunistic application of the attack cycle—*the attack related behavior of a purse-snatcher.* In the case of the purse-snatcher, he's looking for an easy mark.

Purse Snatcher		***Attack Cycle Steps***
1	Looks for a soft target with an easily accessible purse.	**Look**
2	Chooses her by noticing soft target indicators (appears weak, unaware, alone).	**Choose**
3	Verifies that she is in fact a valid target and then plans on the best way to close in.	**Stalk**

Table 2.4 Purse Snatcher Attack Cycle *(continued on next page)*

4	Following his plan - which may take only a matter of seconds to devise —he closes in from his initial position.	**Close**
5	Snatches the purse.	**Attack**

Table 2.4 Purse Snatcher Attack Cycle (continued)

The steps of the attack cycle are identical in the case of a sexual predator or child abductor.

Kidnapper Or Sexual Predator		***Attack Cycle Steps***
1	Searches for a soft target that is unaware and/or alone.	**Look**
2	Selects his target by observing soft target indicators.	**Choose**
3	Stalks the child for a time to ensure she is his best choice and makes plans on the best way to close.	**Stalk**
4	Following his plan—which may have taken only a matter of seconds, he closes in from his initial position.	**Close**
5	Abducts the child.	**Attack**

Table 2.5 Child Abduction Attack Cycle

Now that you understand how the attack cycle works—you have a blueprint for how an attacker must act in order to the attack you! They must complete each step in the process in order to be successful. You only need to break the cycle at *any step* to stop the attacker. In other words, your attacker has to get everything right—you only have to get any one part right!

Tying everything together, when you apply the OODA Loop to the attack cycle you can get a better look into the mind of a predator.

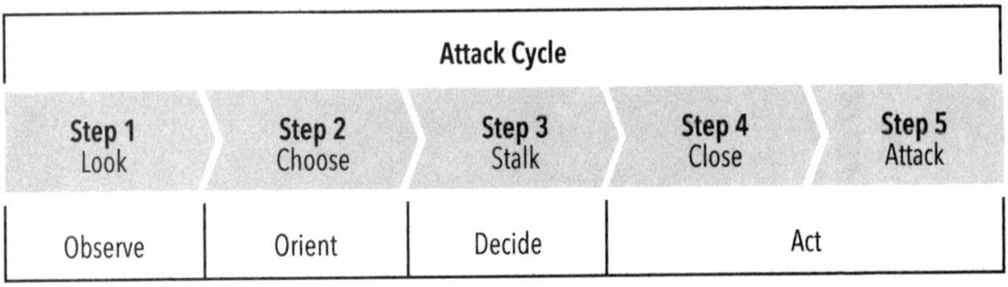

Attack Cycle				
Step 1 Look	**Step 2** Choose	**Step 3** Stalk	**Step 4** Close	**Step 5** Attack
Observe	Orient	Decide	Act	

Fifty percent of an entire threat progression is described by the attack cycle:

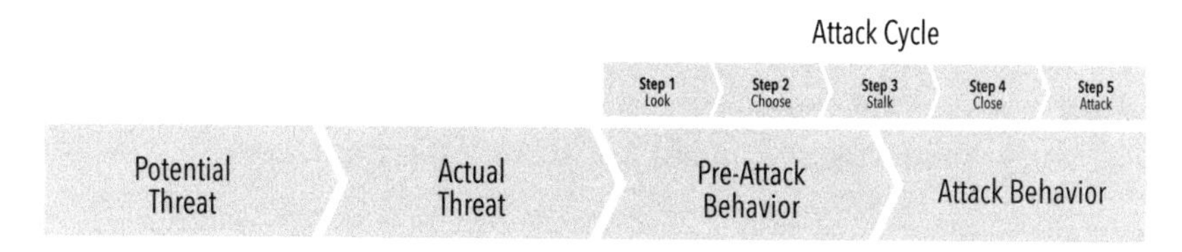

So far we've discovered some interesting observations about a successful attack:

1. A physical attack doesn't just pop out of the blue.
2. An attacker needs to run his OODA Loop *twice*—one time through to move from a potential threat to an actual threat and then again to run through the attack cycle.
3. Not only does attack-related behavior require a minimum number of events that must occur in sequence, that behavior can be observed in quantifiable steps—referred to as the attack cycle—making it predictable and thus further manageable.

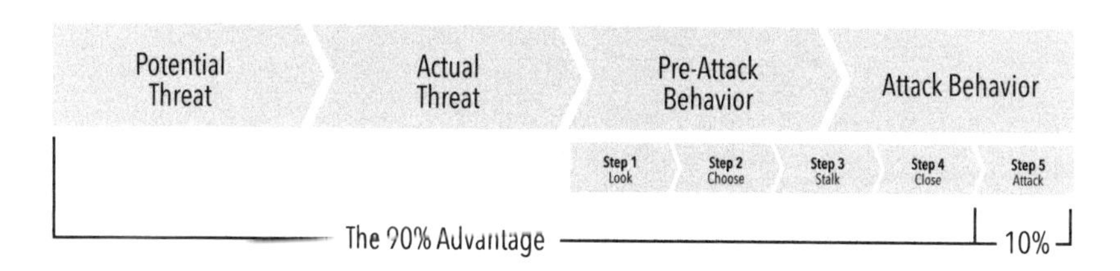

A physical attack—if it ever came down to it—can *only* happen during the last one fifth of an attack cycle, which accounts for only ten percent of the entire threat progression. Most people focus only on this "dreaded ten percent" as they are completely unaware that it is only at the tail end of a much more manageable series of events. Why would you ever want to put yourself or those you care about at the disadvantage of this tail end ten percent?

So what about the majority 90 percent of an entire threat progression? Why not take full advantage of all that valuable time and opportunity? Leveraging the *PreFense® 90% Advantage* allows you numerous options for solving problems without the need for a karate chop or a gun. The remaining chapters of this book are designed to teach you to use this decisive advantage in exactly how and where to break the attack cycle.

CHAPTER 3

Threat Management

"An Ounce of Prevention is worth a Pound of Cure."
Benjamin Franklin[1]

In This Chapter You Will Be Introduced To...

...the four principles of threat management which use the anatomy of a threat to help prevent bad things from happening. These established principles are used by government agencies and private security experts to safeguard their most valuable assets—their people. You can apply these same principles to your everyday life, protecting yourself and your family.

At A Glance

Criminals are not superheroes. In fact, although cunning, most are not the sharpest tools in the shed. As we now know, they *must* follow specific cycles of action for them to be successful.

Bound by the natural mechanics of both the OODA Loop and the attack cycle, they are further relegated to a limited menu of options. Understanding these options allows you to effectively manage the realistic threats that they may present.

Intelligence professionals in the military and other agencies have numerous people dedicated to evaluating an enemy's offensive capabilities which allows them to understand how to better defend against realistic threats. Similarly, you can use the principles of threat management to make educated decisions to keep your family and the things you care about safe.

How Do I Use This In Real Life?

In addition to the tools you already have, which are common sense and good habits, the four principles of threat management that may be

1 *February 4, 1735 edition of the Pennsylvania Gazette writing anonymously as an "old citizen."*

applied to your daily routine as part of a successful strategy to avoid, mitigate or defend against a threat are: 1) Options and Opportunity, 2) Time and Effort, 3) Protective Intervention, and 4) Evaluation and Response.

What The Pros Know

The first step in leveraging *The 90% Advantage* is to understand how to manage and protect against real world threats.

Sharing the same concerns you do about safeguarding against real world threats, federal agencies such as the Secret Service, hire and train experts to evaluate the relevant and realistic threats so limited assets can be effectively employed to protect their people. Evaluating and mitigating risk is referred to as "threat management" whereas the physical defense of people against a threat is referred to as "protection."

Threat Management And Protection

Threat management is a professional's tool used to apply the right protective concepts and measures to avoid and/or reduce the impact of an actual threat. You can think of this as the administrative aspect of dealing with bad guys—similar to the architect of a construction project.

Protection is a professional's tool to apply the right protective concepts and measures to physically defend against an actual threat. You can think of this as the *hands-on* aspect of dealing with bad guys similar to the workers on the construction crew for the same project. They both work together as a team—architect and crew, to provide you with every tool you need from the top down to handle almost any threat a bad guy can throw at you. The difference between you and the professionals is that you will have to be both the architect and the crew—which you can do very effectively!

Threat Management

Fortunately threat management is something that's already a part of your everyday routine. For example, you use common sense and good habits to check the gas gauge in your car to ensure that you have enough gas in the tank. You make and confirm reservations at your hotel ahead of time so that upon arrival you avoid the threat of being stranded.

However, not all threats are as easily managed and the higher the threat level, the greater the information and skill needed to manage it. The first step in threat management is to clearly define and dissect exactly what is considered a threat.

Anatomy Of A Threat

You can't manage something you don't understand, so for purposes of threat management, it's necessary to understand the anatomy of a threat.

To simplify our understanding, a threat is anything or anyone that can physically harm us. While emotional or financial pain is real and significant, it is outside the scope of this book. If it can physically harm you or your family, it is a threat.

Risk managers[2] further classify threats into two general categories: natural and manmade. Natural threats typically come straight from Mother Nature whereas manmade are adversarial in origin and can come from terrorists, extremists, activists, anti-nationalists, criminals, foreign intelligence services, disgruntled employees, corporate/industrial spies and emotionally unstable persons.

Using the threat progression and the OODA Loop, we find that manmade threats such as individuals or groups require motivation, opportunity and the capability to act. If they lack any of these requirements, then they will remain only a potential threat. Conversely, their having all three can put you at the beginning of an attack cycle.

Potential Threat	Actual Threat	**Step 1** Look	**Step 2** Choose	**Step 3** Stalk	**Step 4** Close	**Step 5** Attack

The Principles

There are four established threat management principles that are used as guidelines by government agencies and private security experts to safeguard their most valuable assets—their people—which you can use to safeguard yourself and those closest to you.

Guideline 1—Options and Opportunity

Options matter—the greater your number of options, the greater your opportunities to avoid or mitigate a threat. A threat progression runs

2 Risk managers are professionals in charge of assessing, minimizing and preventing damage or loss to a business.

on a timeline, which is further exacerbated by an accelerated attack cycle timeline.

Attack Cycle Timeline

Attack Cycle Timeline Accelerates As An Incident Moves Toward The Later Steps.

The timeline of an attack cycle may vary from minutes to years. An opportunist looking for soft targets, such as a purse-snatcher's attack cycle, completes the entire attack cycle from start to finish in just a matter of seconds. Compare this very rapid timeline to that of the attack cycle used on the World Trade Center, which ran for over five years! Although all attack cycle timelines vary in overall timespan, they all share one common denominator; regardless of overall timespan all attack cycles rapidly accelerate at Step 4—Close and Step 5—Attack.

Example	*Step 1 Look*	*Step 2 Choose*	*Step 3 Stalk*	*Step 4 Close*	*Step 5 Attack*	*Total Time*
Terrorist Act	3 years	2 years	1 year	1 month	1 day	More than 6 years
Purse Grab	3 minutes	2 minutes	1 minute	30 seconds	5 seconds	Less than 7 minutes

Table 3.0 Attack Cycle Timeline

There exists a relationship between the amount of time you have to the number of options you have available to you. The more time you have available the greater your number of options. Conversely the lesser amount of time the fewer your options ending with only three remaining—run, fight or give up—which is covered in detail in later chapters. Table 3.1 illustrates this relationship as applied to the entire threat progression.

Guideline 2—Time And Effort

Everything in our lives depends on some expenditure of time and effort. In the world of protection, these are two equally precious commodities and are critical to the handling of any real world threat. A very realistic example of this is when the attack cycle further accelerates at Step 4—

Potential Threat	Actual Threat	**Step 1** Look	**Step 2** Choose	**Step 3** Stalk	**Step 4** Close	**Step 5** Attack
Threat Management	Unlimited Options				Limited Options	3 Options

Table 3.1 Threat Management Guideline 1 As Applied To A Threat Progression

Close and Step 5—Attack reducing the amount of time and increasing the amount of effort required for response.

If you wait until Step 5 of the attack cycle to respond, then the threat—not you, is in the driver's seat. The longer an event is in progress, the fewer options you have to manage it, the less time you have available at your disposal and the more effort it takes for you to break the attack cycle!

Potential Threat	Actual Threat	**Step 1** Look	**Step 2** Choose	**Step 3** Stalk	**Step 4** Close	**Step 5** Attack
Threat Management	Unlimited Options				Limited Options	3 Options
	Maximum amount of time/ least amount of effort				Less Time/ More Effort	Least Time/ Max Effort

Table 3.2 Threat Management Guideline 2 As Applied To A Threat Progression

Timing is everything—the sooner the better—as threat management is about avoiding, mitigating or defending against a threat *before* it turns into a physical attack.

Protective Intelligence

"Protective intelligence" is the art and science of understanding potential threats by collecting and assessing relevant information about adversaries who have the motivation, capability and opportunity to mount attacks against a target. Looking at it from the predator's perspective—you and anyone or anything of value or importance to you, can be considered targets. The purpose of protective intelligence and of *PreFense®* is to help you identify and effectively manage real-world threats.

Protective intelligence is the evaluation and construction of the range of options available to an assailant. The fact is criminals all have a menu of choices from which they must choose. Fortunately for us, that menu is limited. You cannot bomb the World Trade Center without explosive materials and you cannot take money from a victim who fails to show up for your robbery.

The important part of protective intelligence is that it allows you to make realistic threat-based assessments and the more effective your assessments, the better your ability to apply the right protective measures against a potential threat.

One of the core principles of protective intelligence is that if you can accurately assess and act on that assessment early in the attack cycle, then you hold all the cards. This principle helps to set your threat management and protection priorities.

Guideline 3—Protective Intervention

The professionals use protective intelligence to guide interventions by primarily avoiding, mitigating or defending against a threat.

- Avoid
    - Don't even be there
- Mitigate
    - De-escalate—reduce the intensity of a threat
    - Divert—deflect or distract a threat
    - Defuse—slow or stop the progression of a threat
    - Deter—discourage any threat efforts
- Defend
    - Disrupt—cause a break in the attack cycle

Avoid

One of the most often overlooked, yet easiest to understand, preventative concept is to altogether avoid a potential threat.

> *Don't be there in the first place—do not purposefully place yourself in harm's way!*

As easy as it may sound, you would be surprised at how many people will not follow this simple admonition of the professionals. They generally blow it off and say such things as "Well, I'm going anyway," or "Nothing's going to happen."

A potential threat, say confronting an intoxicated, aggressive young male, may not manifest into an actual threat. Of course there exists a higher probability that it will, if you are in a bar district at 2:00 AM, and much less likely if you are asleep in your bed at home—so simply leaving the bar scene early or not going reduces this threat significantly.

Mitigate

Failing avoidance, the next best thing you can do is to mitigate or reduce the likelihood of being successfully attacked. If for some reason you MUST drive through an extremely high-threat neighborhood, the next best thing you can do is to try and mitigate the threat by taking some elementary precautions such as: keep your windows rolled up, doors locked, stay off your phone and pay attention to your surroundings. If you cannot avoid a threat entirely, you must be hypervigilant for the period of time you are intentionally exposing yourself to this threat. We will discuss this in "mode skills" in later chapters, but mitigation means you expect to be attacked and have a plan to minimize the impact.

Body armor is another example of mitigation that may be appropriate in extreme circumstances. Buying more effective locks, shatterproof glass, or a heavier door that cannot be easily broken down are all examples of mitigation.

Defend

Although falling under the domain of "protection" and covered in much more detail in following chapters, failing avoidance and mitigation of a threat your only remaining option is defending against one—generally this ends up being physical protection. The best you can do is to break the attack cycle.

For example, if you can't avoid an argument with someone and they start to raise their voice, don't shout back at them and add fuel to the fire. Try to do everything and anything you can to mitigate the situation to lower the probability of the threat progressing to a physical attack. However, the second events move to Step 5, then your only remaining option is to break the cycle by using one of only three remaining options: run, fight or give up.

	Potential Threat	Actual Threat	**Step 1** Look	**Step 2** Choose	**Step 3** Stalk	**Step 4** Close	**Step 5** Attack
Threat Management	Unlimited Options					Limited Options	3 Options
	Maximum amount of time/ least amount of effort					Less Time/ More Effort	Least Time/ Max Effort
	Avoid					Mitigate	Defend

Table 3.3 Threat Management Guideline 3 As Applied To A Threat Progression

Guideline 4—Evaluation And Response

Avoidance, mitigation and defense against a threat are supported by evaluation and response using the APA Process, Assess and Respond, and React options.

The APA Process

The purpose of the APA Process is to better prepare you to manage an anticipated threat—actual or potential—and may be applied to almost any anticipated event. This very useful tool is considered a proactive measure in threat management and can be broken down into three easy-to-follow steps:

1. Assess—once a threat is identified, evaluate the potential risk

2. Plan—make best preparations to avoid, mitigate or defend against that risk.

3. Act—if necessary, take affirmative action by implementing these plans.

Let's take a closer look at each individual step.

(A)—Assess—Identify any potential or actual threats you may encounter. Let's say you're running errands in your neighborhood. In assessing your "potential threat environment," there are very few threats that you may encounter. Based on this assessment, you might consider this to be a low-threat environment without need for additional planning or defensive measures.

If your errands take you to inner city gang turf or overseas to a war zone, then your potential threat environment changes drastically. In high-threat environments, you would need to consider attacks from hos- tiles. These two potential threat environments are on opposite ends of the threat management spectrum and each carries with it a completely different set of planning considerations.

(P)—Plan—Make best preparations to avoid, mitigate or defend. Just like the Boy Scouts of America, whose motto is "Be Prepared," all protection professionals recognize the importance of preparation. Preparing or planning is considered the golden rule of threat management; that is, simply "be ready."

The best management of any number of threats is proper planning. Lack of planning exposes you to higher risk and greater vulnerability. Let's say that you had to travel to Grand Forks, North Dakota—one of the coldest destinations in America—in the dead of winter. Would you wear a t-shirt and shorts? Do you already have a ride from the airport? Exposure to sub-zero weather for any length of time could kill you; thus, you would need to plan accordingly.

Allow yourself adequate time to prepare and figure out as much as you are able about where you're going and what you'll be doing. Firefighters must prepare before answering an alarm. Doctors must prepare before performing an operation. The same applies to your threat management and that of your protectee(s)—the better prepared you are, the greater likelihood of success. Conversely, the less prepared you are the less likely you are to succeed.

(A)—Act—if necessary take affirmative action. Part of your initial threat assessment would be to calculate the probability of the event actually occurring. Given all of the above, you can use the combination of your own observations, common sense and your personal experiences to determine the probability of a threat. A good example of this is the threat of sexual harassment.

Unfortunately, most females are aware, at some point in their lives, they are at greater risk of sexual harassment then males. For example, if you are a female, and you must travel on foot to a neighbor's house several city blocks away in July wearing summer clothes and know that your chosen route takes you through a potential threat area, for instance a crew of rowdy and intoxicated young males—actual threat—who regularly party in the front yard of their frat house, choosing that route is likely to result in harassment.

Based on all of the above, you **A**ssess the situation and determine that "Yes, there's a good chance I'm going to be harassed by those guys." Based on this assessment you then make plans commensurate with your available options to avoid the threat: 1. select an alternate route, 2. drive instead of walk, 3. wear different attire, 4. walk with male friends—whichever you **P**lan to be the best course of action to adequately avoid or mitigate this threat. Based on those plans you may then **A**ct accordingly. The above three separate activities follow in chronological order—Assess, Plan, and Act.

Failing to run the APA Process during your everyday life will spell disaster. Unaware and unprepared, you would place yourself at the mercy of the potential threat progressing into verbal harassment or worse—a physical attack.

The APA Process allows you plenty of time and preparation for where you're going and what you may be doing, taking into consideration your assessment and decisions.

Assessment And Response

As an anticipatory threat management tool to help you prepare for an activity or an event, the APA Process is made up of three easy-to-follow steps affording you unlimited time and opportunity to manage any *anticipated* threats that you may encounter. However, there are such circumstances where you may not be afforded the luxury of time.

For example; crossing the street on foot and running your OODA Loop you **O**bserve a driver failing to see you and continuing to drive their car through the stop sign. You Orient to this observation in that you've only got two solutions—get out of the way or get hit. Deciding to get out of the way you then immediately Act on that decision—all of which transpires in less than two seconds.

Applying the APA Process to imminent danger is not the right tool for the job. When physically moving out of the way of an oncoming vehicle or getting hit are your only two options there's not a heck of a lot of planning involved. Such exigent circumstances effectively cancel out any opportunity to plan. Extracting the *plan* step from the anticipatory APA Process, one is left with rapid assessment and immediate response to that imminent danger, or simply "assessment and response."

Denied the luxury of planning time, assessment and response allows you to make accurate assessments resulting in appropriate response. Applying this to a threat progression your options and opportunities decrease as the potential threat progresses toward attack behavior, further compressing your response time. The faster and more acute your observation—the more accurate your assessment will be, resulting in a timely and appropriate response.

React

Failing both the APA Process and assessment and response as threat management options, your only remaining option is to simply *react*. Here you don't have a choice. If you didn't see it, hear it, smell it or sense it coming then you are so far behind the power curve that you're literally blindsided by the incident and can only defend against it.

For example, getting out of your car, fumbling with your bags, looking down at your keys while talking on your cell phone—your attention completely withdrawn from your surroundings, when all of a sudden "out of the blue" two unsavory characters—who've been stalking you since you pulled into that parking lot 15 minutes ago, place their hand on your shoulder.

Shocked to discover you've been caught in the very last step of the attack cycle, any time or opportunity for accurate assessment followed by appropriate response has unfortunately been eliminated from the equation rendering you completely dependent upon only your physical skills.

Although the least desirable of the three options, all is not lost to react. It is still possible to defend against an attack as is covered in upcoming chapters.

	Potential Threat	Actual Threat	Step 1 Look	Step 2 Choose	Step 3 Stalk	Step 4 Close	Step 5 Attack
Threat Management	Unlimited Options					Limited Options	3 Options
	Maximum amount of time/ least amount of effort					Less Time/ More Effort	Least Time/ Max Effort
	Avoid					Mitigate	Defend
	Assess, Plan, Act–*The APA Process*					Assess & Respond	React

Table 3.4 Threat Management Guidelines As Applied To A Threat Progression

The principles provided for you by threat management—and recommended by protective intelligence, for use against a threat progression timeline may be readily adopted and applied. In summary these include:

Guideline 1—Options And Opportunity

1. Unlimited Options
2. Limited Options
3. Three Options—run away, fight, or give up

Guideline 2—Time And Effort

1. Most Amount Of Time/Least Amount Of Effort
2. Less Time/More Effort
3. Least Time/Maximum Effort

Guideline 3—Protective Intervention

1. Avoid
2. Mitigate
3. Defend

Guideline 4—Evaluation And Response

1. APA Process—Assess, Plan, Act where you have all the time and opportunity
2. Assess And Respond—you no longer have the luxury of planning
3. React—you no longer have the time or opportunity to assess

PART 2
Protection

CHAPTER 4

Introduction To Protection

"The wise man avoids evil by anticipating it."
Publilius Syrus[1]

In This Chapter You Will Be Introduced To...

...the domain of protection. Topics covered in this chapter include the purpose and fundamentals of this domain which are comprised of protective concepts, proactive, active and reactive measures, and the protection envelope.

At A Glance

Protection is defined as "the act of saving someone from any source of potential harm, affording you an ample supply of options and opportunities at your disposal to stop an attack."

In the event you didn't see it coming or failed to identify, assess, plan for and prepare to defend against a potential threat, it may develop into an actual threat and further develop into an attack. Again, all is not lost. Although not as advantageous as avoiding an attack, you still have opportunity to stop the attack using protection.

How Do I Use This In Real Life?

Protection helps provide a stable and relatively predictable environment, one where we may be at home, work, or school, seek recreation and travel without fear of disturbance or injury. In other words, protection allows you to be both safe and comfortable.

Viewing protection like a fire extinguisher or first-aid kit, you can use it to manage and defend against any number of threats. In doing so you may discover which protection tools work best for which job. You can

1 Publilius Syrus—a Roman first century BC writer of maxims contemporary with Cicero noted for his collection of versified aphorisms.

then leverage the experience and skills of the professionals by adopting the concepts and measures available in the "fundamentals of protection."

What The Pros Know

Although we may not anticipate fighting a three-alarm blaze, we don't need professional firefighter training to put out an easily manageable kitchen fire. If we find ourselves in a minor medical emergency we can certainly use a first-aid kit without having been to medical school. However, professional training is extremely useful to have and understanding the "tools of the trade" allows you to benefit from them if needed.

What Is Protection?

Protection is any concept, method or practice, which prevents someone or something from suffering harm. In ancient times there were protection programs such as clearing brush and other concealment options for 200 feet on either side of the king's roads as a precaution against robbery or other assaults. Personal guards such as the Praetorians of ancient Rome and the Samurai of ancient Japan were additional insurance against bad things happening to a VIP. The same concerns of the ancients are equally as applicable in our time.

The world isn't as safe a place as we'd like. It never has been. Given the frequency and intensity of emerging worldwide threats—protection should be a matter of personal responsibility. If you choose to abdicate that responsibility to professionals like police, military and security guards, you are choosing to believe that they will be there when you need them.

How can you protect your daughter who is going off to college this year and living away from home for the first time? As a business owner, what can you do to provide protection assurances for your employees and your business? If you're the President of the United States, then you are protected by the Secret Service. If you're a celebrity or a very high-ranking corporate executive, then you are protected by what's called a professional or "executive protection" detail—a team of bodyguards skilled in the tradecraft of protection.

Most of us do not live in a threat profile that requires that level of protection and successfully defend ourselves and our family by simply applying the principles of threat management and learning the protective measures presented in this book.

Protective Measures

In the world of protection there exists a large body of knowledge built squarely on lessons learned from the field by professionals. These are comprised of the best protection methods and practices gleaned from literally centuries of trial and error.

Spanning far back into history and filling the myriad requirements for protection of royalty, dignitaries, celebrities and high-profile affluent families, these methods and practices have been proven to be the most effective by professionals worldwide.

Protective methods and practices incorporate similarly derived protective concepts that are functional ideas which, when applied, achieve a specific protection objective. An example of this is the idea of securing your home when you're not there—accomplished by locking your doors and closing your windows prior to your departure.

These traditional and time tested methods and practices incorporating protective concepts are referred to as "protective measures."

Protective measures are very diverse, flexible in application and can also be applied proactively, actively or reactively based on any number of conditions and circumstances, which will be covered in their entirety in following chapters.

Protection professionals draw upon a repository of protective concepts and measures used every day to identify and manage bad things before they happen—these are called "proactive measures." Although less than ideal for managing events while they are happening—proactive measures do work with practice and the appropriate tools. Once the attack has commenced you are left reacting to the attacker's plan and the only protection option you have left on the table is "reactive measures"—the least optimal of the three.

The Fundamentals Of Protection

In addition to this repository of concepts and measures, the professionals devote time and effort to improving and refining their observation skills. They additionally dedicate time and effort to learning how to appropriately communicate with each other when moving a protectee[2] safely from one place to another (verbal skills). This and many other specialized skills are referred to as "protective skills." A number of these skills are introduced throughout this book, for example, having a family duress code is a

2 A protectee is someone that you wish to keep safe from harm.

verbal skill used by professionals, which you can easily adopt and immediately apply.

In addition to protective concepts, measures, and skills, most professionals have at their disposal an array of physical protection tools such as flashlights, communication devices, and weapons that they may use to support their protective efforts. This comprehensive repository of concepts, measures, skills and tools is considered the fundamentals of protection.

> *Protection is comprised of the thoughts, actions, skills, and tools used in anticipating, preventing, or limiting any action or situation which may cause danger or harm.*

The fundamentals of protection are categorized by their defining functions:

1. Thought—Protective Concepts
2. Action—Protective Measures
3. Skills—Protective Skills
4. Tools—Physical Protection Tools

Of these categories protective concepts are the most frequently used, most reliable and the greatest resource of the protection professional. They are the bedrock of *PreFense*®— and the cornerstone of the fundamentals of protection.

Just like the professionals, once you understand the fundamentals of protection and how they work you may immediately apply them to become more successful at avoiding, mitigating or defending against an attack.

The Protection Envelope

One of the key concepts of protection is that in order for physical injury to occur, an assailant must be able to make contact with the victim. If we can stop physical contact from occurring, there will be no injury. Ideally this is an "invisible blanket" of threat protection around yourself and your loved ones. This is a protective concept commonly referred to as the "protection envelope."

All protection professionals are trained to make and keep a 360-degree protection envelope around their protectee(s) in order to protect against as many threats as possible. The idea is to keep that 360-degree envelope wrapped, like a bubble, around yourself and your protectee(s) regardless of the environment. While impossible to protect against all threats at all times, this protective concept will lead to forming good habits if incorporated into your daily routine.

A "controlled area" is a secure location such as an airport, bank, corporate or federal building and the like; there are plenty of security doors, locks, secured elevators, security guards and surveillance cameras to help keep certain threats at bay. Controlled areas provide the *physical* means for creating that blanket known as the 360-degree envelope of protection or protection envelope.

The protection envelope is only one of a plethora of tools available to the professionals, and now you, in the fundamentals of protection. All of these tools are covered in subsequent chapters.

	Potential Threat → Actual Threat → **Step 1** Look → **Step 2** Choose → Verify → **Step 3** Stalk → Plan	**Step 4** Close	**Step 5** Attack
Threat Management	Unlimited Options	Limited Options	3 Options
Threat Management	Maximum amount of time/ least amount of effort	Less Time/ More Effort	Least Time/ Max Effort
Threat Management	Avoid	Mitigate	Defend
Threat Management	Assess, Plan, Act–*The APA Process*	Assess & Respond	React
Protection	Proactive Measures	Active Measures	Reactive Measures
Protection			
Protection			

Table 4.0 Protective Measures Applied To A Threat Progression

CHAPTER 5

Situational Awareness

"It's not what you look at that matters – it's what you see."
Henry David Thoreau[1]

In This Chapter You Will Be Introduced To...

...the single most relied-upon protective measure used by the professionals —"situational awareness." Knowing *how* to pay attention to your immediate environment is the common denominator of all threat management principles and protective measures and as such is paramount in the world of protection. You will also be introduced to how to optimize your situational awareness by adopting the protective mindset, powering up your "radar" and knowing how to observe like the professionals.

At A Glance

Situational awareness is essentially paying attention to the details of your immediate surroundings. It also means that the more unfamiliar your surroundings the greater your attention needs to be applied.

The key to effective threat management and protection is to collect relevant information. Situational awareness is simply developing the habit of filtering out irrelevant information and collecting relevant information.

How Do I Use This In Real Life?

Choosing to adopt and optimize your situational awareness will allow you to develop the habit of observing your environment from a practical perspective.

By understanding and incorporating situational awareness into your already existing good habits you gain the capability to raise your awareness, affording you far more accurate and timely assessment and

1 *Henry David Thoreau—(b.1817 - d.1862) American author, poet and philosopher.*

appropriate response. Situational awareness enables you to assume positive control of your surroundings and use your environment as an extension of your awareness.

What The Pros Know

To identify a threat you must first be made aware of it. The very first step of the APA Process—**A**ssess requires it. The very first step in the OODA Loop—**O**bserve, requires it as does the very first step in assessment and response. Situational awareness is less about what to look for, and more about what to ignore. We receive literally millions of sensory inputs every day. We cannot possibly process them all. Learning to filter in the relevant stimuli is the key to developing situational awareness.

Developing Awareness

Developing awareness starts from a baseline level. To illustrate fundamental situational awareness, let's take an example of a responsible parent who maintains a commonly acceptable level of awareness about her children.

While mom is reading, her daughter is playing nearby. She loses control of her ball, which rolls across the park into a busy city street. Excited, the little girl runs toward the street after the ball.

Mom, acutely aware of her daughter's activities observes the potential threat and makes an accurate assessment followed by an appropriate response to avoid and prevent an actual incident. By maintaining a satisfactory level of awareness about herself and her protectee in a public place, mom was able to step in and avert a catastrophe.

To effectively apply it as a proactive measure *anywhere* along a threat progression timeline, it's necessary to build upon this fundamental level and further develop your situational awareness by first differentiating between event and threat indicators.

Event Indicators

An "event indicator" may be anything you observe about your environment that tells you what's about to happen.

Every event that occurs has indicators that precede the event. Before someone speaks, they take a breath; before someone applies the brakes, they move their foot over the brake pedal; before someone throws a punch, they make a fist. The key to situational awareness is learning to filter in the event indicators on which we can base decisions and filter out the competing background noise. You have already developed the basis of these skills throughout your life.

Developing situational awareness is simply a matter of learning which indicators to filter in and which to filter out.

It doesn't take a master spy to notice an aggressive glance, excessive observation or unusual attention from a stranger. These indicators are frequently ignored by much of society. "Don't look at him and maybe he'll go away," "if you go looking for trouble, you're sure to find it," and "I choose to see only the good in people." These attitudes are counterproductive to developing situational awareness. It takes a conscious effort to choose to observe your environment as it is, not how you want it to be.

A mother becomes acutely attuned to the sounds of her child through experience. What may sound like a cry for help to an inexperienced new mom will simply sound like a normal cry to an experienced mother.

Machinery that appears dangerous to one person is completely non-threatening to an experienced equipment operator. We are each experienced in our own environment. We got that way through systematic trial and error and learned to filter in indicators that we subsequently process and ignore those that are irrelevant. What differentiates a protective professional from most other people is they have applied the same systematic approach to learning to identify a specific range of event indicators in their everyday lives. The key to avoiding threatening situations is to become adept at identifying threatening event indicators or more precisely threat indicators.

Threat Indicators

A "threat indicator" is anything you observe about your environment triggering a concern that conditions have changed from non-threatening to threatening and needs your immediate attention.

Most of us already have the innate ability to distinguish threatening situations and threatening people from their non-threatening counterparts. We frequently exercise this ability when driving. How many times have you noticed a car swerving out of its lane? Why do those particular driver's actions capture your attention and place you on alert? Regardless of the reason, that driver is distracted and is a threat to others—including you. You are able to observe certain indicators—car swerving, other drivers reacting—which alert you that this is a threatening situation.

In short, situational awareness is remaining observant of any threat indicators and being prepared to appropriately respond.

When you identify threat indicators, it allows you to take proactive actions to avoid the threat and/or mitigate the severity of its impact—and the good news is, you already do it every day. Upon collection of this relevant information you may then accurately assess the situation based on that information. Critical to threat management—as we discussed previously—accurate assessment leads to appropriate response.

To further develop rapid and acute observation of threat indicators—which in turn results in accurate assessment and appropriate response, requires understanding the *"why,"* the *"how,"* and the *"what"* of situational awareness. Let's start with the *"why."*

Action Reaction Power Curve

An action will always occur *before* you can react to it. Reaction always follows action and is thus dependent on that action to exist. When you are reacting, you are responding to an event, which has already transpired in your immediate environment and in most cases has limited many of your options.

For example, on foot, and with the right of way at a major intersection, you step out onto the crosswalk. Suddenly, a car is headed straight for you—the event has occurred. Realizing this *event is in progress*—oncoming vehicle—you have *limited options to react to the event.* Situational awareness tells you, "This guy is headed straight for me!" which spawns the motivation to get out of the way, immediately followed by your committed effort *(response)* to get out of the path of the oncoming vehicle before impact.

Reaction can never start at the same time an event begins. When an event occurs, no matter how quickly you react, that reaction will *always* follow action placing you behind the action reaction power curve.

Reaction may begin only after an event begins and *only after you become aware of it.* The sooner you become aware the sooner you may respond. It is only by *awareness* that you are allowed response—without awareness there can be no response.

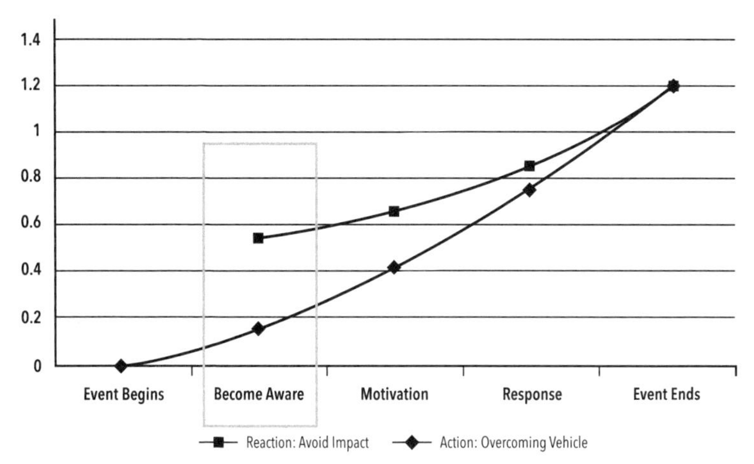

Table 5.0 The Action Reaction Power Curve—Reaction Always Follows Action

In terms of threat management and protection all observations and assessments are time sensitive efforts, meaning that the sooner you become aware of a threat the sooner you may respond to it. In fact there is a functional relationship between awareness and response—the "how" of situational awareness, giving you the decided advantage in managing or protecting against any real-world threat.

Awareness Response Relationship

The "awareness response relationship" starts with becoming aware of threat indicators. Once you learn which indicators are associated with which threats, you can act to avoid them or mitigate their impact much more effectively than if you are placed at the mercy of the action reaction power curve.

Rather than waiting for events to occur, you can use threat indicators to shape your actions which allow you to exert a measure of control over your environment, rather than reacting to events as they occur. This subtle difference is the essence of situation awareness.

For every action there is an equal and opposite reaction. If *you* take action against the threat as opposed to waiting for the threat to action against you, it places your adversary in the unenviable position of reacting to your actions and places your adversary at the mercy of the action reaction curve. Referred to in protection community parlance as "gaining and maintaining the initiative," if you are aware you can *act*. If you are unaware you can only react once you become aware, which is inherently inferior. Hence the most important part of any effective response is to first become aware.

The awareness response relationship works like this: the better and faster you can observe and the more relevant information you can collect about a threatening situation the more accurate your assessment, resulting in appropriate and timely response.

People who are "situationally aware" have a tremendous advantage over those who are "generically aware" as they have already engaged their awareness and as such gain several distinct advantages over those who don't.

They have gained the initiative in:

1. The *Action Reaction Power Curve*
2. The *Awareness Response Relationship*
3. Identification Of *Threat Indicators*
4. Effective *Assessment And Response*

The key here is to *enhance* your level of awareness. You may ask, "OK, I get all that, but how can I enhance my level of awareness? Isn't awareness a subjective term?"

Optimizing Situational Awareness

Optimization translates to further development and control. Human beings are by nature capable of collecting an incredible amount of sensory information. We cannot possibly process all of it.

Choosing to process more information is a tradeoff between volume and energy—the more information you choose to process, the more energy you will have to expend. This is especially true when we do not have the experience to filter out irrelevant event indicators and filter in the relevant threat indicators. Regardless of your experience level you cannot remain hypervigilant at all times as it's not only exhausting but effectiveness suffers and it becomes completely counterproductive. The key is choosing *when* and *where* to power up your awareness.

There are three core components available to help you develop and further control your situational awareness. They are "protective mindset," "mode skills," and "observation skills." These elements work together to help you increase or decrease your situational awareness at will, allowing you to establish an optimum level of awareness based on your environment.

Your level of awareness functions just like the volume setting on your cell phone. You control when and how much information to filter in and process. Controlling this volume allows you to monitor your environment as an extension of your awareness.

Protective Mindset

As a protective agent candidate, I was attending a certain high-profile protection course when one of my instructors shared a pearl of wisdom with our class that stuck with all of us: "Gentlemen, maintaining situational awareness is as much a state of mind as it is part of your skill set." That opened my eyes to the concept that it was as much about choosing to look for threats as it was about knowing what to look for.

In other words, we all learn from our own personal experiences, but that education begins with our viewpoint or perspective or, as my instructor would say, our *"mindset."*

The mindset of someone who chooses to optimize his or her awareness differs greatly from that of someone who does not. That stark differentiation is best illustrated by studying and understanding the essential components of the protective mindset.

There are four essential components of the protective mindset that lead to the development of awareness—these are: motivation, responsibility, reality, and acknowledgement.

1. **Motivation**—Be predisposed to win! As mentioned earlier, motivation is a critical factor in the awareness response relationship. People who have survived life-and-death threats share this same protective mindset as those who practice extreme sports. Adopting a predetermined mindset that you will prevail no matter what gives you a decisive readiness advantage over any number of real-world threats.

2. **Responsibility**—Protection is my responsibility! The need to take responsibility for our own protection is a critical component of the protective mindset. Safe and secure communities rely on responsible individuals to support that safety and security in an ever-changing

social landscape. A consequence of this changing landscape is the fact that certain inner-city police departments, understaffed and with limited resources, are forced to respond to calls at an ever slower rate and in some cases unable to respond. As concerned citizens we make the decision that we alone, not others, are ultimately responsible for protecting ourselves, our loved ones, and our communities.

3. **Reality**—Threats are real! A critical component of the protective mindset is accepting that bad things do happen to good people. Denial or ignorance of a threat indicator because you think, "Hey that stuff never happens to me," or "Oh, I can't believe this is happening to me," significantly reduces your chances of managing or protecting against a threat. Complacency, ignorance, denial or apathy toward real-world threats plays no part in the protective mindset.

4. **Acknowledgement**—Uhhh, I have this gut feeling! Just go with it. Most people ignore that initial "spider sense" or "hair raised on the back of your neck" genetic-level perception or feeling. This is a subliminal aspect of our human awareness sending you a primal warning of imminent danger. DO NOT disregard this—acknowledge it! Take advantage of this primal warning, if it doesn't feel right, smell right, sound right, look right, then it probably isn't. You're not being silly, you're being safe. It's far better to feel foolish for being too careful than suffer the repercussions of being too careless.

Adopting the protective mindset doesn't require any training other than simply your decision to adopt the protective mindset.

Mode Skills

Although critical in its effectiveness, adopting the protective mindset makes up only one-third of the three recommended elements to optimize your—situational awareness. Another component is the ability to appropriately change your state or mode of awareness based on your environment and your observations.

Each of us experiences various states of awareness or Awareness Modes based on the conditions of our environment and mindset. For example, when we are at work we switch our mental state to "work mode." Similar to changing channels on your TV, most of us employ certain filters and monitor our outward actions and appearances to ensure appropriate communications and activities in the workplace. Once we leave work and get away from the work environment we switch to "non-work mode." When on vacation we switch over to "vacation mode" and so forth.

The ability to change or switch awareness modes—"mode skills"—is what enables us to appropriately dial in the most suitable level for the applicable situation. Let's take a look at these different awareness modes and the importance of being able to switch between them at will.

A grandmother at home in the winter with the doors locked, frost on the windows and baking holiday cookies with her grandkids, finds herself in a very different state of awareness than an 18-wheel truck driver carrying a volatile payload driving in extremely hazardous ice and snow conditions on a highway. Other than her concern for the kids touching the hot cookie tray right out of the oven, she is at a very different setting than that of the truck driver who is constantly trying to avoid a catastrophe. There are varying states or modes of awareness between the two extremes.

To help illustrate the ability to change between modes there are four general modes[2] of awareness or awareness modes which can be referenced. You can think of these as "settings" that you can "click to" when powering up or down your environmental awareness radar.

Home Mode—This awareness mode can be illustrated by Grandma in the above example. She's at home, in a safe environment, the doors are locked, and the windows are closed. This mode is a very relaxed state.

There is absolutely nothing wrong with being in home mode in a relaxed environment. However, you raise the potential for problems when you assume this same mode in public, unfamiliar, or potentially unsafe environments.

Public Mode—As the title implies, this is the recommended state of awareness to assume anytime you find yourself in public, not behind the

2 *The four modes of awareness are a derivation of what I was taught long ago by one of my instructors, Col. Jeff Cooper (b. 1920 – d. 2006) who originally created them and referred to them as "Awareness Color Codes."*

safe walls of your home or a similar safe or intimately familiar nonpublic environment.

All professional first responders maintain public mode in the monitoring and awareness of their immediate environment as part of their job responsibility. There is no paranoia here—you can still enjoy a cup of coffee or a conversation with a friend. It's just a matter of powering on your radar and maintaining a very comfortable level of public awareness. You must, however, make the conscious choice to periodically observe your environment from a practical perspective, which can become a good habit.

Alert Mode—The next higher state of awareness after home mode and public mode is alert mode. In this awareness mode, something of interest has caught your attention. Registering as a blip on your radar, perhaps you noticed a shadowy figure lurking nearby. Or maybe you observed an unfamiliar car or a stranger in your neighborhood. Something looks out of place or just doesn't seem right. You enter alert mode and focus all or your attention on this potential threat to collect as much information as possible. If you confirm it's a potential threat, you take action to mitigate it. If you determine it's nothing, you go back to the appropriate mode.

Act Mode—Alert mode is also illustrated by the above example of the 18-wheeler truck driver trying to manage a potentiality hazardous situation. If another driver swerves out of control in front of him, he now enters act mode. In this mode of awareness you're looking straight down the barrel of very realistic potential threat; what had originally captured your undivided attention has now gone from a blip on the radar (in alert mode) to a confirmed clear and present threat. You now need to do everything in your power to minimize the chances of the threat impacting you or mitigate the effects of it.

Awareness Mode	*Application of Your Attention*	*Radar Setting*
Home	On an activity—TV, phone, cooking.	Radar Off
Public	On your environment.	Radar On
Alert	On a specific subject (potential threat).	Blip on the radar
Act	On your immediate physical actions.	Blinking lights and buzzers blaring

Table 5.1 Awareness Modes

Mismatching environmental and conditional changes with inappropriate awareness modes gets you into trouble. For example, some folks will stay tuned out in home mode with radar off even when walking alone to their car late at night across a poorly lit parking lot.

Still others will establish a mindset where they deny that they can be victimized, as they do not believe threats are real. They are also tuned out.

Equally as unacceptable is mismatching environmental and awareness modes at the opposite end of the spectrum. You don't want to be sharing thanksgiving with grandma while in act mode, right?

You should be able to switch modes quickly and easily to match any changes in your environment you sense. The key to honing that ability is the development of observation skills, which are covered in the next section.

Observation Skills

The next recommended component to optimizing your situational awareness is "observation skills." There is nothing more to this element than simply knowing *what* to look for and *how* to observe more accurately. Observation is also the art of filtering in threat indicators that may indicate an attack.

When you drive to the grocery store or to work or school each day, you pass any number of moving vehicles. Although you may notice there is a car in the right lane next to you, unless you observe some type of threat indicator—its color, make, model, size and position remain irrelevant. You have filtered the indicator out the millisecond you determined that is was irrelevant.

Some of the data points we collected on our drive were relevant. Stoplights, speed limit signs, and detours are all examples of relevant data that cause us to develop a plan and act on it. Filtering in relevant data allows us to create a plan. Filtering out the irrelevant data allows us to move on to the next data point. This filter is the assessment portion of the assessment and response process. The more relevant data we can filter in, the better our plan is likely to be. The better our plan, the more effective our actions are likely to be.

An observant person can accurately assess his or her surroundings by taking mental note of things that look right and don't look right. Event and threat indicators abound in the natural environment. One way to increase your observation skills is to occasionally run a basic surveillance exercise by carefully watching and taking in the surrounding environment during daily activities.

Surveillance is commonly defined as "close observation." Professionals trained in the art of surveillance exercise this skill as part of their job responsibilities, and in doing so over time develop excellent observational skills. These observation skills can be practiced on an ongoing basis, and will sharpen your assessment and response by increasing your ability to more accurately assess your environment. Doing so allows you to proactively identify threats early in the attack cycle and possibly prevent an attack.

At the earliest steps of the attack cycle predators are relegated to looking for and monitoring their targets, which makes them vulnerable to detection. This vulnerability is one of the weakest links in the attack cycle for any predator. By exploiting this weakness you are afforded the opportunity to successfully manage a threat prior to its developing into an attack.

In fact, the longer the predator spends looking or choosing or stalking his target, the greater their chances of being observed, as they must place themselves in a physical location where they can see the target and also be seen.

What are you looking for in others when you are observing? You want to look for anomalies—things that just don't fit it, things that don't look or feel right, such as someone that may be acting unnaturally or looking blatantly suspicious. It could be someone exhibiting poor demeanor in that they just don't look like they belong. If someone moves when you move—on foot or in a vehicle, avoids eye contact with you, makes sudden starts and stops or otherwise starts acting funny around you it is possible that they may be evaluating you!

When you have observed the number of people present, their activities, your distance from them and the nearest doorway, stairwell, elevator, and windows, you can use this visual information to determine an efficient exit strategy if needed. By making this determination based on your observations, you have taken visual control and harnessed your skills to use the environment to your advantage.

Having established visual control, you can then take audio control. Listen for warnings, listen to conversations, listen for gunfire, explosions, people screaming, car tires screeching. These environmental sounds, combined with visual observations, afford you a more comprehensive awareness of your immediate environment.

Electing to adopt the protective mindset or select an awareness mode, you can similarly choose to develop your observation skills whenever you're waiting in a line at the supermarket or sitting in a waiting room at the doctor's office or even for just 90 seconds while waiting at a red light.

Armed with the capability of your new observation skills, it becomes easy to survey your environment and assume positive control of your immediate surroundings. Try it sometime, you may even burn a predator at Step 1 of his attack cycle—have fun with it!

The Middle Path

The more secure you make something, the less convenient it becomes—including your lifestyle. This security vs. convenience dilemma has been around since the very first locking door. It was just as much an issue then as it is today. The key to balancing this conundrum is learning how to find the middle path.

Potential Threat	Actual Threat	**Step 1** Look	**Step 2** Choose	Verify	**Step 3** Stalk	Plan	**Step 4** Close	**Step 5** Attack

Threat Management	Unlimited Options		Limited Options	3 Options
	Maximum amount of time/ least amount of effort		Less Time/ More Effort	Least Time/ Max Effort
	Avoid		Mitigate	Defend
	Assess, Plan, Act–*The APA Process*		Assess & Respond	React
Protection	Proactive Measures		Active Measures	Reactive Measures
	Home Mode	Public Mode	Alert Mode	Act Mode

Table 5.2 Situational Awareness Applied To A Threat Progression

Optimizing your situational awareness with its three recommended elements, 1—adopting a protective mindset, 2—developing your mode skills—appropriately matching your mode with your environment, and 3—developing your observation skills, is completely a matter of personal choice and the more often you practice the sooner it becomes habit.

Deciding to take advantage of these three components affords you the benefit of scalable optimization. When dialing in your situational awareness to the level you want, there is the consideration of "how much is too much" and what would be considered "not enough." The extreme of either end of this spectrum is not without personal cost.

Your ability to maintain an optimized situational awareness predisposes you to effective response, should it be needed. However, if your dial is set too high—you anticipate a threat behind every closed door—then that's just plain paranoia! The price for being wound so tight is needless restriction of your lifestyle and unwarranted mental duress. On the other hand, if your setting is too low then you pay for it by becoming a soft target. The answer is to find which setting works for you in accordance with your environment and your current lifestyle.

CHAPTER 6

The Anatomy Of An Attack

"You have to think an awful lot about...people's behavioral intentions or what their body language can indicate or what's really going on or what makes people...do the irrational things they do."
Ron Silver[1]

In This Chapter You Will Be Introduced To...

...how to recognize and defeat an attack by exploiting the vulnerabilities of an adversary. Topics include the predator's optic, the anatomy of an attack, eliminating soft target indicators, and denying adversarial opportunity.

At A Glance

Understanding the mechanics of the anatomy of an attack, it is possible to directly influence or control attack related behaviors and disrupt the functionality of each element. After reading this chapter you will be able to answer the questions: "Why would a predator go after me as opposed to somebody else? What exactly do they look for when choosing a victim? How can I maintain control of a threatening situation?

What exactly makes a successful attack work and how can that be used to defeat the attack?

How Do I Use This In Real Life?

Either you control an attack or an attack controls you. What gives you the ability to control an attack is the combination of your understanding of the anatomy of an attack—its component parts, how they work together and how to influence them at any time.

---

1 Ronald Arthur "Ron" Silver (1946-2009) New York actor, director, producer, and talk-radio show host.

What The Pros Know

Converting yourself, your loved ones and your home into unattractive targets cause predators to shift their focus to less-protected targets. In addition to situational awareness, understanding a predator's motives and their attack-related behaviors is critical to assessing, managing and ultimately defending against any manmade threat.

Your knowledge of what a predator looks for and the other critical elements of the anatomy of an attack empower you to eliminate those indicators and defeat the attack.

Behavioral Management

Behavioral management reaches beyond mere observation and works by not only understanding the *"why,"* but also the *"how"* and the *"what"* of adversarial motives and the natural mechanics of attack related behaviors.

The "why" is the reason(s) an adversary would want go after *you, your* family, and *your* home, as opposed to your next-door neighbor.

The "how" is the mechanics of pre-attack behaviors encompassing the step-by-step behaviors of an adversary planning to carry out a successful attack against you or your family.

The "what" is the adversary's target such as you, your spouse or significant other, your kids, your home, your car, your identity, or your property.

With the desired end-result of training you to influence and ultimately *disrupt* such behavior, let's first start with taking a close look at the "why."

Why Me?

Predators observe their environment or what they call "the playing field" and collect information that they can use to make a best-guess assessment of their next potential victim—you! And any other target they estimate will make an easy mark.

But why you?

Why would an adversary or opportunistic predator come after you as opposed to your next-door neighbor?

In this case, the "why" is answered by the "how" and the "what":

1. *How* a predator views the world around him.
2. *What* a predator specifically looks for.

Let's first understand how the predator views the world.

The Predator's Optic

The professionals break down our society into two types of targets: Those who are aware that bad things do happen to good people and are prepared to do something about it are labeled "hard targets" and those who are not are labeled "soft targets."

Perception is reality and hard targets perceive real-world threats very differently than soft targets as illustrated in the following table.

Thought Process	***Perspective***	***Reason***
Bad things happen to victims.	I can make it much harder for a predator to victimize my or my family.	Educated
Bad things happen to good people.	Sooner or later it could happen to me.	Realistic view
If something bad happens.	I'm prepared to do something about it.	Responsibility
Somebody should do something.	That somebody is me.	Self-reliance
Bad things can and do happen.	I'm aware of this and ready to deal with it if need be.	I care about my personal security and that of my family.

Table 6.0 How Hard Targets View Real-World Threats

Regardless of your worldview, a predator also divides our society into the very same categories of the hard and the soft. Bad guys tend to shy away from hard targets and are drawn to soft targets, as they are much easier to victimize. This viewpoint of adversarial attraction to easier prey is called the "predator's optic."

The following statement, an excerpt from the United States Department of Homeland Security US National Strategy for the Physical Protection of Critical Infrastructures and Key Assets[2] (schools, sports arenas, malls, concert halls, high-rise residences, office buildings, places of worship, special events), further describes the predator's optic:

"[they] are relentless and patient...[they] are also opportunistic and flexible. They learn from experience and modify their tactics and targets to exploit perceived vulnerabilities and avoid observed strengths. As [protec-

2 *http://books.google.com/books?id=0l0O7fYxn_8C&pg=PR1&dq=The+National+Strategy+-for+the+Physical+Protection+of+Critical+Infrastructures+and+Key+Assets&ei=5CNTTLSp-KZq2ywS7rYiiDg&cd=1#v=onepage&q&f=false Executive Summary "Understanding the Threat", p viii*

tion] increases around more predictable targets, they shift their focus to less protected [targets]."

In plain speak—bad guys go after soft targets! Let's focus our study on what a predator specifically looks for.

Soft Target Indicators

Predators look for the path of least resistance and continually monitor the playing field for signs from potential targets to guide them down this path. When you see a turn signal on the freeway, you can respond accordingly. Similarly a predator will look for "indicators" or signals from the playing field to *indicate* which is a more suitable or *softer* target.

In a study conducted by a prison psychologist where dozens of convicted felons were interviewed, the psychologist played videos or presented several snapshots of random crowds of people in shopping malls, subway stations, and busy city streets and asked each of the inmates to point out for him the softest target in the pictures—that is the individual that they would most likely attack if given the opportunity. All responses were carefully recorded. The study concluded that nearly every inmate selected the same people in each segment for similar reasons—these reasons form the baseline definition of soft target indicators (STIs).

Examples that help describe a soft target indicator come from snippets of those recorded study responses, and include "looks sheepish," "eyes were looking down," "obviously lost," "an easy mark," "looks out of place," "not paying attention," "distracted," and the most common—"unaware of their surroundings." Soft target indicators can be anything along these lines that a predator might outwardly observe about you from his optic that sends him a clear message that you are easy prey.

As every case is unique according to its own specific set of circumstances, there are no hard and fast rules to unequivocally define a soft target indicator other than any appearance or activity that tells a predator, "Hey look over here, I'm an easy target, pick me!" Although they predominantly seek weakness, lack of awareness and exposure, throughout the remainder of this book you will be presented with details from other real-world incidents, which will provide actual case examples of soft target indicators, affording an in-depth understanding to help you avoid or eliminate them altogether.

Similarly, your car, your home and even your online presence may exhibit soft target indicators—these will be covered in following chapters.

Further illustration of personal soft target indicators via the predator's optic can be gleaned from our earlier example of a purse-snatcher where he spots an unsuspecting woman *standing alone* with her *purse easily accessible, completely absorbed* in her phone conversation and totally unaware of her surroundings—including the predator and that she hadn't realized that her cash-flashing wallet was hanging out of her purse.

In most cases two or three solid STIs are more than enough to capture the attention of a predator. Thus, per the above example, a summary list of STIs presented to a hardened street-experienced predator might read:

1. Unsuspecting Female
2. Apart From Others
3. Clearly Observable Value (cash hanging out of wallet)
4. Completely Distracted (deeply absorbed in her phone conversation)
5. Unaware Of Her Surroundings (including the predator)
6. Target (what the predator wants) is easily accessible

Remember that for every move there is a counter and for every threat there is a response so let's take a close look at how using threat management can convert you from a *soft target* to a *hard target.*

Primary And Secondary STIs

We know it's not possible to control the intentions or thoughts of a predator. However, it is possible to convert a soft target into a hard target by gaining an even deeper understanding of the soft target indicators from the predator's optic. Use this to your advantage in controlling whether or not you or your loved ones or property appear as a soft target to a predator. STIs may be further distilled into two categories:

1. **Primary Soft Target Indicators**—*awareness-based* those STIs that grab the attention of the opportunistic predator at "first glance". Primary STIs are what *initially* captures the predator's interest—you are unaware, distracted (lack of situational awareness), clearly not paying attention to your immediate surroundings, including them watching you.

2. **Secondary Soft Target Indicators**—*preparedness-based* those STIs noticed by the predator which firmly place the soft target on the selection list. Secondary STIs are what secure the predator's interest—you appear to be weak, easily accessible, exposed, or some or all of the above.

A predator may look at many potential targets and in doing so may find two or three equally suitable candidates. As he studies what appear to be three equally qualified soft targets—all whose primary soft target indicators initially caught his attention—the predator makes his final decision based on their secondary soft target indicators.

The two categories of STIs follow a rule of thumb when an opportunistic predator observes a soft target: primary soft target indicators are predominantly awareness-based, that is the outward appearance of your awareness as publicly observed by a predator.

Secondary soft target indicators are preparedness-based, that is the outward appearance of your actions or activities including the control—or lack thereof—of your personal belongings or those who may be with you—elderly, kids, et al.

Per the previous purse-grabbing example, if you were that purse-snatcher and you were viewing the above two images from the predator's optic you might observe several examples of soft target indicators, which would include:

Primary Soft Target Indicators (Awareness-based)	Distressed female.
	Standing alone away from others.
	On her cell phone - facing away from the street.
	Distracted by her conversation.
	Unaware of her surroundings.
Secondary Soft Target Indicators (Preparedness-based)	Purse is easily accessible.
	Exposed wallet - hanging out of purse.
	Cash visible in exposed wallet.

Table 6.1 Example Of Primary And Secondary STIs

Further illustrating primary and secondary soft target indicators is another real-world example of what was later reported as a corporate espionage case. A well-dressed travelling male executive was waiting for his flight at the airport.

Seated in an empty waiting area, immersed in his work, he was completely tuned out to his surroundings when he was spotted by a predator who noticed that the exec was wearing a very expensive business suit, tuned out, working on something obviously important and every now and again kept getting up and walking away from his briefcase while intently absorbed in conversation on his mobile phone. At this stage the predator was figuring out how he could abscond with the briefcase while moving to a blind spot in between surveillance cameras.

Examples of soft target indicators to a corporate espionage opportunist may include but are not limited to:

Primary Soft Target Indicators (Awareness-based)	Very well-dressed executive.
	Standing alone away from others.
	On his cell phone facing away from the crowd.
	Distracted by work and intense conversations.
	Unaware of his/her surroundings.
Secondary Soft Target Indicators (Preparedness-based)	Briefcase periodically unattended - not in his/her immediate control or vicinity
	Observable contents.
	Case and/or contents appear to be valuable.

Table 6.2 Awareness-Based STIs And Preparedness Based STIs

Eliminating Indicators

Now that we've covered the "why"—that is the reason(s) an adversary would be more attracted to you, your family, your home, as opposed to your next-door neighbor, let's take a close look at the "how." This means the inner workings or mechanics of adversarial pre-attack behaviors and how you can use this knowledge to influence and further disrupt such behaviors.

Taking Control

Taking control of anything means that you must first take control of what makes that thing work. For example controlling a car means that you control the steering wheel, the brake pedal and the gas pedal. Losing control of any one or all three of these devices would result in your losing control of the vehicle.

Conversely, gaining control of all three devices gains you control of the vehicle. Drawing an analogy from this "controlling a car" example, we can take control of a predator's behavior in much the same way by taking control of what makes up a "successful attack." To do this we must fully understand what makes an attack work. That is to identify the "steering wheel," "gas pedal," and "brake pedal" of a successful attack.

Only after you have a working knowledge of all three devices may you begin to take control of "the vehicle." Stopping an attack requires an understanding and familiarity with the anatomy of an attack—its component parts, how it all works and of course how to stop it.

Let's start with how an attack works and then we will reverse-engineer it from there.

Anatomy Of An Attack

How an attack works is much like archery. If you wanted to hit the red dot in the middle of a target with an arrow, you'd need three required items to make that happen. First, to hit a target you would need a target.

Second you would need an archer, and lastly you'd need a means by which the archer may hit the target—a process to accomplish this task—in this case working a bow and arrow.

It's important to understand that minus even one of these three items it's not possible to accomplish the task.

Target—Bad Guy—Process

The same applies to executing a successful attack. If the bad guy wants to execute a successful attack then he would need three required items:

1. A Target
2. A Bad Guy
3. A Means Or Process By Which To Carry Out That Attack

Analogous to our archery example, without any one of these three support legs it would not be possible for a bad guy to execute a successful attack. This critical piece of protective intelligence technology is something that you can use every day to help maintain that 360-degree envelope of protection.

Defeating The Anatomy Of An Attack

Remember that a bad guy has to get everything right in order to be successful in his planned attack. It only takes breaking any one of the tripod legs to defeat the anatomy of an attack.

The secret to knocking out any one or all three of these tripod legs is found in disrupting their functionality.

Listed in threat progression order, first is the target—person(s), place, or items such as your home, wallet, the World Trade Center, your laptop, purse or briefcase chosen by a plotting adversary based on soft target indicators.

Second is the bad guy who is capable, motivated and intends to carry out his attack plan—provided he is given the opportunity.

Lastly, the attack cycle—the process by which the predator has no other choice but to follow, per the mechanics of nature, in order for his attack to be successful.

Looking at these legs from a functional perspective each has certain characteristics or attributes which are essential to their functionality—that is what makes them work. The following table illustrates these characteristics, what makes them work and how to stop them from working.

Anatomy of Attack	*Characteristics or Attributes*	*Functionality - What Makes It Work*	*Disruption - What Stops It From Working*
Target	Exposed Vulnerable.	Person, Place or Thing perceived by a predator as a soft target.	**Eliminate Indicators**
Bad Guy	Motivated Capable.	Given the Opportunity.	**Deny Opportunity**
Process	Steps Of The Attack Cycle.	The only means of carrying out a successful attack.	**Break The Cycle** at any step as early as possible.

Table 6.3 Disrupting What Makes The Attack Anatomy Work

Eliminate Indicators

You can easily influence the target by eliminating its soft target indicators. Removing a target's STIs effectively removes it from the selection list of a predator who is specifically looking for them. Taking the target off that list is equivalent to knocking out a tripod leg from under the *anatomy of an attack* resulting in the defeat of that attack.

Given that it takes *all three* legs to support a successful attack, eliminating any one of them eliminates the possibility of a successful attack. You may ask "If I was able to eliminate my soft target indicators before I leave home then why should I be concerned with the other tripod legs—the bad guy or the attack cycle? Didn't I already disrupt the anatomy of an attack by converting myself from a soft target to a harder target?"

The answer is yes—you may have successfully converted yourself from a soft target to a harder target by eliminating your STIs before you left your home[3] and in doing so made yourself a less attractive target to opportunistic predators. Unfortunately, there are many other factors appealing to a predator; some of which are out of your control such as your gender, height, weight, the condition of your environment—they observe you *from their perspective* to determine weakness, awareness or if you are exposed.

Deny Opportunity

All predators are opportunistic, convenience-oriented; and are attracted to soft targets, but not all are common street thugs. Some are professional criminals, experienced repeat-offenders and determined threats such as violent thrill-seekers, psychopaths, sexual offenders, professional kidnappers and well-organized terrorists who will reach beyond ad hoc opportunity and make aggressive attempts at probing for weakness—above and beyond observable soft target indicators. In some cases they have the resources to create an opportunity where none exists prior to their intervention.

Running their OODA Loop, predators, capable and motivated to apply their craft, pose only a potential threat. Adding *opportunity* to their existing *capability* and *motivation*—is the combination that results in the decision to begin pre-attack behavior. If these behaviors are not detected and stopped they will further develop into attack behavior.

---

3 *Although believing you've eliminated all your STIs from your perspective, out of seven potential targets in an elevator a predator may have to choose from, you may still be the most appealing from his optic.*

Predators can be very cunning and motivated, and every situation is unique unto its own set of circumstances. You may have taken great care in controlling your outward appearance, eliminating your soft target indicators, but all environments are dynamic and certain variables in a dynamic environment may attract unwanted attention.

Such environmental variables—over which you don't always have control—can be a determining factor in any protective equation. In other words, the conditions of your environment can change as well as the condition of the threat.

You may very well have disrupted the *anatomy of an attack* by eliminating your soft target indicators before leaving home, at which point the attack cycle will cease to exist. When that solution works, in most cases you will never even notice its success!

However, a determined predator will use whatever means he has at his disposal, such as distraction techniques and the like to carry out his plan of attack. All he needs is the opportunity and denying him that opportunity is one key aspect that pulls the plug on his attack plans.

For example, let's take the real-world incident of three female college students attending a party after school. Arriving as part of a group, even after having taken care to eliminate any STIs before leaving their dorm, they are assuming risk. Despite these precautions, they are entering an environment in which the chances of sexual harassment and/or sexual assault are much higher than had they stayed at home (by the way I am not advocating that everyone lock themselves in their rooms, but that we all make realistic risk assessments based on our choices). The volume of date-rape drug cases is staggering and many go unreported. Knowing this allows us to create a plan that minimizes the chances of being attacked and mitigate the effect of the attack.

Our three young ladies have chosen to enter an environment where alcohol and drugs are frequently used to impair the judgment of selected targets. Knowing this provides us with three key pieces of information we can use to break the cycle.

- Impaired judgment is a key component of the problem.
- Alcohol contributes to impaired judgment.
- Drug use contributes to impaired judgment.

Date rape drugs and spiking drinks with excess alcohol is common at college parties. Regardless of whether these ladies choose to imbibe and limit their consumption, they may not be aware of the quantity ingested. Knowing this can help them create a plan to deal with this environmental risk. Lastly, physically, women are generally not able to stop a determined male attacker. Being alone in this environment may well result in being selected for sexual assault.

In order to be successfully attacked by the common means of attack at college parties there are three factors that will create opportunity:

1. Isolation.
2. Intentional alcohol or drug use.
3. Unintentional alcohol or drug use.

We can remove these opportunities by:

1. Staying together with the group.
2. Not drinking or assigning one of the groups to stay sober and monitor the other two.
3. Maintaining physical control over their drinks, drugs, and/or ingestion mechanisms (pipes, syringes, etc.) at which point number 2 becomes even more critical.

If one of these three young women is aware, in control of her faculties and ensuring the other two adhere to their plans, their chances of being successfully attacked is reduced dramatically for two reasons. First, the opportunities to attack this group has been reduced or eliminated. Second, there is a high likelihood that there will be many easier opportunities at the party who are more likely to have been selected.

Opportunity to the predator is critical to his successful attack.

You can influence the bad guy by denying any opportunity, which disrupts his planning. Being denied an opportunity means that the bad guy cannot move to the next step in the attack cycle. Disrupting the functionality of this tripod leg results in the defeat of a successful attack.

Break The Cycle

In the previous examples you can see that influencing either the target or the bad guy defeats two out of the three supporting legs—and you only need to break one for the anatomy of an attack to collapse. However, given that every case is unique unto its own set of circumstances based on adversarial motives and ever-changing environmental dynamics, you cannot determine every possible variable.

In certain circumstances the options of eliminating soft target indicators and denying opportunity may have been absent, or the opportunity missed, or it wasn't effective, or you were engaged by a determined adversary in which case you may need to disrupt the attack cycle itself—the third and final option of defeating an attack.

You can break the process by exerting your influence along any step of the attack cycle by using proactive, active or reactive measures to disrupt the predator's only means of carrying out his intentions. Learning how to do this is covered in its entirety in the next chapter.

CHAPTER 7

Breaking The Attack Cycle

"We need others to say 'no' to unacceptable behavior."
Jan Peter Balkenende[1]

In This Chapter You Will Be Introduced To...

...how you can break the attack cycle at each step along the threat progression using proactive, active and reactive measures.

At A Glance

Impacting the steps of an attack cycle provides you with the ability to stop an attack at any point—the sooner the better. Working knowledge of the concepts and measures presented in this chapter enable you to successfully influence attack related behaviors, putting you in the driver's seat in defeating a planned attack.

How Do I Use This In Real Life?

Almost anyone has either personally experienced or knows of others who have experienced the devastating effects of personal violence. Fortunately, empowered with the information in this chapter you can dramatically reduce the chances that you will become a victim. The very best way is to break the attack cycle as soon as possible.

What The Pros Know

Your ability to influence the individual steps of the attack cycle enables you to break them at any time resulting in the defeat of an attack.

---

1 Jan Peter Balkenende former Prime Minister of the Netherlands 2002 – 2010 and Professor of Political Science at the Eramus University Rotterdam.

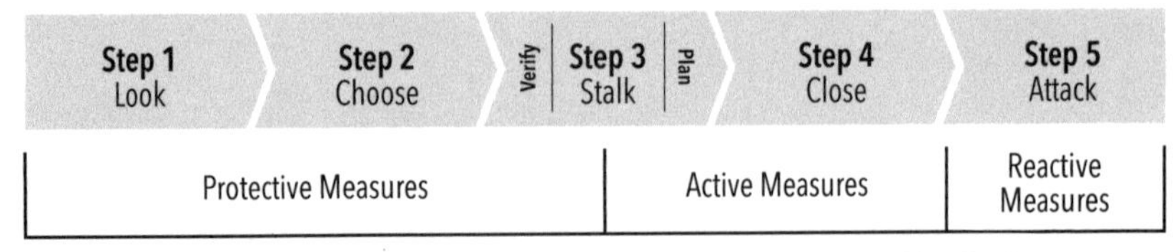

Table 7.0 Three Types Of Protective Measures To Break The Cycle

Throughout the attack cycle you have at your disposal three types of protective measures—proactive, active, and reactive that you may use to break the cycle at any step along the way. Let's start with the first of these—proactive measures.

Proactive Measures

Beginning at "Step 1—Look," running all the way through and including the first half of "Step 3—Stalk/Verify," and in public mode you have the opportunity to avoid the threat entirely by applying proactive measures.

You can take advantage of unlimited options and opportunity by using the likes of situational awareness and the APA Process to help you eliminate soft target indicators.

Step 1 Look · Step 2 Choose · Verify · Step 3 Stalk
Unlimited Options
Maximum amount of time/ least amount of effort
Avoid
Assess, Plan, Act–*The APA Process*
Proactive Measures
Public Mode

Breaking The Attack Cycle At Step 1

The *very best* time to break the attack cycle is at the earliest stages of the cycle—specifically at Step 1—Look, when the predator is scanning the playing field for primary soft target indicators in his search for prey. At this earliest stage of the attack cycle you are afforded plenty of time and the least amount of effort needed to proactively eliminate the appearance of soft target indicators.

To illustrate this, let's take the example of a real-world physical assault case. At the time of this writing there was a case of a well-dressed young woman carrying multiple shopping bags in each hand who decided to walk alone on a deserted street in an unfamiliar area. Allegedly she was in a hurry because it was getting dark and she thought she should take what she considered to be a quick shortcut to her destination.

The predator, at Step 1—Look, already in the process of searching for an optimal soft target in this particular unsavory neighborhood, was scanning the street looking for his next victim. He observed the woman, who appeared unfamiliar with her environment, was walking alone at dusk, appeared to be lost and—as he determined by her well-dressed physical appearance, affluent. She also had both of her hands full of department store bags. She appeared uncomfortable and had a worried look on her face. The predator's search is over as he has found his prey.

What was the predator's optic and why did he continue on to Step 2—Choose? What made him settle on this particular soft target was that she exhibited not only one or two but at least a half-dozen soft target indicators:

Primary Soft Target Indicators (Awareness-based)	Appears to be uncomforable.
	Appears to be distracted.
	Appears to be in an unfamiliar environment
	Appears to be distraught.
	Appears to be trapped and looking for a way out.
Secondary Soft Target Indicators (Preparedness-based)	Walking alone at dusk in bad area of town.
	Carrying many department store shopping bags.
	Both her hands are occupied.

Table 7.1 Primary And Secondary Soft Target Indicators As Viewed By The Predator

The woman could have easily applied the APA Process, and taken a few seconds to evaluate her travel itinerary. Based on her assessment she could have made a new plan and then the wise decision to act by avoiding the threat area altogether.

Armed with her knowledge of the attack cycle and soft target indicators and how they work, she could have determined it wouldn't be such a great idea to walk alone down an isolated dark alley.

Between Steps 1 and 2 is your very best option to avoid the threat altogether. This can be accomplished by taking the time to appropriately prepare for any anticipated activity. Failing this it is still possible to remain in public mode and use your observation skills to monitor your environment and continue to make yourself an unattractive target.

Step No.	*Step*	*Soft Target Indicator*	*Predator's Optic*
1.	Look	Primary STI	Target Appearance
2.	Choose	Secondary STI	Target Condition

Table 7.2 Relationship Of Attack Cycle Steps To The Predator's Optic

Breaking The Attack Cycle At Step 2

The predator, upon completing Step 1—Look, moves on to Step 2—Choose when he identifies secondary STIs, as she is alone, carrying many bags and with both her hands occupied. The predator is now ready to move to the next step in the cycle.

The victim failed to realize she was a potential target. She didn't know anything about the attack cycle, primary soft target indicators, secondary soft target indicators, or the predator's optic. She didn't know that she could have converted herself from a soft target to a hard target in less than a few seconds by eliminating soft target indicators.

How could this woman have stopped the predator at Step 2—Choose and prevented being a victim? At any time she could have applied her situational awareness—clicked her radar into public mode, stopped and easily removed a few soft target indicators.

She could have walked toward other people or a well-lit area, blended in to a nearby restaurant or store or called a friend. Had she known the mechanics of the attack cycle used situational awareness and taken proactive measures she would have avoided presenting the soft target indicators that got her in trouble.

Learning from your own experience is one thing but how much more beneficial to learn from the experience of others. Understanding how to convert and control an attack enables you to avoid presenting primary and secondary soft target indicators to a potential threat, thus gaining the ability to break the cycle at Steps 1 and 2.

Breaking The Attack Cycle At Step 3 (Verify)

If for some reason you have failed to stop the attack cycle at Step 1 or at Step 2, there is still a pretty good chance for you to stop it at the first half of Step 3—Stalk/Verify, using the same proactive measure of eliminating soft target indicators.

Late at night on October 7, 1998, two strangers approached 21-year-old university student Matthew Shepard at a public lounge and offered him a ride home. Accepting their offer he clearly verified for these predators that he was in fact a qualified candidate. The two assailants drove Shepard to a remote rural area and proceeded to rob, pistol-whip and torture him by tying him to a fence and leaving him to die.

Shepard suffered fractures to the head, severe brainstem damage, and his injuries were too extensive for doctors to operate. Shepard, the victim of a hate crime, then in a coma, was pronounced dead on October 12, 1998.

Matthew Shepard was harassed by members of his class for his sexual orientation. He was aware of the fact that he was not accepted by certain members of the community. At the point they were offering him a ride they were in the last half of their stalk phase having confirmed he was the right victim and planning to move to the next step.

Let's take a look at another example. If we are aware of Step 1—Stalk/Verify of an attack cycle, we can maintain our situational awareness as in this case of a would-be child abduction, where a pedophile cruising in the vicinity of an elementary school in a pickup truck, was searching for an optimal target at Step 1.

He noticed what appeared to him to be a soft target walking alone about to walk under a bridge.

Taking into consideration what appeared to be several soft target indicators—young child, alone, walking under a bridge in a secluded area—he made his selection—Step 2—Choose, and he began to stalk the unsuspecting child—Step 3—Stalk/Verify.

He was then planning for his best attack—Step 2—Stalk/Plan—when the elementary school girl using her situational awareness noticed the stranger which triggered a proactive measure provided by her mother: "Don't talk to strangers and never walk alone—always walk with someone else when you can—preferably an adult."

Running her OODA Loop and observing the stranger, the young girl, oriented to her precarious situation and remembering the words of her mom, instantly ran away from the bridge and found another child to walk with, this time on the sidewalk and near other adults in the neighborhood on the way home.

In this example, even though she eventually did observe the predator, she had unknowingly fallen victim to Step 1—Look and Step 2—Choose, and was at the very beginnings of Step 3—Stalk/Verify.

However, because of her maintaining her situational awareness she hardened herself against the attack by finding companions and adult attention, successfully breaking the attack cycle at Step 3.

Active Measures

Given less time and requiring more effort, now past midway of the attack cycle you are afforded limited options and opportunity to break the cycle from the latter half of Step 3—Stalk/Plan, all the way through and including all of Step 4—Close, to mitigate the threat.

You can take advantage of this opportunity by using active measures such as assessment and response and situational awareness to deny a predator his or her opportunity.

Step 3 Stalk | Plan	Step 4 Close
Limited Options	
Less Time/ More Effort	
Mitigate	
Assess & Respond	
Active Measures	
Alert Mode	

Breaking The Attack Cycle At Step 3 (Plan)

Immediately after the point where a predator has verified that you are indeed his confirmed target, you are no longer afforded the proactive measure of eliminating soft target indicators as he moves to the latter half of Step 3 in which he devises his plan of attack to close in on you and complete his successful attack.

Breaking The Attack Cycle At Step 4

It is possible to break the attack cycle and therefore throw a wrench into the predator's plans at any time; however, the earlier you handle it the more likely you are to succeed.

The initial step of the attack cycle also provides the best opportunity to stop it. If you don't catch the attack cycle until the second step, your opportunities are still excellent. By the time you get to the onset of Step 3—Stalk, your options are still pretty good, believe it or not, as you still have a sufficient amount of time, options and opportunity to use proactive measures.

However, if the attack cycle is allowed to run its course toward the latter part of Step 3—Stalk/Plan through Step 4—Close those options and opportunities to break it are significantly reduced in time and increased in effort because of the timeline accelerating toward the final steps.

Additionally, you are no longer afforded the opportunity of utilizing proactive measures and are relegated to active measures at best. One of these active measures is to *deny opportunity.*

There are 4 general categories of active measures that deny opportunity:

1. Deter—discourage any threat efforts
2. De-escalate—reduce the intensity of a threat
3. Deflect—distract a threat
4. Defuse—stop the progression of a threat

An easy way to remember these is "The Four D's"—for *deny opportunity!* Let's take a look at how they work at Step 4—Close of the attack cycle.

> **Deter**—If I am driving and have to stop my car, at which point I see anyone approaching for any reason, simply rolling up the car windows, and locking the doors is active deterrence.
>
> **De-escalate**—Active de-escalation is demonstrated by a man and his friend who stepped out of a bar pausing to have a cigarette before heading home for the night. A heavily intoxicated and belligerent patron also outside began to give them a rough time. Assessing the distance between them and his car, the man interrupted the aggressive dialogue between his friend and the unknown patron, excused them both politely and urged his friend to his car.
>
> When questioned by his friend as to why he didn't use his self-defense training to make the drunk leave them alone, he replied, "*I did use it. I was able to stay calm and assess the situation. I saw that we had a possible escape from what could be a bad situation without escalating it. One thing I learned from these classes is that once you go physical, anything can happen.*[2]"
>
> **Deflection**—in an example of deflection; a woman, waiting for a bus, was approached by a stranger

2 *Source: http://www.impactboston.com/impack-success.html—Assessing the Situation, A Man's Success Story.*

asking the time. She provided an answer; however, he continued to approach. She made a comment about the police car she just saw and how safe it makes her feel to see so many of them in the area. She can challenge him with a clear and direct "back off!" statement—not what a predator expects from a soft target. She can comment on his appearance, which will subconsciously acknowledge that she will be able to identify him to police. Something as simple as: "You look exactly like my brother, except he has a scar under his right eye, same brown hair, same hazel eyes, and almost identical frown lines." Anything that forces the attacker to reevaluate his decision to complete Step 4—Close is use of deflection. The bus arrived, she boarded and he did not[3].

Defuse—The following covers an example of defusion in everything our three young ladies at the party (hopefully) chose to do. Let's see how that works at Step 4. Despite their best efforts, a predator has chosen one of the women and is actively looking to separate her from her two friends. He may use his buddies to assist him or any number of other means at his disposal. Assuming he has somehow been successful, and she is not alone with the would-be attacker, she can further deflect him by simply explaining that her friends and she are concerned about exactly this type of situation, and she must return immediately or they will not only look for her, but also call the authorities.

Reactive Measures

Given the least amount of time and requiring maximum effort, now at the very last step of the attack cycle you are afforded only three options and limited opportunity to break the cycle at Step 5—Attack to defend against the threat.

You can take advantage of these three options by using reactive measures and situational awareness to either get away from, temporarily fight or surrender to your assailant(s).

3 Source: http://www.strategicliving.org/success-stories.php—Beth: Telling a Stranger to Back off

Breaking the Attack Cycle At Step 5

The longer it takes for you to identify and manage a threat, the greater its chance of progressing into an undesirable incident. In fact, once the attack occurs you can no longer break the cycle—only react to it with your physical skills. You might overcome it or you might not, but the physical risk is certainly elevated. Up to that point you have proactive and active measure options to break the cycle. Once you hit Step 5, however, the cycle is complete—you can no longer break it, only defeat the attack or become victim to it.

Step 5 Attack
3 Options
Least Time/ Max Effort
Defend
React
Reactive Measures
Act Mode

At this very late and final step you are faced with a physical attack and have only three remaining options—all of which are considered reactive response.

Flight, Fight Or Freeze

Stuck in the last 10% of the attack cycle, your only three options are listed in order of best to least effective:

1. **Flight**—involves running away with the goal being to place as much distance and if possible objects between yourself and the threat while moving to a more advantageous location.

2. **Fight** (or counterattack)—meaning do whatever it takes — using whatever tools are at your disposal—to put yourself in a condition where you can eventually move away.

3. **Freeze**—submit, give up, surrender. If you were able to run a short distance, hiding may be a suitable version of "freeze," but it is by far the least preferred response and nearly always leads to the attack being completed.

The first option, flight, is the safest because it immediately lowers your risk of physical harm and provides you with more space and time to solve the problem. Tossing the cash from your wallet on the ground in front of a robber and moving away is likely to eliminate physical harm from the equation.

The second option, fight,—although increasing your potential for physical harm due to proximity—is still only temporary, and if properly trained only momentary. The goal of fighting is to give you the opportunity to use your best reactive measure—flight—get away. The first and second options—flight or fight—result in the most beneficial outcome.

The least beneficial is to freeze.

If you freeze, you are subjecting yourself to the whims of the attacker, and relying on their mercy. We have no natural defenses and must use our most powerful weapon—our mind and its ability to make us safe. Even if you freeze, it does not limit your ability to attempt to mitigate or minimize the impact of the attack by using your verbal skills and conversing with the assailant.

Armed with situational awareness and your working knowledge of how and when to break the attack cycle at any step along the way using proactive, active and reactive measures—you now know how to defeat a successful attack.

<table>
<tr><th></th><th>Potential Threat</th><th>Actual Threat</th><th>Step 1 Look</th><th>Step 2 Choose</th><th>Verify Step 3 Stalk Plan</th><th>Step 4 Close</th><th>Step 5 Attack</th></tr>
<tr><td rowspan="4">Threat Management</td><td colspan="5">Unlimited Options</td><td>Limited Options</td><td>3 Options</td></tr>
<tr><td colspan="5">Maximum amount of time/
least amount of effort</td><td>Less Time/
More Effort</td><td>Least Time/
Max Effort</td></tr>
<tr><td colspan="5">Avoid</td><td>Mitigate</td><td>Defend</td></tr>
<tr><td colspan="5">Assess, Plan, Act–The APA Process</td><td>Assess & Respond</td><td>React</td></tr>
<tr><td rowspan="3">Protection</td><td colspan="5">Proactive Measures</td><td>Active Measures</td><td>Reactive Measures</td></tr>
<tr><td colspan="2">Home Mode</td><td colspan="3">Public Mode</td><td>Alert Mode</td><td>Act Mode</td></tr>
<tr><td colspan="5">Eliminate Soft Target Indicators</td><td>Deny Opportunity</td><td>Flight, Fight, Freeze</td></tr>
</table>

Table 7.3 Breaking The Attack Cycle As applied To A Threat Progression

CHAPTER 8

Defensive Principles

"There is no approved solution to a tactical situation."
George S. Patton[1]

In This Chapter You Will Be Introduced To...

...how to more effectively respond to a threat at this last stage of the attack cycle—which inherently takes more effort, increases your risk, and significantly decreases your options and opportunity. There are no rules and you certainly don't want to rely on either hope or luck to provide you with protection solutions because they won't—but you can rely on established defensive principles.

This chapter adds recommended protective concepts such as the scale of injury, the reactionary gap, and the two-second rule to your ever expanding personal security toolkit. Also introduced are the reactive measures of moving off the "X," and having a plan, to give you that last minute decisive advantage in effective reactive response.

At A Glance

Finding yourself at the end of the attack cycle means the attacker has now moved in on you and it would be very helpful to have a few extra tools in your kit to solve the problem. Well, you've turned to the right page.

Yes, your timeline of options and opportunity is significantly compressed. Yes, the attack cycle, further progressing toward the latter steps has carried you across a line where your options and opportunity are diminished and you are relegated to the application of only three remaining options. But fortunately, there exists a repository of established protective guidelines—defensive principles, which can help tilt the scales in your favor toward the most beneficial outcome of engaging in a physical attack.

1 *George Smith Patton, Jr. (November 11,1885–December 21, 1945) was a general in the United States Army, best known for his command of the US Army in the European Theater of World War II.*

How Do I Use This In Real Life?

Armed with your understanding and working knowledge of the additional defensive measures and skills presented in this chapter, you gain greater capability to directly confront the rapidly unfolding conditional changes of a physical attack.

What The Pros Know

Step 5
Attack

3 Options
Least Time/ Max Effort
Defend
React
Reactive Measures
Act Mode
Flight, Fight, Freeze

Even though you may only have three remaining options and the least amount of time requiring the maximum amount of effort—you can still stack the odds in your favor by arming yourself with reliable defensive principles to assist in your running away, fighting or surrendering.

In reality, when it comes down to the dreaded ten percent, there are no rules. If you decide or it's decided for you by the bad guy or the threat environment—you suddenly find yourself at the dead end of an attack cycle, then it will happen without a referee or a rulebook. Limited only by the creativity and cunning of your adversary, the event will unfold rapidly allowing you very little response time or options.

However, there are established sets of defensive principles that can be used as guidelines to assist with those few remaining options so let's take a close look at each one in detail.

Scale Of Injury

In the event of a physical attack, it is imperative to keep your bodily injuries, and that of those who may be with you, to a minimum. In any physical altercation, injury can be a significant factor. To minimalize personal injury, it's important to understand what you may be up against.

In any physical struggle, there exists the potential for five levels of injury. This is referred to as the "scale of injury" with the lowest being *no* injury, which is of course the most desirable outcome and exactly how you'd want to walk away from any physical encounter.

The next level up from no injury is a minor injury such as bruises, scratches, minor cuts or abrasions; these are uncomfortable and inconvenient but still better than the next level up on the scale, which is a recoverable injury, such as a broken leg, broken arm, broken nose, and the like.

Up one more rung on the scale is a permanent injury, which would include such horrific results as blindness, paralysis, or maiming for life. The last and final step in the scale of injury is a fatal injury—death—your worst-case scenario.

No Injury	Minor Injury	Recoverable Injury	Permanent Injury	Fatal Injury

Your goal in managing any threat engagement throughout the attack cycle, especially at the dreaded ten percent, is to keep any injuries as low on the scale as possible—preferably at the lowest.

Distance-Injury Relationship

The amount of physical distance between yourself and an adversary is a critical factor with regard to your potential injury. A guy in New York City with a shovel in his hand trying to smack you in the face with it will have a heck of a time if you're located in Los Angeles. The distance is too great and there's *no way* he could reach you.

Now put that same guy with his shovel right across the street from you. Although your awareness mode may shift from public mode to alert mode, at this distance he still can't reach you.

Now bring him and his shovel to the distance where you could hold a normal conversation. Not only would you switch from alert mode to act mode, but at this closer distance he can now make contact with you. It is at this conversational distance—otherwise referred to as "contact range," where you could potentially incur injury as all he needs to do is reach out with that shovel and smash your hand.

If he steps in closer to you and takes away even more distance—instead of smashing your hand he's now close enough to break your elbow—a recoverable injury which is the next rung up on the scale of injury. If he steps even closer and smashes it full force against the side of your head just above your ear, this could raise your scale of injury to fatal.

Although a somewhat graphic example, it clearly illustrates the direct relationship between distance and injury or the distance-injury relationship—the closer the physical threat, the greater the potential to incur physical injury.

Reactionary Gap

Aside from a firearm, which can reach out and hit you from well over a thousand yards with accuracy—depending the type of weapon system, any other non-ballistic weapon requires close-range contact to be effective in raising your scale of injury.

Referencing any non-ballistic weapon, the relationship between distance and injury severity is similar to the relationship between distance and time to react. The lesser the space between you and the threat, the less time you have to respond. Conversely the greater the space, the greater the amount of response time. Remember the action reaction power curve? In a nutshell, reaction can only follow an action, and there is a measurable amount of time between an event occurring and any response to that event.

To further illustrate this principle, consider a baseball player in center field who observes that the batter has hit the ball. He watches the ball's trajectory from the point of impact up and over the field toward his location. Because of this greater amount of space he has plenty of time to react and may even need to wait patiently for the ball to come down before catching it in his glove.

The very next play, however, the pitcher may have only a split second to duck out of the way of a ball the batter has drilled straight at him!

This demonstrates the relationship between distance and time. Because the ball traveled through such a great amount of distance the outfielder had plenty of *time* to react to the ball and catch it—whereas the pitcher, due to the tremendous speed of the incoming projectile, had very little time to react.

The more distance you have, the more time you have to react; the less distance available the less time you have to react. This is known as the "reactionary gap."

If someone moves physically as close to you as to have a normal verbal conversation between two people, they have made three changes on the playing field. They have:

1. Closed the reactionary gap.
2. Positioned themselves at a distance where they are capable of making contact with your body, or "moved to contact range," in protection parlance.
3. Increased the potential for raising your scale of injury

The instant an adversary is positioned at a distance where they can make physical contact with your body—"contact range"—is the same instant that your potential for injury increases. In any threat environment there are only two distances or ranges that you can be from a threat:

1. **Non-Contact Range**—that distance which provides you the most space and time and is outside the potential for increasing your scale of injury.
2. **Contact Range**—that distance where you could have a normal verbal conversation between two people—"*conversational range.*" This is the exact physical distance where you move from the safety of "no injury" to the potential of "minor injury" on the scale of injury.

The safer of these two in terms of physical threat management is obviously non-contact range. Your knowledge of the distance-injury relationship and the reactionary gap will give you the advantage in managing a physical threat at conversational ranges.

Two Second Rule

Part and parcel of the reactionary gap is another important protective concept known as the "two-second rule." We've all heard the common phrase, "Keep it simple," right? In the world of professional protection keeping it simple is mandatory. Complex solutions have more moving parts that may fail in any situation, especially under duress.

If you need to get to an exit in a crowded restaurant, we know a straight line is the shortest distance between two points. When confronted by an adversary, the quicker you effectively respond the more of an advantage you gain. If you happen to be engaged by an adversary at conversational ranges, your immediate reaction should take no less than two seconds.

If you can't pull off a response in less than two seconds then it's probably not going to work.

Professionals place a maximum timeline of less than two seconds as part of any effective response. It is strongly recommended that you take advantage of this important rule of thumb by adding it to your growing repository of protective concepts.

Changing Conditions

Know what to expect. A boxer expects to get hit in the face with the gloves of his opponent, a police officer expects to arrest law-breaking subjects, and a firefighter expects to put out a raging blaze. Each of these professionals is conditioned, inoculated, and accustomed to these anticipated threats. The same applies to protection professionals, who are trained to expect the unexpected and are prepared to handle it.

Maintaining situational awareness provides you the advantage of an early warning system for potential threats. It allows you to accurately observe your environment, change awareness modes, use your observation skills as needed and even adjust your own thoughts and actions by raising or lowering your dial based on the conditions of your environment. You may widen the scope of application of these same skills to detect and monitor the continually changing conditions in your environment.

In any real-world threat scenario there are always three conditions that change continuously:

1. Condition Of Your Environment
2. Condition Of Your Threat
3. Condition Of Yourself (and those who may be with you)

Because conditions change constantly—as rapidly as within fractions of a second—it's important not only to observe these changes, but follow your natural OODA Loop and orient yourself to them. If needed you may also make some decisions about them, such as "I'll need to go down that hallway toward the back door, then I need to get to the car, and then..."

Move Off The "X"

The single most critical reactive measure available is the "Distance is your friend" concept. Professionals know that the safest place to be in any physical altercation is as far away from the threat as possible. They make every possible proactive, active and reactive effort to gain distance between the threat and themselves.

Whenever presented with the option to either engage or disengage from a threat, the safer of the two is to disengage—that is, get out of that bad situation as quickly as possible.

By increasing the reactionary gap between yourself and a threat you accomplish three things:

1. You create more space, which allows you more reaction time.
2. You use distance to place yourself outside contact range, which lowers your scale of injury.
3. You disengage from a threat as opposed to engaging, which is far less safe.

Whether your threat is a single adversary, multiple adversaries, or even a natural disaster, the very best response you can have is to immediately get away and increase your reactionary gap.

Although not always the case, usually your very best and most immediate response to a threat is to get away. The professionals call this "moving off the X." Whether using a gas pedal or your two feet you literally "move off the X."

"I get why it's best to disengage and take advantage of creating distance," you may say, "but what in the world is an X"?

In the world of theater, the X is a mark—usually made from two crossed pieces of tape on the ground or the stage floor—upon which the actors are required to stand. That exact spot is where all efforts and energies are focused; right there on that X. The same applies to the protective environment. When faced with a threat, the exact spot where you are located in time and space is where all the action happens.

Military and law enforcement professionals use the term "exfiltration" which means to *get out* or get yourself off the X and move away from the threat as rapidly as you can.

Regardless of the type of threat or where you find yourself in the attack cycle, your good habits and situational awareness will take over, and utilizing your observation skills you will realize that you're standing on that fateful X. Using this reactive measure as an immediate response option, you can quickly move off the X and toward safety.

Why Move Off The X? The longer you stand there on the X, the deeper you fall into the attack cycle. As we have already seen, the further along in the attack cycle the more difficult it is to defeat it.

Always Have A Plan

To defeat the attack cycle in the later steps, it's important to be able to make a plan in immediate response to imminent danger. It doesn't need to be an elaborate ten-step process and it doesn't need to be written down. In fact, most immediate-response action plans are made up on the fly and are often split-second decisions. Such instantaneous planning should be used to accomplish one simple objective at a time such as get to the door, go up the stairs, run into the hallway, get back to the car, and so on.

Developing a plan can happen in a matter of seconds. Sometimes your plan may be contingent upon the actions of others—if *this* happens, then I'm going to do *that* and if *that* happens, I'm going to do *this*. For example, someone you feel looks out of place causes you to switch to alert mode as you observe him enter the convenience store where you happen to be shopping. Running your OODA Loop you decide, "If anything happens I'll move behind that wall and out the door!"

Hope and luck are nice to have on your side but they have never been part of any successful plan. Follow the OODA Loop! Plan to use your natural attributes such as your physical size, strength, speed, or agility. Use your non-physical training and skills such as the protective mind-set, situational awareness, observational skills and take advantage of the opportunity to use denial techniques to defuse or de-escalate a threat, or distract an adversary just enough to move yourself and your loved ones off that fateful X.

Your ability to instantly create a plan gives you that much more of an advantage if ever you may need to get out of a bad situation.

In addition to these recommended defensive principals, there are a number of physical protection tools available to support these concepts and measures, which are covered in the next chapter.

CHAPTER 9

Physical Protection Tools

"You can never be sure exactly what collection of problems you're going to face... That's why you need your whole toolbox in front of you."
Donald F. Kettl[1]

In This Chapter You Will Be Introduced To...

...physical protection tools classified into six basic categories, with each category supporting a specific application of your protective knowledge and skills. You will also be introduced to warning devices, focusing on the value of threat detection and deterrence.

At A Glance

Part and parcel of your personal security includes physical hand-held tools, which complement and support your ongoing protective efforts. Such tools are classified into six basic categories: communication, illumination, navigation, carry, warning devices, and weapons. The decision to carry any daily carry tools is a personal one. Of course you don't *need* to carry anything besides perhaps the key to your front door, but as no decision is without consequence, when you really need one of these tools and don't have it, well, you don't have it.

How Do I Use This In Real Life?

Understanding and implementing the fundamentals of protection empowers you with the knowledge and skills essential to your protection. These may be further supported with physical protection tools that are applicable to a wide range of personal security situations such as needing to exit a building or alerting others.

---

1 Donald F. Kettl is Dean of the School of Public Policy and a nonresident senior fellow at the Brookings Institution. Prior to his appointment, he was the Robert A. Fax Leadership Professor at the University of Pennsylvania and Professor of Political Science. The quote is from his book "System Under Stress: Homeland Security and American Politics," 2ND Edition (Public Affairs and Policy Administration Series).

Armed with your understanding and working knowledge of these tools, you gain the capability to fully support your everyday protective efforts. It is with these physical tools, which are strongly recommended by the professionals, that you can help make and keep your family and yourself safe.

What The Pros Know

The purpose of protection is to be prepared for and effectively manage any threat situation, with the desired outcome of maintaining that 360-degree envelope of protection around yourself and your protectee(s). To help accomplish this task, it is sometimes necessary to employ certain physical tools.

Physical Protection Tool Categories

You can compare the use of these physical protection tools, as applied to the support of your personal security, to the use of a sewing machine by a tailor or a hammer by a carpenter. As such it's important to understand the tools of each category and their function as applied to your protection efforts.

Category		*Applications*
1	Communication	Tools to send and receive important information.
2	Illumination	Tools to provide you artificial light sources.
3	Navigation	Tools to determine your location and movement.
4	Carry	Tools to support your physical movement
5	Warning Devices	Tools to support your efforts to detect and deter a physical attach in breaking the cycle at Step 4.
6	Weapons	Tools to support your reactive efforts to stop a physical attack in breaking the cycle at Step 5.

Table 9.0 Physical Protection Tool Categories

Communication Tools

Essential to every branch of the military, law enforcement, and federal protective services, communication is paramount in emergency response.

Trained at the highest levels to "shoot, move and communicate," very experienced professionals know that sending and receiving relevant information in a timely manner is an essential part of any effective strategy. Whether it is a simple hand signal to the person next to you, a shout to the kids "Hey, watch where you're going!" or dialing 911 in an extreme emergency, communication is critical in alerting others.

The most common method of communication is by cell phone. Provided that the battery is charged and you have a good signal, the cell phone should instantly connect you to people all over the globe. If you lose your cell phone, run out of battery life, or can't get a signal, then your cell phone essentially becomes a paperweight and you lose your primary communication resource.

To ensure battery life, carry at least one fully charged backup battery for certain mobile phones and/or be sure to keep the current battery charged. Take a charging cable with you. Leave it accessible when you go to bed at night, and carry it with you while traveling.

Many cellular service providers offer international packages that can keep you connected worldwide. Prior to travel you should contact your cell phone provider to confirm your cell phone coverage in the areas you will be travelling. An alternative to the cell phone w/ regards to foreign or remote area travel is the satellite phone, which provides greater range and options for connectivity.

Pay phones are well on their way to extinction, but cannot be discounted from your list of options. You may also have access to landlines. Landline phones in some countries depending upon location may not have long distance capability. It's vital to survey and confirm your communication options prior to travel.

Another recommended communications proactive measure is to store a contact number or numbers **I**n **C**ase of **E**mergency. The idea is that you plug the word "**ICE**" into your cell phone contacts and include the number of the person you would want to be contacted "in case of emergency." In an emergency situation, ambulance and/or hospital staff will be able to quickly find your next of kin or significant other and contact them in the event you are unable to do so.

Illumination Tools

Illumination or "artificial light source" tools include everything from keychain lights to chem-lights to flashlights. Next to communication, illumination is the most critical piece of equipment that should be part of your everyday protection package. Military, law enforcement, and protection professionals alike consider their flashlights essential to their job responsibilities.

Aside from the fact that it gets dark every single night, even in broad daylight there are many homes and buildings that are without windows or skylights.

In the event of a power outage, inclement weather, or a disaster involving dust, smoke, ash or other conditions impairing your visibility, a reliable flashlight with a strong light and power source offers the best protection solution.

Interviews with personnel who were on-site and survived the attacks on the World Trade Center in NYC in 2001 reveal that if other victims had had illumination tools such as glow sticks or flashlights, some of them would likely have been able to navigate through the thick ash to safety.

Certain quality flashlights can also be used in self-defense for both temporary visual impairment and physical detection of the bad guy, if needed. A quality flashlight will allow you one-hand or hands-free operation so your hands are available for more important activities and you can remain completely functional under duress.

When selecting a flashlight consider both form and function. It's strongly recommended that you have at least one flashlight in every room of your home and at least one that is easily accessible in your car. The flashlight you carry on your person should be lightweight, streamlined, comfortable and easily accessible, befitting your clothing. Most flashlights in and around the 200-lumen range are compact, lightweight, and can be found for a reasonable price.

Navigation Tools

Knowing your current physical location and your desired destination is critically important in any physical movement.

Years ago maps, maybe a compass, and a good sense of direction were all you had available to navigate. Along came the Global Positioning System (GPS), a navigation system made up of a network of satellites placed into orbit by the U.S. Department of Defense. GPS was originally intended for military applications, but in the 1980s, the government made the system available for civilian use. GPS works in any weather conditions, anywhere in the world, 24 hours a day.

Most smart phones now offer navigation tools such as Google Maps, Traffic, VZ Navigator, and so on—provided you enable the GPS features and related location access settings. In addition, many common GPS devices are available for travel protection use, including well-known industry products from manufacturers such as Garmin©, SPOT© Satellite GPS Messenger, On-Star©, Hertz Never-Lost© and the like.

Some of these locator and navigational tools have add-on features that in a life-threatening situation you can notify emergency services that you need assistance and pinpoint your exact location.

The benefits of such modern navigation tools are obvious. However, always be ready to go back to the basics as the downside of relying too heavily on technical gear is that if it dies it can literally leave you stranded without direction or bearing. Have a commercial map or research and print directions before a trip. Have a compass (or two) and always maintain a realistic sense of where you are such as cardinal direction. Read signs, check your paper map, and maintain situational awareness of where you are and how to get back should you completely lose signal and or power.

Carry Tools

In exigent circumstances it may be necessary to perform such tasks as break open a window, or unscrew a doorknob or even cut through drywall. All of these things are very difficult to do without the right tool for the job. Since it's impossible to ever know exactly what tool they would need, the pros carry those tools, which have proven themselves useful by experience.

Pocket Knife

A pocketknife is used for myriad daily chores:

- Opening boxes, packages, and letters
- As a gardening tool
- Cutting shoelace or rope
- Loosening wedged objects
- Cutting food
- As an emergency tool to pry open cans or break glass
- In self-defense (covered in the following chapter)

There are two general classifications of pocketknives: fixed and folding. The term fixed blade is applied to a knife that has no moving parts. A folding blade is defined by the fact that it does have moving parts. Fixed blade is synonymous with the term fixed knife, and folding blade is synonymous with the term folding knife. There are advantages and disadvantages with regard to both categories.

The advantage of a fixed blade is that there are no moving parts, which makes it more reliable than a folding knife, but the cost is that in order to carry a fixed blade you need a sheath. Also, it requires that you wear this solid piece of steel somehow affixed to your body. Although some smaller fixed blades will fit behind your waistband, hang from your neck or even fit in your pocket, the folding knife is generally more compact, without the need for a sheath or attachment straps, and is therefore more convenient to carry than its fixed counterpart. The modern production folding knife has also withstood the test of time and is an indispensable utility tool that is strongly recommended for daily carry.

"What is the best folding knife out there?" and "How do I know which is the best folding knife for me?" To answer these two critical selection questions it is important to take into account several considerations with regard to owning, carrying, and utilizing a folding knife. These considerations include, but are not limited to functionality and application, quality and cost, size, legality, accessibility, fit, appearance, policy, aesthetics, and personal preference.

The time-tested adage "form follows function" directly applies to the selection of a folding knife. First and foremost in the selection of any folding knife is functionality. The questions of overall application such as, "What's the right knife for my job? What exactly is this knife to be used for? Can I use it both for utility and self-defense? What is the primary function of my folding knife?" should be paramount considerations to determine the selection of make, model, and style.

Under duress your folding knife may be used as a weapon of opportunity in your protection or that of your loved ones. However, you don't want to carry a folding knife that's sold as "The Widow Maker" or "The Ninja Killer," because if you ever need to use it as a weapon of opportunity for protection and your case goes to court rest assured that such a brand name or product description will attract the attention of a prosecuting attorney.

Cost is a consideration for most of us. As with any physical tools materials and construction determine quality. In most cases there is a direct correlation between cost and quality. When selecting a folding knife there is that fine line of high quality versus too high a cost. Generally speaking, the more expensive the knife the higher the grade—the expression "you get what you pay for" does apply to the world of modem folding knives.

Multi-Tools

Carrying a full-sized toolbox around with you everywhere you go is not possible and also not advisable. Conversely multi-tools are easy to use and convenient to carry. Anyone can carry a multi-tool that includes common tools that may be called for in your day-to-day activities.

If you've never carried or used a small multi-tool, you may be pleasantly surprised at how often it can be useful. Selecting the right multi-tool can seem somewhat overwhelming, given the virtually unlimited array of features and options.

One useful selection tip is to match the tool to the environment in which you will be active. For example, if you spend a lot of time on airplanes and in airports, you need to consider blade length and you will need to limit your choice to TSA-friendly multi-tools unless you place it in checked baggage.

Surprisingly the list of truly essential and basic components is rather short and simple. The basic multi-tool components most recommended are a small blade, a Phillips head screwdriver, a flat head screwdriver, and a pair of pliers. The blade is of course subject to your travel profile.

A compact, lightweight multi-tool convenient to your activity profile is a very useful item to keep handy, and must be considered in any emergency planning. As is the case with most tools, you really do get what you pay for in terms of durability and quality. It will be a worthwhile investment to buy a tool that will last a long time and do everything you need it to do. It is strongly recommended that you have access to a multi-tool should you be likely to find yourself in an emergency situation. Like a knife it may also be used for protection and should be readily accessible, if not on your person.

Pouches, Bags, And Packs

In addition to all of the above and to support your personal protection when at home, at work, while in your car, or travelling, you should have immediate access to an easy-to-carry container of minimal protective equipment that may assist you and your protectee(s) in moving off that X.

As a matter of both convenience and protection you are strongly advised to store, carry, or transport any loose and/or valuable items in a covered pouch, bag, or backpack.

It is also advisable that one container be set up to hold specific items conducive to moving off the X. Such a container is referred to as a "go bag."

Go Bag

An important physical protection tool, the go bag is designed to help you off the X and toward safety. Indispensable to any protection expert, the go bag is a mobile personal protection kit. It's a piece of compact lightweight gear that you can hold in your hand, that affords you options to keep that 360-degree envelope of protection around you both inside and outside of a controlled area 365 days of the year.

Every item in your go bag should bring you one step closer to keeping that protection envelope. Your go bag should be mobility functional, that is either one- or no-hands operation. It should be specifically designed by professionals for your personal protection. When necessary, it should be both airport and airplane-friendly so that you can keep it with you as a carry-on.

Your go bag should have loops on both ends to hang on any style door knob or hook, and should allow you hands-free carry over one shoulder, across the body, or as a fanny pack. It should be easy to store, ambidextrous, and allow you one-handed access to your gear.

Go bag usage is quick and simple. If needed you can literally just grab it and go! When staying at a hotel you simply throw in your critical personal items—any medications, cell phone, wallet, glasses, etc., zip it up and hang it on the doorknob. Should an emergency event occur in the middle of the night you can grab that one go bag which has everything you need in it to support maintaining your 360-degree protection envelope.

The go bag is something that can be given to your son or daughter who is leaving the nest or travelling overseas, and will provide them a recommended physical protection tool that they can hold in their hands.

Contents of your go bag may include communication tools such as cell phone or satellite phone, persons to contact, phone lists of a support network of individuals or organizations, language card (if working or living in a foreign country), and transportation and navigation information.

It should include illumination tools such as a flashlight and glow sticks including easy-to-find replaceable batteries. It should also include any prescription medications, Epi-pens, asthma inhalers, list of allergies and any medical problems, copies of official documents such as your driver's license, passport, credentials, some local currency in the form of cash and change, emergency action planning information and even backup credit cards.

Backup lights are also strongly recommended. You should also have functional clips, tape or carabiners, which can be used to fasten keys to tabs and secure your light source to your gear, your body, or your environment.

Also include a backup or local cell phone, extra cell phone batteries, and your multi-tool and/or pocketknife. To personalize your go bag, you may consider such items as a backup pair of prescription glasses, a couple of protein bars, your own water bottle, extra lithium or alkaline batteries, a dust and particle mask and even ear protection depending upon where you are traveling.

The key qualities of any go bag are for it to be useful, lightweight, compact, and easy to access and carry. Pack only the bare essentials you will need most for the environment in which you will most likely find yourself.

Just as you check the oil on your car before going on a long road trip, it's a good idea to check the contents of your go bag every now and again.

Recommended Daily Carry Tools

The "Friendly Five©" protection tools carried by all protection professionals include: communication (cell or sat phone), flashlight, firearm, pocketknife, and a pen.

Since most people are not protective agents—and most people are not in possession of a permit to carry a concealed firearm—depending upon where you live and what you do for work you may be relegated to the "Friendly Four©" (the same list but without the gun). Either way, it's not advisable to go out into the world minus physical protection tools. At a minimum, you must have a phone, flashlight, and a sturdy ink pen.

Why a sturdy ink pen? Besides being the single most innocuous weapon of opportunity available, you may need to write down names, numbers, and other relevant data that may be useful in the very near future to help you make beneficial decisions.

Certain states have maintained the rights for people to own and carry firearms either concealed (not visible in public) or openly carry (openly visible in public). If you are a resident of one of these states, you are permitted to carry a firearm for self-defense and as such are considered a legal firearm owner.

Certain work environments do not permit the carry of such edged tools as a folding knife or a fixed blade.

As such you would be considered a "non-knife owner."

The following table illustrates the Friendly Five© and the Friendly Four© categorized by what you may be allowed to carry by law or profession.

		Communication	***Illumination***	***Carry Tools***		
Friendly Five©	Protective Agent	Cell Phone and/ or Satellite Phone	Flashlight and Chem-Lights	Firearms and chem-lights	Pocket knife and multi-tool	Sturdy ink pen and pad of paper
	Legal Firearm Owner	Cell Phone	Flashlight	Firearm plus an extra magazine	Pocket knife and multi-tool	Sturdy ink pen and pad of paper
Friendly Four©	Non-Firearm Owner	Cell Phone	Flashlight		Pocket knife and multi-tool	Sturdy ink pen and pad of paper
	Non-Knife Owner	Cell Phone	Flashlight		Pocket knife and multi-tool	Sturdy ink pen and pad of paper

Table 9.1 Recommended PreFense© Daily Carry Tools

Weapons And Warning Devices

Finding yourself at the last ten-percent of a threat progression with limited options and reduced response time, you may consider assistance from the final two categories of physical protection tools—weapons and warning devices.

The usage of weapons is in your final efforts to stop a physical assault whereas the usage of warning devices is to detect or deter a threat at the very last stages of the attack cycle. Let's start with warning devices—used to help you detect or deter a threat.

At your disposal is a plethora of loud attention-getting devices that allow you to conserve energy and more effectively alert those around you, rather than screaming which may encourage the attacker who is now convinced you are afraid.

Warning Devices—Tools To Detect And Deter

When a predator is on the move, you may employ physical protection tools in detecting and deterring a physical attack using what are called warning devices. There are two categories of warning devices. The first one is detection devices, which are designed to warn you of an imminent threat in or near your immediate environment. The other type of warning device is the deterrence device, used to conspicuously attract the attention of others—including your attacker(s).

Detection Devices Warning You		*Deterrence Devices Warning Others*	
Where	**What**	**Device Type**	**Device Example**
Home, Car, Hotel, Dorm	Perimeter Alarm—motion detectors, lighting systems, door alarms.	Audio	High decibel screamer, air horn, loud whistle.
School or Corporate Campus	Early Warning Systems—keychain alerts, public announcements.	Visual	High-lumens flashlight, strobe.

Table 9.2 Examples Of Warning Devices

Detection Devices—Warning You

Warning devices are designed to detect a pending threat and provide you an early warning. These can include perimeter alarms, school or office campus warning system, and personal alarms. Perimeter alarms may be hand-held, quickly and easily installed, and used to protect your living or working space from potential burglary.

Most door alarms range from simple cost-effective single purpose models to those that come with a remote. Certain door alarms such as the electronic doorstop types serve a dual purpose, impeding entry as well as sounding an alert. An instant trigger will alert you if someone breaks the magnetic connection. A disturbingly loud 130 dB alarm ensures the sound is heard and helps deter vandals.

Certain detection devices may be issued to you by school or office campuses as part of a dedicated, 24/7, emergency-only system, monitored by the school or office campus security, providing immediate and simultaneous alerts to make sure students, faculty, and staff are informed about what has happened, what they should do, and where they should go. These alerts are received by a small and convenient key chain device, which vibrates and emits a loud audible alert upon receipt of an emergency message.

Deterrence Devices—Warning Others

Utilized as a deterrent by drawing attention and warning others, there are a vast number of non-contact personal alarms such as high-decibel screamers, personal and mini-personal alarms, air horns, whistles, and bright or flashing lights—all of which can be carried and used to deter assailants. If you are at home you can even keep your car alarm button or fob nearby if it works from inside the house.

Used in breaking the attack cycle these easy to carry and install personal alarms can provide you with an extra measure of security when your ability to defend yourself may be limited.

However, these detection and deterrence devices are not the be-all and end-all of protective solutions. They serve one purpose only, and that is to help provide you with an opportunity to move off that X as quickly as you can and get to safety. There is one remaining category of physical protection tools design to support your reactive efforts in stopping a physical threat, which is covered in the next chapter.

CHAPTER 10

Weapons

"Limiting the capacity of good Americans hinders their ability to protect themselves"
Sheriff Ken P. Campbell[1]

In This Chapter You Will Be Introduced To...

...the world of weapons as used in support of your protective efforts. Weapons are divided into two basic categories—those which are specifically designed as weapons such as a gun or a pepper spray and those which are not—called improvised weapons. Stressing the importance of mechanical compliance over pain compliance, this chapter covers firearms, stun guns, mace and pepper spray, impact weapons, edged weapons, improvised weapons, and personal weapons.

At A Glance

Warning devices differ from weapons in that as opposed to stopping a physical attack they are designed to assist in detection and deterrence of an imminent threat, which could otherwise escalate to a physical attack. Warning devices are not weapons and weapons should not be used as warning devices—such as firing a gun in the air to warn a potential attacker. At Step 5—Attack, where proactive and active measures are no longer an option, it is still possible to apply one of the three reactive measures—fight, using weapons to stop a violent physical threat.

The decision to purchase, carry and deploy a weapon is a personal one. Only you can make that decision based on five considerations beforehand: preparation, legality, accessibility, carry, and deployment. For any weapon to be effective you must be mentally prepared to use it.

---

1 Elected two-term Sheriff of Boone County, Indiana. The quote is from a media interview referencing protection.

There are some people who cannot intentionally inflict pain or injury upon another person regardless of circumstance—even to defend themselves or their family. If you are one of those people, you should not own, carry, or use a weapon of any kind. Finding out everything you need to know about considering a weapon affords you the opportunity of making one of the most important educated decisions about your personal security.

How Do I Use This In Real Life?

An important and commonly overlooked factor when considering ownership and or usage of weapons is training, which is absolutely mandatory if you're going to trust your life to your proficiency in their use. All weapons share one thing in common: they require the time and commitment of personal training needed for you to gain comfort, familiarity and, ultimately proficiency in their handling, storage, carry, access and deployment. Once developed, these skills become perishable over time. Like playing golf, speaking a foreign language or playing a musical instrument, if you don't use it, you lose it, and it requires periodic upkeep for you to maintain a satisfactory level of proficiency.

Armed with your understanding and working knowledge of weapons you gain the capability to fully support your everyday protective efforts. Use of these physical protection tools can help keep you and your protectee(s) safe, especially in the latter steps of the attack cycle.

What The Pros Know

The sixth and final category of physical protection tools is the category of weapons. As previously discussed, the human mind is our most powerful protection tool. Few people realize that it is also the most powerful weapon and warning device given to us by Mother Nature—one that we carry with us every day. Fortunately everybody gets one; unfortunately not everyone uses it. We ought to use it to observe our immediate environment, maintaining optimized situational awareness. Use it to make sound risk management decisions. Use it to rapidly determine protective measures using whatever means are at our disposal.

As the mind is your primary protection tool, protection experts use this tool to think outside the box to address threat management issues. Understanding and applying the proven concepts and measures of the fundamentals of protection is your first line of defense, and remains indispensable in assisting you to both prepare for and manage real-world threats. All else is secondary to your knowledge and skill.

No weapon is a substitute for good common sense, good habits and other sound protective measures.

Relying upon a weapon for protection instead of using the most powerful protection tool available puts you at a strategic disadvantage as it places you far behind the action-reaction power curve. The sole purpose of any weapon should be purely as a support element used in the event of failure to break the attack cycle.

Weapon Deployment

Deployment means pulling a weapon out from its carry-position and using it. To deploy a weapon you must first have one in your possession. A weapon in a drawer or safe at home and not in your hand when you need it is useless. When considering whether or not to own or use a weapon you must first reflect upon the following five-point checklist listed in order of priority:

1. **Preparation**—Are you morally, ethically and mentally prepared to purposefully raise the scale of injury against another person or persons? Specifically, can you take the life of another in exchange for your protection and or that of your protectee(s)? If not then you should not consider ownership or usage of weapons.

2. **Legality**—Is it legal to possess, carry and deploy a weapon in the area where you intend to carry and if need be, deploy. Get on line and check local laws or contact your local sheriff's office or police department. Keep in mind that in certain states a weapon may be legal to possess but not legal to carry or deploy. If you travel on commercial aircraft you will need to review TSA's website (US Department of Homeland Security's Transportation Security Administration) for rules on traveling with weapons[2].

3. **Accessibility**—Fancy term for "where and how I can get to it when I need it." Is it kept only at home? Will it be in your car or on your person? If you keep your

2 *http://www.tsa.gov/traveler-information/firearms-and-ammunition*

gun at home then it can only be used there. If you keep your pepper spray in the car, then that's where it will be should you need it elsewhere.

4. **Carry**—Another firearms term, "carry," means how will the weapon be carried on your person? Will it be carried openly (in plain view of others), inside a pocket, clipped to your belt, stored in your purse or other hand-held bag? You may never need a weapon, but when you do it will most certainly be in a hurry. As such there are two carry considerations. The first is comfort; will it get in the way of your daily activities? The second consideration is accessibility. How accessible will it be when you need it?

5. **Deployment**—Are you currently familiar, comfortable and proficient enough to be safely handling the weapon? Do you feel that your deployment skills are honed to a level of proficiency greater than that of a street-skilled assailant while you are under duress? If not, are you willing to put in the time and effort required to get professional training, develop proficiency and then maintain that proficiency with ongoing training and practice?

Defining Weapons

In the world of protection a weapon is "a physical tool used as a means of gaining an advantage or defending oneself in a conflict." Employed as physical protection tools, weapons are nothing more than hand-held implements available to help you stop a physical attack if needed at the very last step of the attack cycle.

Used as an extension of your knowledge—protective concepts and skills—protective measures, weapons fall into two categories: 1—those which are specifically designed to help you stop a physical attack such as a firearm, stun gun, pepper spray, and 2—those

Specifically Designed	***Opportunistic/ Improvised***
Firearm	Hot cup of coffee
Stun gun	Umbrella
Taser®	Flashlight
Pepper spray	Ink pen
Knife	Purse, belt or necktie
Expandable baton	Fingernails

Table 10.0 Weapon Categories

which are not specifically designed as a weapon but may serve as one in a pinch. This second category is called improvised weapons or weapons of opportunity. An improvised weapon is essentially anything you can grab hold of—including the use of your hands!

If you understand what constitutes an effective weapon and how to use it, regardless of category, weapons are applicable in any threat environment. Whether it's a firearm, a folding knife, a pen or even your fingernails, you are never without physical protection tools available to assist you in stopping a physical attack.

Weapons—Tools To Help Stop A Physical Attack

One of the most commonly asked questions about protection is, "Should I carry a weapon such as a gun or pepper spray?" The answer is, "It is best NOT to carry weapons unless you are willing, qualified and trained to use them." If you're not proficient in their usage, weapons can too easily be turned against you by adversaries who are intimately familiar with them and willing to deploy them against you. Special needs persons should also not carry or use weapons.

In a weapons-assisted response to any physical altercation, the scale of injury increases. That scale applies both to you and your attacker. In terms of scale of injury, the outcome of any physical altercation will be significantly influenced by the type of weapon involved and the skills of its wielder. The outcome of a physical altercation in which an assailant is attacking you with his bare hands is very different than that of an assailant attacking you with an edged weapon, which differs greatly from a situation where an assailant may be attacking you with a firearm.

Moving off the X by itself will solve the vast majority of protection problems at the latter stages of the attack cycle, but for that very small percentage of the time it might not, you may need the support of a weapon to help place you in a position from which you can then move off the X.

Compliance

In protection parlance "compliance" is a term used to describe making an adversary comply with your demands as opposed to you complying with theirs in your surviving a life-threatening situation.

There are two types of compliance—"pain compliance" and "mechanical compliance." Twist your wrist and it might hurt—pain. Break your wrist and you can't move it—mechanical.

Pain compliance is the result of causing an adversary pain by twisting his wrist or hitting a pressure point on his body with the intention of causing that person enough pain to make them comply with your demands.

Mechanical compliance is causing severe physical structural damage such as stopping the heart from beating or the brain from functioning, or breaking a bone to make an adversary comply with your demands.

Usage of a weapon may or may not be painful to an assailant. Pain should never be a consideration in weapon selection or usage. Pain is an insignificant factor in any defensive situation; it is wildly subjective and as such varies in great degree from person to person. What may be considered painful to you may not be so to the next person and vice-versa. From a protective viewpoint, to stake the outcome of a physical altercation on someone else's level of pain tolerance is unsatisfactory.

Weapon Categories

You have a wide range of hand-held weapons available to support your existing knowledge and skill in stopping a physical attack.

Such weapons may be categorized in order of effectiveness and deployment range in stopping a physical attack by one or more assailants. The following are seven categories of weapons, which will be further addressed.

Weapon Categories:

1. Firearms
2. Stun Guns
3. Mace And Pepper Spray
4. Impact Weapons
5. Edged Weapons
6. Improvised Weapons
7. Personal Weapons

To provide comprehensive coverage of every aspect of all weapons in every category would be a daunting task, as each category could be studied exhaustively. However, what follows is intended as a general introductory overview to provide you with relevant information about weapons. It is my hope as an author that such information will elicit further study, discussion and reflection resulting in educated decisions as to your choice of weapons as a means of gaining an advantage or defending yourself in a conflict.

Category 1: Firearms—The 800-Pound Gorilla

OK, let's take a hard look at the 800-pound gorilla that some people don't even want to talk about.

It's important to approach this topic from the bottom line: in a life-or-death defensive situation, a firearm operated by a qualified user is the most effective hand-held physical protection tool available to immediately stop a physical attack—bar none. This same premise explains why military, law enforcement, and federal agents are required to carry firearms and why they are also required to qualify with them.

You may certainly qualify to own and carry firearms. However, to quote a respected colleague and close friend of mine, Tom Rovetuso, who is both a decorated veteran and highly-experienced retired law enforcement professional with more than 30 years on the job: "The decision to use a firearm for the protection of your family is a personal decision unique to each of us and one based in the sum of our morals, beliefs, and experiences."[3]

Many people believe that they can and will simply dial 911 in any emergency. Even if one is successful in contacting a police department or sheriff's office it can take anywhere from a few minutes to a half hour or even longer depending upon location, before response can be expected. Given that the average home invasion consists of two or more assailants, it's safe to say that in a minimal time frame a lot could happen prior to the police arriving.

As professional firearms instructors both Tom and I are often asked to share our views with our students regarding home invasion scenarios: the homeowner handling the situation versus waiting for the police to arrive to handle the situation. With his permission I have elected to share with you our perspective courtesy of Tom's vernacular:

"You are seated at your kitchen table. In front of you are a loaded firearm and a phone. You are advised that in 15 seconds three ruthless criminals will forcibly enter your home armed with handguns. Once inside, these aggressive and violent assailants plan to take control of your house and everyone inside. You and your family will be completely at their mercy

3 *Personal conversation.*

if you allow them to take that control. You are further advised that their intent is to brutally attack and murder every member of your family. One question: When they come through that door, which of the two will you reach for: the gun or the phone?"

A firearm provides any trained person with the ability to use lethal force in a defensive situation against street-hardened attackers. A firearm levels the playing field between that person and an attacker and affords them the optimal means of defending themselves regardless of physical stature or athleticism. However, guns are not for everyone. There are four categories of individuals who should not own or carry a firearm:

1. **Those Who Are Incapable**—e.g., emotionally disturbed, special needs persons and young children.
2. **Those Who Are Disqualified**—e.g., convicted felons, registered violent persons, sexual offenders, persons of interest who may have used a gun to commit crimes, fugitives from the law, and terrorists.
3. **Those Who Are Unwilling**—based on the sum of their morals, beliefs, and experiences will not use a firearm to defend themselves.
4. **Those Who Are Untrained.**

Even for those of us outside those four categories, buying a gun satisfies only one aspect of firearms proficiency requirements for protection. To quote another of my esteemed colleagues, retired veteran, former military intelligence officer and senior firearms instructor Patrick S. Henry (USMC ret.) "The belief that owning a gun makes you safe is as absurd as believing that purchasing a scalpel makes you a qualified surgeon. In both cases, the blind act of owning these items alone without proper training, mindset and planning for the items' use actually makes you less safe."[4] The other two aspects of firearms proficiency requirements for protection include training and maintenance, as you are responsible for safe handling and storage.

Owning a firearm is like owning a car. It's a tremendous responsibility and commitment of time and effort. If you plan on buying, owning, and driving a car you need to acquire a driver's license, which means you need

4 Reprinted with permission from an article written for Aegis Academy—http://aegisacademy.com/

to prepare for and take both a written test and demonstrate proficiency. The same degree of personal responsibility befalls any gun owner—namely the commitment of time and effort to own, maintain, and safely store the gun, and to maintain skills proficiency.

As a firearms owner you assume the responsibility for 1—appropriate mindset, 2—safe gun handling and storage, and 3—marksmanship, or the ability to hit what you're shooting at. A firearm in the hands of a qualified, responsible, and well-trained owner remains an indispensable life-saving physical protection tool.

Police officers use them every day to keep our society safe. Federal agents use them every day to help keep their protectee(s) safe. Qualified, responsible and well-trained citizens use them every day to keep their children and their families safe.

Even though not very often reported by the media, there are countless real world cases of qualified and responsible citizens who have used firearms to save the lives of their family members and children. The following are a couple of examples.

January 5, 2012 9:07AM CBS/AP Report[5]—Blanchard, Oklahoma—Authorities say they won't file charges against an Oklahoma widow who fatally shot a New Year's Eve intruder at her home while she was on the phone with a 911 dispatcher. Sarah McKinley, 18, asked a Grady County dispatcher for permission to shoot the intruder at her Blanchard mobile home. "I've got two guns in my hand. Is it OK to shoot him if he comes in this door?" McKinley asked the dispatcher. "Well, you have to do whatever you can do to protect yourself," the dispatcher is heard telling McKinley on the 911 tape released. "I can't tell you that you can do that, but you have to do what you have to do to protect your baby." McKinley's 3-month-old son was with her when she shot the intruder.

Oklahoma law allows the use of deadly force against intruders, and prosecutors said McKinley clearly acted in self-defense. According to court documents, her attacker was holding a knife when he expired. "Our initial review of the case doesn't indicate she violated the law in any way," said the Assistant District Attorney. According to court documents, both intruders might have been looking for prescription drugs. McKinley said it took the men about 20 minutes to get through her door, which she had barricaded with a couch.

---

5 *http://cbsnews.com/8301-504083_162-57352784-504083/okla-mom-sarah-mckinley-wont-face-charges-for-shooting-intruder*

June 19, 2013—Orange County, California[6]—A 72-year-old grandmother who fired her .357 magnum revolver at a man allegedly trying to break into her Orange County home said that she was trying to defend herself and her 85-year-old husband. Jan Cooper said at a news conference that she fired one shot from her high-powered handgun, according to a report on KTLA-TV Channel 5.

Cooper and husband, a disabled World War II veteran, were alone at the home Sunday when she loaded her gun and dialed 911 as the man allegedly tried to force his way in. On the 911 tape, Cooper can be heard telling the man to leave. "Get the hell out of here," she said. She told the dispatcher that she was going to shoot at the man. "I'm firing!" she said, as sound of the gunshot broke out.

The suspect, identified by authorities as Brandon Alexander Perez, 31, was not hit. He was arrested a short while later. The Orange County Sheriffs Department said Perez was on parole for a burglary conviction.

We would be remiss if we failed to consider that for every action there is an equal and opposite reaction—disarming qualified, responsible citizens of a free republic will not be without consequence.

The following is provided as an abridged primer to help you explore the options for responsible firearms ownership. What type of gun to buy is a matter of "function and fit." Let's start with function.

Function

What exactly will the gun be used for? If for residential and personal protection there are two general categories of firearms, which are considered practical —handguns and long guns, known collectively as "small arms" in industry parlance.

Handguns tend to be either revolvers—generally the older style guns with rotating chambers—or semi-automatic magazine-fed pistols. Both are available in a variety of sizes and calibers, some of which are suitable to carry on your person and some which are not.

Long guns such as rifles, carbines (lighter, more compact rifles), or shotguns (either pump-action or semi-automatic) can be used for self-defense and/or for hunting, but typically cannot be easily concealed and are generally not carried in public without arousing suspicion.

---

6 Robert J. Lopez. 72 year old Grandma Fires Handgun at alleged would-be burglar. Los Angeles Times June 19, 2013—http://www.latimes.com/local/lanow/la-me-ln-grandma-fires-handgun-would be-burglar-20130611,0,5261091.story

For home defense you can't beat a good old-fashioned shotgun versus a handgun. However, in some cases, either the physical stature of the gun owner or the size of the area that the gun is used in may have bearing on which type of gun would be considered optimal. A handgun shoots only one projectile at a time, whereas a shotgun loaded with buckshot shoots from 9-12 projectiles with each cartridge fired. The advantage is both the number of projectiles fired and the shot placement or pattern. Low velocity buckshot is more than adequate to take down an attacker.

Handguns are the best option for concealed carry. They are compact and thus easy to conceal, lightweight, carry a reasonable amount of ammunition, and can be easily transported. Concealed properly, no one will even know you are carrying a firearm, which provides yet another advantage of concealed carry, namely the element of surprise. The downside to a handgun is that it is ballistically insufficient when compared to a rifle or a shotgun.

When it comes to function here are some guidelines: A handgun is a great tool to have to respond to an unexpected attack, but if you knew you were going to be attacked, you would choose a rifle or a shotgun. A handgun is a great tool to use to fight your way to a shotgun or a rifle and is certainly easier to carry around.

Carrying a firearm legally in most states requires an official government document often referred to as a "concealed weapons permit." You can check with your local sheriff's office or police department to find out the requirements.

Remember that you are morally, legally and ethically responsible for the final resting place of every round (bullet) you fire so if you plan to carry a handgun, it is very strongly recommended that you attend a professional firearms training course specializing in the carry, access, storage, maintenance and use of a firearm prior to carrying one.

Fit

If purchasing a handgun, you must meet the most basic of requirements: does the gun fit my hand? The gun should feel comfortable to you. The most important part of fit is the distance from the back-strap (or tang) of the grip to the face of the trigger. You must be able comfortably to place the center of the pad of the index finger on the face of the trigger in order to shoot well. If the gun is too small, you can eventually learn to shoot it, but it will be a struggle. If the gun is too big—you'll never shoot it as well as one that fits your hand. If the gun feels comfortable, learning how to shoot it well is much easier. If the gun feels awkward, that discomfort will be noticed by you every time you shoot.

When selecting a firearm, your local gun store is the last place you should rely on for advice on which gun you should purchase. They undoubtedly have "the perfect gun for you," because like a car salesman, they are there to sell guns. Find a quality trainer and ask their advice or spend some time at a firing range asking range officers questions and learning about guns before you buy one. The NRA First Steps programs can be beneficial, but there are many quality institutions that offer firearms familiarization courses specifically designed to help you make sound purchasing decisions.

When it comes to using a firearm, however, there is absolutely no substitute for professional training. It is strongly recommended that you complete professional firearms instruction to learn the fundamentals of shooting your gun.

Your firearm should be on your person or in a locked container such as a safe and any qualified professional firearms instructor should be able to assist you with a purchase decision.

In case I failed to mention it earlier—there is no substitute for professional weapons training!

Category 2: Stun Guns

A stun gun is a type of electronic device that uses electricity to influence the sensory and/or motor nervous systems of an individual. Individuals seeking to carry a stun gun may be concerned about being seen with an obvious stun gun, causing potential issues with neighbors, co-workers or passersby. This possibility has led to the design of stun guns that look like something else, such as cell phones. This allows you to carry what looks like a cell phone, while keeping the people around you from realizing that you have a weapon.

Hand held stun guns, as described below in the section on TASERs, disperse high voltage with low amperage. Stun guns are considered "contact weapons" in that you actually need to be at conversational ranges to make physical contact with your assailant. Considered a mechanical compliance protection tool in that they can be used to temporarily incapacitate an attacker's nervous system, the brief moments of this incapacitation will provide you the opportunity to move off that X.

As of this writing, stun guns are not allowed to be shipped to the following locations: Hawaii, New York, Michigan, Illinois, Rhode Island, New Jersey, Wisconsin, Connecticut, Baltimore City, Maryland, and Philadelphia. As with all weapons, laws and regulations can change at any time. Therefore, if you are interested in the purchase, carry and deployment of stun gun for defensive purposes, you must check with local law enforcement before buying one.

TASER®

Technically classified as a "stun gun," TASER® technology stands apart from other stun guns in that it offers the benefit of greater range (distance between you and an assailant) and control by affecting both sensory and motor nerves. Other stun guns do not affect motor nerves but only sensory nerves.

A longstanding tool that revolutionized law enforcement less lethal use of force, TASER® weapons have gained widespread acceptance throughout the civilian community. TASER® technology represents a physical protection tool that can immediately incapacitate an attacker with a reduced scale of injury.

TASER® weapons are referred to as Conducted Electrical Weapons (CEWs). It is because TASER CEWs can gain control of a subject at relatively safer ranges that they have been adopted by many military, law enforcement, and federal agencies and are currently available in the civilian market.

How Does A TASER® CEW Work?

When the user presses a button, two small probes fire out of a replaceable cartridge, sail through the air and stick small barbs (similar to fish hooks) either into the assailant or the assailant's clothing. Energy is conducted through the wires to affect the sensory and motor functions of the nervous system of the assailant temporarily incapacitating them affording you the time to move off the X.

Professional training is highly recommended and includes complete instructions on activation, safety release, how and where to aim, and firing your TASER®.[7]

7 For further information contact Rick Guibault, VP-Training & Education, TASER INTERNATIONAL INC., 17800 North 85th Street, Scottsdale, AZ 85255, Email: sarge@taser.com, Phone 800-978-2737

TASERs are not considered firearms because they use compressed gas as opposed to explosives to launch the projectiles. Because they are not firearms they are legal to carry in most states without permits.[8]

Category 3: Mace And Pepper Spray

Also known as CS—a lot easier to remember than its official name, orthochloro-benzalmalononitrile—tear gas was used by the US military during the Vietnam War and, based on certain after action reports from the war, was adopted by law enforcement as tear gas—also called "mace." It is effective for controlling riots and unruly crowds and also used in most corrections facilities for the same purposes.

Although very effective on most people, certain individuals under the influence of drugs and/or alcohol, emotionally disturbed persons, or those individuals with extremely high pain tolerances do not react in the same manner to this chemical.

Pepper spray is a lachrymatory agent, which is a chemical compound that irritates the eyes causing inflammation of the tear ducts—a biological mechanical compliance. Today pepper spray is used by police officers for individual, riot, and crowd control, and by correctional officers to help control inmate violence. It can also be used by civilians for self-defense including defense against dogs and bears. Its inflammatory effects cause the eyes to squint, or close impairing visual acuity. This temporary visual attenuation allows officers to more easily restrain subjects and affords those using pepper spray for self-defense an opportunity to get off the X.

As with all weapons, there are laws and regulations that are associated with pepper spray that you should be aware of before you buy or use it.

It's important that you give some thought in advance to how and where you will carry your pepper spray canister. Make sure you can access and deploy your pepper spray quickly from its carry position.

Pepper spray only works if it is propelled into the attacker's eyes or nose. To be most effective, the canister should be sprayed within 2 to 3 feet of the subject. When spraying, be aware of the wind direction to avoid spraying yourself. The contents should be sprayed in controlled burst of one half to two seconds, continuing until you have the opportunity to get off that X. Remember to stop spraying the OC once you're mobile and have created sufficient distance to non-contact range.

---

8 *http://www.defenseproducts101.com/statesstatuesummary_page2.html*

It is important to note that pepper spray, due to its chemical structure, must be replaced on occasion as canisters do expire.

Category 4: Impact Weapons

Walking sticks and canes are readily available throughout our society. The handling and manipulation of the walking stick or cane in a defensive manner is a highly effective means of protection against physical assault. They both can be carried in a courtroom, on an airplane and in countries where both firearms and edged weapons are not permitted. Utilizing a walking stick or a cane to competently and effectively control an actual threat engagement by employing appropriate technique and protective concepts is an easy-to-learn self-defense option.

Instruction on how to use a stick or cane is available through highly specialized comprehensive knife and baton programs called Kali, Escrima, or Amis (Filipino Martial Arts), combining familiar body movements with specialized principles. Such training affords you efficient usage of walking sticks and canes in self-defense at conversational distances.

Spanning the globe historically, batons and other impact weapons as simple as fire-hardened rattan sticks have been employed predominantly in the Philippines, Malaysia, Southeast Asia, and the Indonesian Archipelago, and were a contributing factor in the fight for independence from European colonialism.

One example is the Battle of Mactan, in the Philippine Islands, where Ferdinand Magellan (c. 1480 - 1521), the Portuguese-born Spanish explorer and navigator, leader of the first expedition to sail completely around the world, was killed by tribal Chieftain Lapulapu in battle on April 27, 1521 while defending the withdrawal of his landing party.

Lapulapu is regarded as a national hero in the Philippines for resisting this first European invasion. The majority of resistance against Elizabethan-era Spanish steel was with primitive impact weapons, which proved highly successful, so much so that these ancient techniques, originally outlawed during early European colonialism, are preserved by the Filipino Martial Arts to the present time. Inspired by these historical events and the traditional effectiveness of utilizing a baton, law enforcement globally adopted the baton as an integral component of their use-of-force options applicable to their job responsibilities.

Examples of everyday available batons include wood or rattan short dowel, short bat, toilet plunger handle, and so on. Expandable batons, which are specifically designed for protective purposes are additionally available.

One of the reasons they are so popular and effective is because they give you a little bit of distance. They can generate a sufficient amount of force upon impact to result in stopping an attacker if you are involved in an assault situation, providing you the opportunity to disengage from the threat. Most street-hardened assailants have an unspoken and healthy respect for impact weapons, as they understand how powerful these weapons can be in the hands of a trained practitioner. As a result, bad guys will generally shy away from full-contact engagement when an impact weapon is present.

When it comes to impact weapons, size does matter. A very heavy two-handed cane or walking stick can be used to block and strike in ways that a thinner, lighter stick cannot. Although six inches of wood, plastic, or metal doesn't seem like much, a dowel not much bigger than the length of an ink pen is among one of the most effective close-quarters self-defense weapons you probably aren't carrying. Innocuous, often legal for the most part and very useful, the pocket stick is a lightweight accessory that you may easily carry and use.

One of the most common questions people ask about pocket sticks after inquiring about how to use them for defense is how to carry them. Everyone is different. Depending on your body type, you may find them uncomfortable to carry in your front pockets. You might choose to carry the pocket stick in the front or inside pocket of a jacket. You might also want to carry it in your hand when out and about.

Another benefit of learning how to use a pocket or palm stick is that so many items can be used as one, including pens, pencils, salt shakers, wrenches, a roll of quarters, and even compact flashlights can be used as a palm stick in self-defense.

Category 5: Edged Weapons

Edged weapons have been around since before the beginning of recorded history. Archeological digs have unearthed proof of man's usage of knives dating back to circa 8,000 BC. Historical evidence suggests that a knife was one of the very first hand-held tools ever created.

As with all useful inventions, the knife was a pretty good idea and has withstood the test of time—possibly ten to twenty thousand years.

Overall knife design has matured through various stages of development. The very first materials were most likely a sharpened bone or stick. Later on, chipped stone and eventually modem metallurgy came into play. Today, in the knife world, there are tens of thousands of models, styles, blades, and handle configurations.

Is the possession and carry of folding knives permissible by law? When traveling abroad it's important to check with local authorities regarding the possession and carry of a folding knife. If you live in Great Britain you would be breaking the law by carrying a folding knife in public. One of the most basic considerations with regard to the law and selection of any folding knife is blade length. What is the optimal size of the blade, the handle, and the overall knife from blade tip to the base of the handle? When considering blade length the first and foremost concern should be compliance with the laws in your state, city, or municipality with regard to the length of a folding knife, predominantly the blade length.

Western European duelists of the 16th century documented that "the length of a blade at only four inches is a most sufficient length [in the hands of an expert] for one man to take the life of another man."[9] From that time on, referencing a knife blade the length of about four inches has pretty much been generally accepted by law as a "substantial length." Many years later, with the establishment of the colonies in America and the subsequent forming of the United States, there were virtually no changes to this notion. Even today a number of states require that the length of a folding knife be no longer than three and one-half inches.

Must your folding knife be readily accessible, or is less accessibility satisfactory? This would be determined by the intended application of the knife. If self-defense is your primary consideration, then like any other weapon, accessibility and rapid deployment is critical.

As a physical protection tool a knife is one of the best. It's compact, lightweight, and concealable, never runs out of bullets, never runs out of battery charge, doesn't need to be plugged in, doesn't expire and usually doesn't require a special permit.

A knife combined with professional self-defense training can be a very reliable combination. Having and knowing how to use an edged tool provides you yet another very useful addition to your physical protection tool kit.

---

9 Giacomo diGrassi was a mid-16th century fencing master from Italy. This quote is from his 1570 treatise on edged weapon fighting—His True Arte of Defence.

Category 6: Improvised Weapons

If carrying a firearm, TASER® or impact weapon is not an option, then improvise with everyday items you normally carry with you, such as an umbrella, rolled up newspaper or magazine, your flashlight, ink pen, nail file. Using these as physical-deterrence devices to get yourself off that X. These are commonly referred to as improvised weapons.

Also known as weapons of opportunity, an improvised weapon is anything you can hold in your hand in exigent circumstance that, should the opportunity present itself, you could use to defend yourself against a physical assault.

An improvised weapon can be any object not specifically designed to be a weapon, such as a crowbar or hammer. The concept here is to make useful what will work for you and disregard the rest.

If you're indoors, you have kitchen appliances, utensils, office furniture, power cords, scissors, picture frames—all kinds of stuff. If you're outside, there are rocks, sand, sticks, fallen tree branches, dirt, leaves, trash, and countless other items placed in the vicinity by man or by Mother Nature. The working principle here is to just put something in your hands—anything—that can be employed to further support your existing knowledge (protective concept) and skills (protective measures) by helping you to deter and even stop a physical attack.

If there is very little or no time to react, then the only option is reaching out for whatever happens to be within your arm's length to defend yourself with. However, in some circumstances you may have time to consider your options. In such circumstances improvised weapons can be judiciously selected. The list of objects you're reviewing in your mind is called a resource assessment list and it only takes a split second to add one or two items to that list.

To facilitate a more effective resource assessment list, all improvised weapons may be classified into four specific categories: *(see Table 10.1)*

When you walk into a new environment, whether it is an indoor room or an outdoor area, it takes only a few seconds to do a quick resource assessment listing in your mind.

Now whenever you walk into a new environment, not only will you notice—using your observational skills where the exits and entrances, windows, stairs, doors, and so on are located, but you now also know how to compile a quick resource assessment listing at will.

	Improvised Weapon Category	*Examples Of Improvised Weapons In This Category*	*Applicable To Which Target Areas On Assailant*
1	Edged Weapons	Kitchen knives - can also be found at your restaurant dinner table, broken piece of glass, scissors, ink pen, car keys, fork.	Soft tissue areas of the attacker(s) such as the eyes, throat, and groin as well as hands, wrists and forearms.
2	Impact Weapons	Rolled up magazine, fallen tree branch, umbrella, stiletto heels, rock, ball bat, edge of your briefcase, a hammer, three-hole-punch, corner of table, flashlight, tea kettle, your car.	Hard bony areas of the attacker(s) such as the head, clavicle, ribs, knees.
3	Flexible Weapons	Length of rope, t-shirt, belt, purse-strap, shoelaces, printer cable, extention cord, dishcloth.	Neck and throat - specifically the trachea area of the attacker(s).
4	Personal Weapons	Closed fists, open palms, knees, fingernails, shins, elbows, head butts, stomping w/your boots, teeth.	Both soft tissue areas of the attacker(s) such as the eyes, throat and groin and hard bony areas such as the head, clavicle, ribs, knees.

Table 10.1 Improvised Weapon Categories

One more advantage of knowing how to identify and apply improvised weapons is that there's no need to bring them with you—they are already there waiting for you when you arrive! Also keep in mind that your personal weapons should be with you at all times. Looking at it from this perspective you are never unarmed.

Category 7: Personal Weapons

The concept of using your bare hands as weapons in self-protection has been around since the first caveman tried to slap the second one upside the head. The ability to defend yourself with only personal weapons—hands, feet, elbows, knees—is a specialized skill which, like any other developed skill takes time and commitment to learn. Such skills may be acquired by at least one of three disciplines of study: martial arts, self-defense or defensive tactics.

Most of us have heard of martial arts or self-defense whereas those in the national defense and law enforcement communities are more familiar with the term defensive tactics. Although all three of these disciplines of study may seem interchangeable they are not.

The martial arts are exactly that—an art. Like any other art, it takes a tremendous amount of time (years) and dedication (many repetitions) to master. The classical martial arts such as Karate, Judo, and Aikido can improve your ability to protect yourself using your hands and feet and other tools as weapons. It can make you more confident and able, but the price tag attached to that confidence and capability is a tremendous amount of practice and dedication before classical martial arts techniques may be used in practical street defense.

Self-defense encompasses any and all means of protecting oneself. Throwing a scalding hot pot of coffee across a room at someone to protect your life or limb is considered self-defense. Firearms are considered a life-saving tool used in self-defense.

Self-defense techniques are not designed to strictly follow traditional forms or take years to master. Many modern martial arts academies offer such self-defense classes specifically for the purpose of immediately applicable street defense in addition to their traditional curriculum.

Conversely defensive tactics are specifically designed to support military, law enforcement, and other first-responder communities in the performance of their job responsibilities which could include arrest and control and to maintain a level of safety for all persons involved—including those wearing the handcuffs!

Whether you train in the martial arts, self-defense, or defensive tactics —repetition is the mother of all skills. As with learning how to play an instrument or proficiency in a second language, regardless of any discipline, it takes plenty of time to learn a new skill.

To convert this to street-applicable proficiency, you must then be able to demonstrate that skill under duress. Only then, can you truly have that skill. The experts claim that it takes nearly 3,000 repetitions for a novice practitioner to gain proficiency in a new physical skill.

Regardless of which discipline of study, the secret three-step formula to gaining street-effective skills is:

- Demonstrable Familiarity
- Supervised Repetitions
- Performance Under Duress

Unfortunately even after you finally develop an effective level of proficiency if you don't use it you lose it. Hence the reason military, law enforcement, and other such communities rely on in-service training, affording community members the opportunity to maintain standardized levels of proficiency.

Hey, what about boxing, UFC (the ultimate fight challenge), and MMA (mixed martial arts)? All that looks like it really works in the ring, with those hard-hitting knees, elbows, fists, shins and feet—wouldn't that work in the street? The answer is yes! The only caveat I will offer is that in the street there are no rules, no referees fouls or penalties. UFC/MMA regulations do not allow for driving a screwdriver into your opponent's eye, or deploying a firearm.

Keep in mind that in addition to traditional curriculum, martial arts schools do offer self-defense programs and techniques designed for immediate street application. With regards to the development of personal weapons, of the three disciplines martial arts, self-defense and defensive tactics the most readily accessible is the martial arts.

When asked, "Which is the 'best' of the martial arts to learn?" what I generally recommend to those who have the interest and inclination, is to focus on two areas of proficiency: stand-up defense and ground defense

To satisfy stand-up proficiency all you need are old-school stand-up skills such as traditional western boxing, kickboxing, or Muay Thai. To support ground defense all you need are some old-school ground-fighting skills such as Grecco-Roman wrestling or Brazilian Jiu-jitsu. Either way it's a VERY good idea to keep yourself physically fit, based on your own healthcare provider's recommendations. As an earnest practitioner you can't allow yourself to get too soft!

Fortunately as most folks are not afforded the time and inclination to "take up an art" there are many one-time self-defense courses, training seminars and self-defense workshops, which are offered at local martial arts schools and elsewhere.

Many of my clients also ask me about their kids. Without hesitation I advise them to get their kids involved in the martial arts as early as possible and through their teens. Activities like Tae Kwon Do, Kung Fu, and Aikido are a fun way for both boys and girls to achieve fitness and mental focus.

Some people may think the martial arts promote violence, but in my more than three decades of hands-on experience both as a teacher and a lifelong student I know this to be a myth. The martial arts actually help teach self-discipline, self-control, and appropriate socialization skills. Ironically, the martial arts teach reasons why NOT to fight, and further provides children with the confidence that they can defend themselves if necessary.

Last Word On Weapons

Whether you end up owning a firearm, a TASER®, pepper spray, a stun gun, a baton, a knife, or plan to use improvised weapons, they all have their advantages and disadvantages. Let's take a look at some of these in the following comparative table of weapons listed in order of capability and effective range in stopping a physical attack:

Weapon	*Effective Range*	*Power Source*	*Legislative Considerations*	*Required Training*
Firearm	Over 7,500 feet, depending on type of firearm	Primer, powder, and bullet seated in cartridge	Federal, state, municipal, and local. The most controversial and legislated weapon in America.	Extensive. A familiarization course covering gun safety, mindset, loading, unloading, storage, assembly, disassembly, maintenance. An entry level course on grip, stance, recoil management, sight picture and alignment, trigger control, carry and deployment, shot placement.
Taser®	15 feet; further for law enforcement models.	Compressed gas (no explosives) and lithium batteries	Somewhat restricted; legal in most states. Check online and with your local sheriff's office or police department.	Manufacturer's recommendation is to attend a training course. As with all weapons, there is always the chance for a missed shot, especially in a dynamic, stressful situation, and you must be prepared to take alternative actions to protect yourself in case of a missed shot or reduced effectiveness.
Pepper Spray	15 feet	Propellant	Legal in most states. Check online and with your local sheriff's office or police department.	Professional training is strongly recommended, followed by continued access and deployment practice.

Weapon	*Effective Range*	*Power Source*	*Legislative Considerations*	*Required Training*
Stun Gun	Contact Distance—where you can reach assailant with your hand	Battery powered	Legal in most states. Check online and with your local sheriff's office or police department.	Training recommended.
Impact	Contact Distance—where you can reach assailant with your hand	Your hand and arm strength.	Somewhat restricted. Legal in most states. Check online and with your local sheriff's office or police department.	Professional training is recommended, followed by continued access and deployment practice.
Edged	Contact Distance	Hand coordination. Strength not as much of a requirement as impact weapons.	Legal in most states. Check online and with your local sheriff's office or police department.	Professional training is recommended, followed by continued access and deployment practice.
Impro-vised Weapon	Contact Distance	Arm strength and hand coordination.	Subject to laws referencing weapons of opportunity.	Professional training is recommended, followed by continued access and deployment practice.
Personal Weapons	Contact Distance	Full body coordination and conditioning	Legal in all states.	Training recommended plus continued practice.

Table 10.2 Improvised Weapons Categories

After reviewing these charts, note that the greater the range, effectiveness, and capability of a weapon in stopping a physical attack, the greater the restrictions and legislation and the greater amount of training required. This is not by coincidence.

Nobody wants violence, but unfortunately our world has not yet evolved to where it has been eradicated. You can click on the news and find moment-by-moment evidence that violence is VERY much a part of our global society. As long as this remains the case, there will always be the need for the use of weapons to defend against violence.

PART 3

PreFense® Applied

Part III Overview

In Part III all six remaining chapters are structured in an easily accessible format directly applying PreFense®.

For each chapter you will see the blueprint of how to break the attack cycle divided into its three component parts, introducing each division of protective measures as applied to that section of the attack cycle:

Step 1 Look · Step 2 Choose · Verify · Step 3 Stalk	Step 3 Stalk · Plan · Step 4 Close	Step 5 Attack
Unlimited Options	Limited Options	3 Options
Maximum amount of time/ least amount of effort	Less Time/ More Effort	Least Time/ Max Effort
Avoid	Mitigate	Defend
Assess, Plan, Act–*The APA Process*	Assess & Respond	React
Proactive Measures	Active Measures	Reactive Measures
Public Mode	Alert Mode	Act Mode
Eliminate Soft Target Indicators	Deny Opportunity	Flight, Fight, Freeze
Applied to Step 1 through the first half of Step 3	Applied to the last half of Step 3 through Step 4	Applied to Step 5

CHAPTER 11

Active Shooter Management

"It is part of our reality that we have to think about what we would do if we were to be caught in an active shooter event."
Peter Anders[1]

In This Chapter You Will Be Introduced To...

...how to manage an active shooter attack. Following the natural flow of a threat progression an active shooting can be stopped proactively, actively, or reactively by breaking the attack cycle at any step—this chapter addresses these in order of safest option first.

At A Glance

The very last thing you'd expect is to get shot at. Nonetheless, it does happen. It happens often and can happen anywhere—including your own home. As such we are motivated to seek protection against an active shooter attack. The concepts and measures included in this chapter will help you prepare for and prevent an attack, as opposed to waiting for an attack to already be in progress only to react.

How Do I Use This In Real Life?

You have the right to know what you and your family are provided, by way of facility and organizational support, with regards to protection against an active shooter. Most of us cannot directly impact, or are at the mercy of, management policy and procedures.

Nonetheless, attackers are deterred by hard targets and drawn to soft targets. From the predator's optic, there are two considerations in determining where a target is on that scale from soft to hard—people and the

1 *Source: Millersville University, Millersville, Pennsylvania, newspaper The Snapper: April 3, 2013, in an article entitled "Student Teachers Get a Dose of Intruder Training." Written by Carissa Slawecki. The quote is from Millerville University Police Chief, Peter Anders. http://thesnapper.com/2013/04/03/student-teachers-get-a-dose-of-intruder-training/*

facilities they occupy. To a would-be active shooter, each is considered a predictable target. In maintaining the envelope of protection, it's imperative to understand how to harden both of these predictable targets.

You can decide to sit back and completely ignore the persistent issue of active shooter attacks now permeating every sector of our society, or you can choose to do something about it. Rather than being purely reactive, this chapter offers you the viable option of a holistic approach to your protection and that of your family from such a volatile and pervasive threat.

Empowered by the protective measures presented here, you will be armed with the threat management and protection tools needed to address and defeat an active shooter attack in your home, at work, or just about anywhere.

What The Pros Know

Running errands, at work, at school, or even sitting at a movie, the very last thing you'd expect is to get shot at—right? Nonetheless it does happen. It happens often and can happen anywhere—including your own home.

The U.S. Department of Homeland Security (DHS), defines an active shooter as "an individual actively engaged in killing or attempting to kill people in a confined and populated area; in most cases, active shooters use firearms(s) and there is no pattern or method to their selection of victims."[2] In other cases such individuals use knives or other weapons.[3]

Active shootings occur all over the globe—China, Finland, England, Germany and other countries with very strict gun control laws have not been exempt. The US is not without its share of incidents:

Sandy Hook Elementary School—Newtown, Connecticut, December 14, 2012. casualties: 26 dead; 2 wounded.

Century 16 Movie Theater—Aurora Colorado, July 20, 2012, casualties: 12 dead; 58 wounded.

Virginia Tech—Blacksburg, Virginia. April 16, 2007, casualties: 32 dead; 17 wounded—and the list goes on.

---

2 *Active Shooter - How To Respond; USDHS, October 2008; http://www.dhs.gov/xlibrary/assets/archive/active_shooter_booklet.pfd, Page 3*

3 *http://www.foxnews.com/story/2009/01/22/virginia-tech-student-stabbed-to-death-on-campus-was-decapitated/*

If you and your family never frequent such facilities[4] as restaurants, movie theaters, parking lots, office buildings, beauty salons, supermarkets, health clubs, schools, hospitals[5], then you have no need to worry about confronting an active shooter in public. However, the rest of us, regardless where we live, are certainly motivated to seek protection against an active shooter—protection afforded by effective measures.

Although knowing how to run, hide or fight[6] may be quite useful as a reactive measure to surviving an active shooter incident at Step 5, in terms of the overall attack cycle timeline this represents only a third of your available options. In addition to reactive measures, you would be far better served in managing an active shooter incident by applying both proactive and active measures.

In taking this holistic approach, we will first analyze the anatomy of an active shooter attack and then use it to apply our knowledge of breaking each step of the attack cycle using appropriate proactive and reactive measures. Let's begin with proactive measures.

Proactive Measures

Beginning at Step 1—Look, running all the way through and including the first half of Step 3—Stalk/Verify, and in public mode you have the opportunity to avoid an active shooter threat entirely by applying proactive measures.

---

4 *To aid in our studies, the word "facility" or "facilities" refers to your home, restaurants, movie theaters, parking lots, commercial buildings, schools, medical offices and such. Additionally the word "occupant" or "occupants" refer to you, members of your family and other protectees.*

5 ***L.A. Fitness**—Collier Township, Pennsylvania, August 4, 2009. Casualties: 3 dead; 9 wounded. **Pathmark Supermarket**—Old Bridge, New Jersey, August 31, 2012. Casualties: 2 dead. **Family Dental Care Center**—Simi Valley, California, July 2, 2009. Casualties: 1 dead, 3 wounded. **M&M Beauty Salon**—Casselberry, Florida, October 9, 2012. Casualties: 3 dead, 1 wounded. **Accent Signage Systems Office Building**—Minneapolis, Minnesota, September 27, 2012. Casualties: 5 dead, 3 wounded. **Café Racer Coffee Shop**—Seattle, Washington, May 30, 2012. Casualties: 5 dead, 3 wounded. **Parkwest Medical Center** parking lot—Knoxville, Tennessee, April 19, 2010. Casualties: 1 dead; 2 wounded. **Chardon High School**—Cleveland, Ohio, February 27, 2012. Casualties: 3 dead; 3 wounded. **University of Pittsburgh Medical Center**—Pittsburgh, Pennsylvania, March 8, 2012. Casualties: 1 Dead; 5 Wounded. **Oikos University**—Oakland, California, April 2, 2012. Casualties: 7 dead; 3 wounded. **Azana Spa**—Brookfield, Wisconsin, October 21, 2012. Casualties: 3 dead; 4 wounded. **Clackamas Town Center**—Happy Valley, Oregon, December 11, 2012. Casualties: 2 dead, 1 wounded. **Howard County Shopping Mall**—Columbia, Maryland, January 25, 2014. Casualties: 3 dead; 5 wounded.*

6 *Run, Hide, Fight—Surviving an Active Shooter Event is a DHS Grant Funded Project of the Regional Catastrophic Planning Initiative produced by the City of Houston Mayor's Office of Public Safety and Homeland Security and is an excellent protection resource available through http://www.readyhoustontx.gov/videos.html.*

You can take advantage of unlimited options and opportunity by using the likes of situational awareness and the APA process to help you eliminate soft target indicators.

Step 1 Look	Step 2 Choose	Verify	Step 3 Stalk

Unlimited Options

Maximum amount of time/ least amount of effort

Avoid

Assess, Plan, Act–*The APA Process*

Proactive Measures

Public Mode

Eliminate Soft Target Indicators

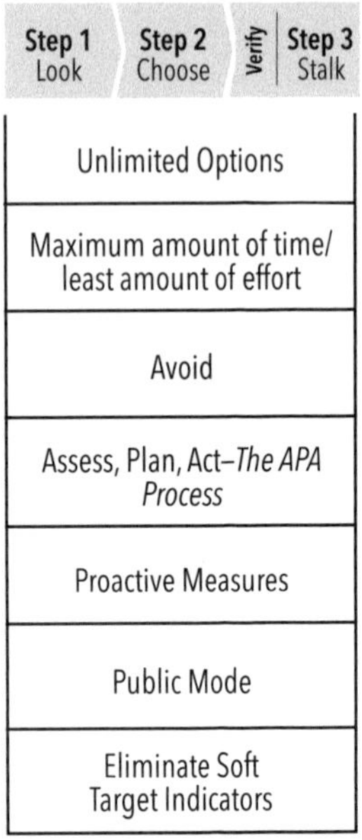

Anatomy Of An Active Shooter Attack

Active shooter attacks are dynamic incidents that vary greatly from one attack to another and DHS notes in their active shooter booklet that, "there is no pattern or method to their selection of victims."[7] Given that there is no identifiable pattern or method available to analyze, we can use PreFense® to effectively manage and protect against such a threat.

Study of each of the three essential items composing the anatomy of an attack required for an active shooter to carry out an attack, will lead to effective protective measures which can be used to manage and protect both facilities and their occupants against such attacks.

Applying the anatomy of an attack to an active shooter incident we end up with the usual tripod legs supporting any "successful" attack: 1—the target—facility and/or its occupants, 2—the bad guy—active shooter, and 3—the process—the attack cycle. Absent even one of these legs it is not possible for an active shooter to carry out a successful attack.

With the desired outcome of defeating an active shooter attack using a proactive approach, let's begin by examining the first leg of our tripod —the target.

In looking at the entirety of protecting a target we must first understand what makes up the target and who is doing the protecting. The target, in this case, is comprised of both a *facility*—the building, and its *occupants*—people.

Those who would be in charge of protecting the target, if it were a commercial building, might be the likes of operations managers and security administrators. In the case of schools it might be campus police, dean/ principal and teachers. In the case of your home then it is *you* who would be in charge. Like any security administrator, you would need to know the most effective protective measures available.

7 http://www.dhs.gov/xlibrary/assets/active_shooter_booklet.pdf

To accommodate both perspectives—one from a facilities (to include your home) management point of view and the other from a non-managerial point of view—the following analysis is presented from both viewpoints to provide the widest scope of understanding.

Analysis For Risk Mitigation

The 2012 Edition of the New York City Police Department's (NYPD *Active Shooter: Recommendations and Analysis for Risk Management,* was released in the wake of the shootings in Newtown, Connecticut. This new edition includes an updated analysis and compendium of active shooter incidents nationwide through December 21, 2012, incorporating 43 incidents (including 5 foiled attacks) that occurred in the approximately two-year period since the release of the 2010 Edition. The analysis is an accurate representation of verifiable data and a tremendous resource from which the majority of the following statistics and information is derived. The NYPD organized attack locations in the active shooter data set into five categories:

1. Schools
2. Office Buildings
3. Factories and Warehouses
4. Open Commercial Areas
5. Other Facilities

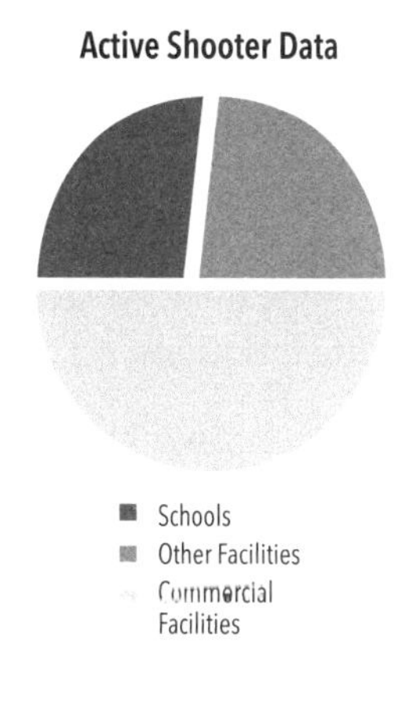

The NYPD's analysis demonstrates that less than one-third of attacks included in the active shooter data set took place at schools; roughly one-half occurred at commercial facilities, such as office buildings, factories and warehouses, and open commercial areas.

For convenient reference, we will divide the data into two general categories: shootings at schools and shootings at non-schools.

Prepared with the information from this analysis, let's get back to addressing our first leg of the anatomy of an active shooter attack—the target, beginning with eliminating indicators.

Eliminate Indicators

The importance of eliminating soft target indicators cannot be stressed enough. The instant you present yourself as a harder target, the less interested a predator will be. How can we convert a predictable target to a hardened target? What does it take to eliminate indicators for a facility as well as for its occupants?

According to the NYPD study[8] within the last five years of the 2012 edition, there were at least 15 high-profile, high casualty-producing active shooter incidents. Most of these cases have occurred in locations where the shooter has been undeterred from carrying out his or her attack. The incident locations are described as soft targets with limited active security measures or armed personnel to provide protection.

Whether at a school or non-school location there are certain proactive measures which may be taken to harden facilities and occupants in such a manner as to deflect the interest of a would-be active shooters and cause *"them to shift their focus to less protected [target(s)]."* [9]

Let's directly address the hardening of this target by its two constituent parts—facilities and occupants.

Hardening The Facility

Again considering that the facility can be your home, office, or the kids' school, the following proactive measures referencing facilities are recommended by DHS, NYPD, and other authoritative federal and state organizations:

- Conduct a realistic security assessment to determine the facility's vulnerability to an active shooter attack.
- Identify multiple evacuation routes and practice evacuations under varying conditions; post evacuation routes in conspicuous locations throughout the facility; ensure that evacuation routes account for individuals with special needs and disabilities.

8 *Active Shooter: Recommendations and Analysis for Risk Mitigation, NYPD, 2012; http://www.nypdshield.org/public/siteFiles/documents/activeshooter.pdf*

9 *United States Department of Homeland Security, US National Strategy for the Physical Protection of Critical Infrastructures and Key Assets, p. viii; http://www.dhs.gov/xlibrary/assets/Physical_Strategy.pdf*

- Designate shelter locations with thick walls, solid locking doors, interior windows, first-aid emergency kits, communication devices, and duress alarms.
- Designate a point-of-contact with knowledge of the facility's security procedures and floor plan to liaise with police and other emergency agencies in the event of an attack.
- Vary security guards' patrols and patterns of operation.
- Limit access to blueprints, floor plans, and other documents containing sensitive security information, but make sure these documents are available to law enforcement responding to an incident.
- Establish a central command station.

Access control is a proactive measure, which facilities need to establish as part of their operational planning. However, proactively hardening the facility itself represents only 50% of the effort in converting a target. The other half is to harden your people.

Hardening Your Occupants

Controlling access is a mindset as well as a physical reality. You must have a mindset of exactly who you want to allow in and who you want to keep out—then build barriers around that. If you set up walls but let everyone in then what's the use?

Any layered protective solution consists of hardening your buildings with armored glass, locks, alarms and cameras; however, even the most hardened facility remains vulnerable to threats targeting untrained personnel. Your people are your most valuable asset as well as the first line of awareness, proactive and active defense. An active shooting, child abduction, harassment, physical assault and or other violent acts can happen to anyone moving to and from your building(s) or while occupying your building(s).

As a homeowner or a facilities manager, you realize that an essential element in effective security is to harden your people. You know that if your family (teachers, employees, students, etc.), are not trained to meet the demands of such a potentially lethal threat as an active shooter attack then they remain unprotected. It is incumbent upon you to provide a means by which to harden your people.

That means is training—the only way to convert your family/people into hard targets. Such training or "preventative defense," must include proactive, active and reactive[10] measures.

Given the wide variety of available programs there is no excuse for exposure to known threats due to negligence. Training is a low-cost, minimally intrusive and recommended protective measure that is critical to converting your family/people to hard targets.

Educated people, made situationally aware and prepared with protective measures as covered in this chapter, make hardened occupants. A hardened facility and its hardened occupants—stripped of soft target indicators—send a loud and clear message to any would-be active shooter that this is a hard target.

Using proactive measures you can eliminate soft target indicators by hardening your facilities, educating your people and preventing the actuality and appearance of being a soft target to avoid an active shooter threat.

The sooner pre-attack behaviors can be perceived, the sooner they may be stopped. Hence, the use of behavioral management as part of your proactive measures is strongly encouraged. Referencing the active shooter and with the desired outcome of defeating an active shooter attack, let's move forward with our capabilities in breaking each step of the active shooter attack cycle by starting with the facts, organizing them, and then making accurate assessments based on verifiable data.

Step 3 Stalk / Plan	Step 4 Close
Limited Options	
Less Time/ More Effort	
Mitigate	
Assess & Respond	
Active Measures	
Alert Mode	
Deny Opportunity	

Active Measures

Given less time and requiring more effort, now past midway of the attack cycle you are afforded limited options and opportunity to break the cycle from the latter half of Step 3—Stalk/Plan, all the way through and including all of Step 4—Close.

10 *The introduction of drills into your emergency preparedness such as ALICE and others: http//. www.una.edu/psi/docs/Alice%20Training*

Nonetheless, you can use active measures to deny a motivated and capable active shooter their opportunity by observing and acting upon pre-attack threat indicators to mitigate an active shooter threat.

Further Analysis

The NYPD's analysis demonstrates that the preponderance of active shooters are male. The age distribution for active shooters at schools is from 15-19 years old, and in non-school facilities 35-44 years of age.

The analysis further demonstrates that 98% of active shooter incidents were carried out by a single attacker. Some active shooters did little or no planning and attacked impulsively, while others did extensive planning, including pre-operational surveillance (prior observation of the intended location of the attack).

Studies[11] show that some active shooters begin surveillance, careful planning, researching, acquiring supplies and equipment, and testing or rehearsing plans weeks, months, or sometimes years before an attack. Thus, efforts to manage this risk must also begin long before an attack.

The NYPD's analysis reveals that active shooters are often members of the communities they target and shows that the majority of active shooter attacks occurred when the perpetrator had either an academic (schools) or professional (non-school) relationship with at least one of the victims. However, in 26% of attacks in the active shooter data set, the shooter had no prior relationship to the victims, confirming that active shooter attacks can occur even without any prior altercation or grievance. Moreover, of the 87 attacks studied that involved professional relationships less than one-third were perpetrated by individuals who were no longer employed by the organization at the time of the attack, implying that the threat from active shooter attacks is not limited to disgruntled former employees. In many cases, these attacks resulted from disagreements among current employees of the organization. Such cases provide clear examples of pre-attack behavior threat indicators, which have proven to be the denominating precursor in each incident.

11 For example, the Secret Service conducted a study of the thinking and behavior of persons who attacked, or tried to attack, a prominent public official or public figure in the U.S. between 1949 and 1996. The study is referred to as the Exceptional Case Study Project (ECSP). The goal of the ECSP was to identify what was known (or knowable) about assassins and would-be assassins leading up to an attack that could be useful in prevention. For more information see http://www.secretservice.goc/ntac.shtml

Active shooter attacks are the product of organized thinking and behavior. Active shooters consider violence an acceptable or permissible solution to a problem. These are not random, spontaneous, or impulsive acts; rather they are methodically planned over a period of days, months, and years. Active shooters have a range of motives, which include a desire for fame and notoriety, to bring national attention to a perceived problem, to avenge a perceived wrong, or to seek law-enforcement assisted suicide. They rarely direct threats to the target or to law enforcement. They do, however, communicate their intentions and/or unusual interest in the target to friends, co-workers, and loved ones.

A recommended active measure is to identify such threat indicators. A noteworthy resource in pre-attack behavior threat indicators hails from a study entitled *"The Role of Warning Behaviors in Threat Assessment: An Exploration and Suggested Typology"* [12]

The authors of this study put forth what they call a "typology" outlining eight warning behaviors, essentially threat indicators or red flags, to help identify pre-attack behavior. These warning behaviors must be actively watched for, if they are to be used as part of a holistic approach to protection.

If a warning behavior is actively identified it should raise the level of concern about an individual who may be predisposed to become an active shooter.

The eight warning behaviors are listed by the authors in the following excerpt:

1. **Pathway Warning Behavior**—any behavior that is part of research, planning, preparation, or implementation of an attack.

2. **Fixation Warning Behavior**—any behavior that indicates an increasingly pathological preoccupation with a person or a cause. It is measured by: (a) increasing perseveration (uncontrollable repetition of a particular response) on the person or cause; (b) increasingly strident opinion; (c) increasingly negative characterization of the object of fixation; (d)

12 The Role of Warning Behaviors in Threat Assessment: An Exploration and Suggested Typology. Meloy, JR et al. Behav. Sci Law 30: 256-279 (2012). Available online at http://forensiceuropa.files.wordpress.com/2011/11/2011_theroleofwarningbehaviorsinthreat.pdf impact on the family or other associates of the object of fixation, if present and aware; (e) angry emotional undertone. It is typically accompanied by social or occupational deterioration.

In an actual incident in Santa Monica, California—the Santa Monica-Malibu Unified School District superintendent confirmed the gunman who killed five [June 7, 2013] was removed from a continuation high school in 2006 after being identified as at risk of committing violence. Superintendent Sandra Lyon told The Times that a teacher observed disturbing behaviors from John Zawahri around his discussion of weapons and violence. District officials contacted law enforcement, she said, and Zawahri was eventually removed from the public schools. "He did demonstrate some threats towards students and we did act immediately on that, called law enforcement, and at that point they took over," Lyon said. "He clearly had exhibited interest in weapons; the teacher saw that, and acted on it.[13]

3. **Identification Warning Behavior**—any behavior that indicates a psychological desire to be a "pseudo-commando," identify with previous attackers or assassins, or identify oneself as an agent to advance a particular cause or belief system.
4. **Novel Aggression Warning Behavior**—an act of violence which appears unrelated to any pre-attack behavior which is committed for the first time.
5. **Energy Burst Warning Behavior**—an increase in the frequency or variety of any noted activities related to the target, even if the activities themselves are relatively innocuous, usually in the days or weeks before the attack.
6. **Leakage Warning Behavior**—the communication to a third party of intent to do harm to a target through an attack.

13 Los Angeles Times "Santa Monica College gunman was expelled over violence fears" Matt Stevens June 21, 2013 http:..www.latimes.com/local/lanow/la-me-ln-santa-monica-college-shooter-schools-20130611,0,7906795.story

An example of "leakage" occurred in Chelan, Washington, on March 4, 2010 Charles Mustoe was arrested for planning an attack at Chelan High School. Mustoe planned to carry out the attack on April 20, 2011, the anniversary of the Columbine High school shooting. Reports state that Mustoe was angry about being bullied at school. The plot was foiled when the parents of a girl with whom Mustoe had discussed his plans alerted authorities.[14]

7. **Last Resort Warning Behavior**—evidence of a violent "action imperative," increasing desperation or distress through declaration in word or deed, forcing the individual into a position of last resort. There is no alternative other than violence, and the consequences are justified. The subject feels trapped.

8. **Directly Communicated Threat Warning Behavior**—the communication of a direct threat to the target or law enforcement beforehand. A threat is a written or oral communication that implicitly or explicitly states a wish or intent to damage, injure, or kill the target, or individuals symbolically or actually associated with the target.

This behavioral assessment approach is echoed by the US Department of Homeland Services in this excerpt from its active shooter course materials.[15]

Recognizing Potential Workplace Violence

An active shooter in your workplace may be a current or former employee, or an acquaintance of a current or former employee. Intuitive managers and co-workers may notice *characteristics of potentiality violent behavior* in an employee. Alert your Human Resources Department if you believe an employee or coworker exhibits potentially violent behavior indicators of potential violence by an employee. Employees typically do not just "snap," but *display indicators of potentially violent behavior over time.* If

14 *http://www.columbian.com/news.2010/mar/04/brewster-teen-charged-alleged-school-shooting-plot/*

15 *Active Shooter—How To Respond; USDHS, October 2008; http://www.dhs.gov/xlibrary/assets/active_shooter_booklet.pdf, p.11*

these behaviors are recognized, they can often be managed and treated. Potentially violent behaviors by an employee may include one or more of the following (this list of behaviors is not comprehensive, nor is it intended as a mechanism for diagnosing violent tendencies).[16]

- Increased use of alcohol and/or illegal drugs
- Unexplained increase in absenteeism; vague physical complaints
- Noticeable decrease in attention to appearance and hygiene
- Depression/withdrawal
- Resistance and overreaction to changes in policy and procedures
- Repeated violations of company policies
- Increased severe mood swings
- Noticeably unstable, emotional responses
- Explosive outbursts of anger or rage without provocation
- Suicidal; comments about "putting things in order"
- Behavior which is suspect of paranoia, ("everybody is against me")
- Increasingly talks of problems at home
- Escalation of domestic problems into the workplace; talk of severe financial problems
- Talk of previous incidents of violence
- Empathy with individuals committing violence
- Increase in unsolicited comments about firearms, other dangerous weapons and violent crimes"

16 *http://www.dhs.gov/active-shooter-preparedness*

Deny Opportunity

Actual cases of active shooter plots that were foiled illustrate the effectiveness of using behavioral management to deny opportunity.

Posting on a website—College Park, Maryland, on March 11, 2012 Alexander Song was arrested after posting on a website that he planned to "kill enough people to make it to national news." Song did not obtain weapons prior to his arrest.

Suspicious behavior—Covington, Louisiana, on August 5, 2011 Jacob Keller, Todd Singleton, and Daniel Hopkins planned to shoot fellow Lakeshore High School students during the first day of classes. Police foiled the plot when other students at the school alerted them to the students' suspicious behavior.

Immediate Environment Threat indicators

One more active measure that can be applied while the assailant is still at Step 3 or 4 is to use your situational awareness to watch for not only the unusual (e.g., sound of gunfire) or the obvious (e.g., bad guy walking in the back door waving a firearm), but for immediate environment threat indicators to include any ad hoc obstructions, barricades, or blockades of access points (doors, stairways, exit routes, etc.).

In an off-line communication with authorities who requested anonymity, referencing the April 26, 2007 Virginia Tech massacre; "when law enforcement responded to the incident already in progress, they found all three entrances chained and locked and found out later that he [the active shooter] had chained and locked the interior doors TWO DAYS prior. People noticed, but no one notified the police.

The doors are 2.5" thick and it took several valuable minutes for an entry team to shoot out the lock and gain access."[17]

Active shooters, after looking for and selecting their target, have been known to set up pre-planned blockades as part of their stalking phase, intending to trap victims and prolong their attacks.

17 *It's interesting to note additional observations from the same case: "[We were] amazed how many times he [the active shooter] showed up on everybody's radar and no one acted. In the two years leading up to the shootings, two different female students filed harassment complaints against him; they were both later dropped by the accusers. Two professors were worried enough about his sanity that they brought it to the attention of the campus authorities. They worried about his rights and did nothing. He had also gotten four speeding tickets in those two years."*

An active shooter is vulnerable to active measures.

Reactive Measures

Step 5
Attack

3 Options
Least Time/ Max Effort
Defend
React
Reactive Measures
Act Mode
Flight, Fight, Freeze

Given the least amount of time and requiring maximum effort, now at the very last step of the active shooter attack cycle you are afforded only three options and limited opportunity to break the cycle at Step 5—Attack, and defend against the threat.

You can take advantage of these three options by using reactive measures, situational awareness and defensive principles to either get away from, temporarily fight or surrender to your assailant(s).

In a commendable effort by a woman working at a school in Atlanta, Georgia an active shooter already at Step 5 started shooting. The woman reacted swiftly and engaged the attacker in conversation as part of her strategy to defend against the threat. Her actions de-escalated the situation to where the shooter ended up being taken into custody and no one inside or outside the school was hurt, despite the gunfire. School staff regularly trains for such threats involving trespassers and emergency protocol.[18]

The desired and beneficial outcome in reactive response to any active shooter attack is to keep any casualties to a minimum, and keep your scale of injury as low as possible. The best way to attain this desired outcome is to immediately and effectively stop the active shooter. Let's focus on this single and critical point of stopping an active shooter.

Stopping An Active Shooter

Back to the facts: according to NYPD statistics, 43 percent of active shooter incidents are ended by the application of force by police or security, 40 percent end in the shooter's suicide, 16 percent of the time the shooter

18 http://www.cnn.com/2013/08/21/us/georgia-school-gunshots/index.html

surrenders, and in less than one percent of the violence ends when the attacker flees.[19]

Paraphrasing the NYPD analysis, research has determined that aggressive action by even a single police officer is the most effective countermeasure in stopping an active shooter:

1. Shooting an assailant—or "aggressive action" (politically correct law enforcement terminology)—is the most effective countermeasure in stopping an active shooter.

Referencing Chapter 10—Weapons, in any life-or-death use-of-force defensive situation:

2. A trained individual operating a firearm is the single most effective means available to immediately stop a physical attack by single or multiple attackers intent on taking human life, *bar none.*

Given 1 and 2 above, one may logically conclude that the very best defensive response against an active shooter is a firearm operated by a qualified individual. Absent such optimal defensive response, you are unfortunately relegated to less effective measures.

Minus optimal defensive response you are relegated to less effective measures.

In lieu of the most effective countermeasure in stopping an active shooter—all remaining countermeasures available to stop an active shooter are inferior options. In that inferior defensive options may be all you are allowed, let's focus our study on these.

Inferior Defensive Options

In the event you find yourself in an active shooter situation at Step 5, remember that you are already behind the power curve in that you are reacting to an action. The condition of your environment, the condition

19 *Active Shooter: Recommendations and Analysis for Risk Mitigation, NYPD, 2012; http://www.nypdshield.org/public/SiteFiles/documents/Activeshooter.pdf*

of the active shooter—where he is, what he is doing, and the condition of yourself and those around you, are in constant flux.

It is important to be able to continually assess these conditions and be able to appropriately respond. The best way to accomplish this task is by using the reactive measures you already have in your toolkit starting with the OODA Loop. Starting with taking flight which we know is the safest, once you start moving off that X, you begin the OODA Loop all over again. Basing your decisions and your actions on your observations and situational awareness, it's time to make a plan. Such a plan doesn't have to be elaborate.

In fact, the more complex the plan the less likely it would be followed under duress. One reactive measure you should consider as part of your plan is to move and communicate.

Move And Communicate

In response to an active shooter attack, your plan should include the two most important principles of surviving a gunfight without a gun: move and communicate. Optimally, both should be done concurrently. Let's address each one.

"Move" means move off the X as covered previously and toward a position of safety. Normally distance is a really good thing, as plenty of space between yourself and the attacker(s) widens the reactionary gap and lowers your scale of injury.

"Communicate" means to use your verbal skills to inform or warn others or provide direction to others to assist you, move with you or just get out of the way. Your cell phone, voice and even hand signals are all valid methods of instantly relaying real-time information while under duress.

Get In Or Get Out

Although it's true that targets are more difficult to hit at greater distances, especially if they're moving erratically, and moving targets are far more difficult to hit than stationary targets, you don't want to risk the chance of a skilled or lucky shot. You want to create distance but not across wide-open space with nothing intervening between you and incoming rounds (bullets).

Given an active shooter in a physical structure, there are only two options for your movement in avoiding flying lead: one is to get *out* of the building, and the other is get *in*.

Plan A—Get Out

The safer of the two is to get out; or exit the building. Move directly away from the high-threat area. Putting plenty of space between yourself and the attacker(s) widens that reactionary gap and lowers your scale of injury. To do that you need to know where the building exits are and the path to get to them.

Cover And Concealment

Once you're outside the building you should continue to move beyond the line of sight of the shooter and away from the sound of gunfire until you have gotten behind suitable cover. Cover is something that will actually stop incoming bullets such as a concrete or brick or solid steel wall or door, the wheel well of a large truck or vehicle, and so on. Cover will also conceal you from the shooter's line of sight.

If cover is not immediately available, then your other option is concealment. Concealment will not stop bullets but will at least hide you from the attacker(s). If the shooter can't see you then he cannot take aim at you. Remember that wide-open spaces are less than optimal in a gunfight. Also note that cover will provide concealment whereas concealment will not provide cover.

In the event that you are outside the building and behind cover or concealment, and the opportunity to call 911 presents itself, do so if it will not compromise your position or give away your hiding place.

Plan B—Get In

If you can't get out, then get or stay in. If for whatever reason you can't exit the building, then movement to a safe position inside the building is your next best option. The guidelines of surviving a gunfight without a gun apply just the same inside the building as they do outside the building: move to a position of safety away from the shooter's line of sight and the sound of gunfire, and seek cover or at least concealment.

When moving be sure to keep your head down below windows and half-partitions. Look where you're going before you move. A good way to ensure you look first is to say to yourself, "OK, that looks clear, I'm going over there..." in your mind (not out loud) and then move off the X. In the event that you are inside the building and behind cover or concealment, and the opportunity to call 911 presents itself, do so if it will not compromise your position or give away your hiding place. Failure to move to a better position due to indecision (i.e., not completing the OODA Loop) may lead to disastrous results. Time is not on your side. When you've made the decision to move, then move.

Verbal skills are considered the use of vocal ability to assist in completing an objective. These can be used to tactfully defuse a heated argument, to succinctly communicate information, or to avoid divulging sensitive or too much information.

Move and communicate means whether you decide to get out or get in, use simple hand signals, or where appropriate, verbal skills to help keep the group moving and assure those with you that it's going to be alright. Insist that they go with you, but if they remain fearful or stubborn and won't move, you must make the decision to leave them behind or use physical force to bring them along with you. Similar to an aircraft exit emergency, you cannot waste precious seconds collecting personal items. Getting yourself and your family out of immediate danger and behind cover is your highest priority.

Barricade Option

When moving you should try to get outside the building, but if you have no other choice and are caught in a room, then lock the door if it locks. If it doesn't, place a barricade between yourself and the threat by moving a large heavy object in front of the door such as a heavy table or file cabinet that you're physically able to move, and then turn out the lights. Get behind a heavy object (take cover). If you have your cell phone, tum off all sound and continue to communicate by text or email. If others are with you try to keep them calm and quiet behind cover and/or concealment—and don't forget to breathe. The object of this plan is to hide from your attacker(s) by staying out of sight, protected by cover (something that might stop bullets), and remaining silent.

Plan C—Get Him

If you've run out of options and you're down to Plan C—you have done everything right but somehow you end up facing an active shooter who is breaking his way into your barricaded room and you have nowhere else to go. Trapped and with no further options to get away, there remains yet one possible action and that is to take down the shooter using any means. If possible use a weapon.

Remember there are no rules. Your only objective is to take down the attacker(s). Here are your three possible outcomes:

1. Get Injured
2. Get Killed
3. Get The Shooter—and maybe get any other able-bodied bystanders to assist you.

It's down to either you or him. Again, there are no further options.

The end result of dedicated armed conflict is either he gets you or you get him. If you're not up for the fight, then don't get in the way of or prevent others from doing what it takes to stop a deadly threat.

Keep in mind that the person with the gun always has the advantage so you need to meet force with force, commit to violent action in keeping with your protective mindset, doing whatever it takes to win.

What To Do

The following is somewhat graphic in nature as is an active shooter attack. However, there comes a point in a physical conflict where it's down to you or him or them. Yes, as some people are inclined or even taught to do—you can always give up, but those of you who refuse to accept this option, please read on.

The very best defensive weapon in any lethal-force encounter is a firearm. If you have a firearm and are trained to use it, then be mindful of your backstop or what's behind the active shooter and proceed to stop the threat.

If no firearm is available then what other weapons are available? Is there a TASER®, pepper spray, a stun gun, an impact or edged weapon available? If no traditional weapons are available, the next best thing is an improvised weapon such as an edged weapon—kitchen cutlery, screwdriver, piece of broken glass, sharp piece of metal, or an impact weapon—chair, baseball bat, corner of a heavy book, fire extinguisher. Run your resource assessment listing. What's available to you and readily accessible as a weapon of opportunity? Most buildings, unless they are completely unfurnished, have all kinds of improvised weapons lying around at your disposal.

If your resource assessment listing comes up empty, don't forget about your belt, a pen, your shoes, and even your shirt, which can be used as a flexible weapon. For example, you could wrap your shirt around a steel paperweight and swing it at the back of the head of an active shooter with all your strength. Even in the absolute worst-case scenario, you still have your personal weapons: fists, knees, elbows, fingernails, and teeth—you are never without those. The combined physical force of two, three, or more determined people, even with bare hands, is capable of overwhelming even an armed assailant.

In this real-world practical example a 74-year-old retired U.S. Army Colonel decided to tackle the Tucson gunman after watching him shoot Arizona Congresswoman Gabrielle Giffords. "Something had to be done," Bill Badger said on "Good Morning America." Badger wasn't the only one who risked his life to stop the carnage. One man clobbered gunman Jared Loughner on the back of the head with a folding chair. A 61-year-old woman wrestled a fresh magazine away from Loughner as he tried to reload. Others jumped on him and held him down, ripping the gun from his hands.[20]

Counterattack

In protection terms, counterattack simply means fighting back—exactly as did the 74-year-old man and the 61-year-old woman in the Giffords case. It describes "fighting fire with fire" that is force against force, and is always the last ditch effort to survive any nasty situation.

When is a good time to counterattack an active shooter? In an active shooter attack the majority of casualties or injuries accumulate in the first ten minutes, so you need to run your OODA Loop as quickly as possible and act immediately upon making your decision. The faster the better.

Unless you have a firearm your best opportunity for effective defense is at conversational distances. To effectively raise his scale of injury you must close the reactionary gap. In a barricaded room where he is coming for you this won't be a concern as he's trying to do the same.

The active shooter in the process of using his weapon may also present opportunity for counterattack. Although transpiring quite rapidly, there are a few technical aspects of a gunfight that you can use in your favor:

1. **Finger Not On The Trigger** - to send bullets in your direction, his finger MUST be on the trigger. If you see his trigger finger anywhere other than on the trigger then he is unable to fire the gun which would present an opportunity for counterattack.

20 *http://abcnews.go.com/US/heros-rep-gabrielle-giffords-shooting-tucson-arizona-subdued/story?id=12580345#.UcTIAIDn-M8*

2. **Weapon Not Ready** - to discharge rounds at you there are a few firearm mechanics that need to be in place:

    - The gun must be in battery (slide forward, or chamber lined up with barrel) with any safety or de-cocking lever in correct position (if these are engaged, it could prevent him from firing). If you see that he's pressing the trigger and no bullets are discharging, this presents an opportunity for counterattack.

    - The gun must be loaded (a cartridge seated in the chamber). If he has run out of bullets or is in the middle of reloading this could present an excellent opportunity for counterattack. Other than on TV and in the movies, all guns eventually run out of bullets! Unlike the movies real firearms may be reloaded once the source of ammunition has been depleted. Reloading a firearm, especially under duress, can take several seconds. You can use this valuable time to take him down.

    - The gun must be pointed at you. If you see the muzzle—business end of the gun—pointed toward the ceiling, toward the floor, or away from you and/or others, this presents another opportunity for counterattack.

    - The gun has malfunctioned. All firearms can malfunction, or fail to shoot due to mechanical or operator error. Either way if you see him trying to manipulate the weapon, without discharging projectiles, then this presents an opportunity for counterattack.

3. **A Lull In The Action**—if he's not shooting, then he's not shooting! Anytime you see him not shooting this presents an opportunity for counterattack.

4. **While He's Distracted**—a pen driven into his eye or throat, spraying him with insect repellant, or

flinging scalding hot water into his eyes will distract him from his shooting spree and can cause mechanical compliance. Slide a lightweight desk toward him or fling a chair at him—he has to deal with it. If you notice that he's distracted, this presents an opportunity for counterattack.

5. **While He's Moving**—you're moving, he's moving, the weapon is moving, it's hard enough to hit a stationary target let alone a moving one especially if the shooter and the gun are also moving around. If you notice that he's moving around and not shooting, then this presents yet another opportunity for counterattack.

Don't wait for him to take up a better shooting position. The only place you need to worry about being is directly in front of that muzzle—anywhere else at that close distance is fair game. Anytime you can safely launch a counterattack is an excellent opportunity!

Throw things at him like books, shoes, canned beverages, food, backpacks, a stapler, purse—any object you can lift up and throw that will reach him will help distract him. Attack him from behind or above. Impair his visual acuity by targeting the eyes—shining a bright flashlight in his eyes is enough, even in broad daylight.

In a firefight there are no rules except for one—
no matter what it takes—you win.

Regardless of which plan you follow or whatever your position, inside or outside the threat area, when law enforcement arrives remain calm, do not shout, keep your hands where they can be seen. Upon initial arrival on scene the authorities' one and only objective is to stop the shooter—follow their instructions and do not get in their way.

In any physical attack, when you move off the X you are immediately getting yourself away from someplace really bad. When you move and communicate you are in transition off the X and toward safety while notifying others with the end result of either getting in or getting out.

Your decisions and actions in defense against an active shooter threat are critical—especially in those precious moments at the beginning of the active shooter attack cycle. By the time events progress toward the end of the cycle you must be prepared to do whatever it takes for you and those around you to come out of it alive.

Step 1 Look · **Step 2** Choose · Verify · **Step 3** Stalk · Plan	**Step 4** Close	**Step 5** Attack
Unlimited Options	Limited Options	3 Options
Maximum amount of time/ least amount of effort	Less Time/ More Effort	Least Time/ Max Effort
Avoid	Mitigate	Defend
Assess, Plan, Act–*The APA Process*	Assess & Respond	React
Proactive Measures	Active Measures	Reactive Measures
Public Mode	Alert Mode	Act Mode
Eliminate Soft Target Indicators	Deny Opportunity	Flight, Fight, Freeze

CHAPTER 12

Residential Protection

"For a man's home is his castle, & domus sua cuique est tutissimum refugium; for where shall a man be safe, if it be not in his home?"
Sir Edward Coke[1]

On the pleasant summer afternoon of July 22, 2007, in a quiet New England neighborhood Mrs. Jennifer Hawke-Petit and her eleven year-old daughter Michaela went to a local grocery store in Cheshire, Connecticut, shopping for the evening meal, which would be prepared by Michaela. Both of them, along with Jennifer's other daughter Hayley (age 17), would be brutally raped and murdered just hours later in an invasion of their home.

While shopping, Mrs. Petit and Michaela had been targeted by a predator—Joshua A. Komisarjevsky—who followed them home, and planned to later rob the family by home invasion. An additional predator—Steven J. Hayes, was an accomplice who later attributed the infamous outcome of their killing spree to a change in plans.

Upon their arrival on the morning of July 23, 2007, Komisarjevsky and Hayes found the kids' father, Dr. William Petit, asleep on a couch on the porch. Komisarjevsky noticed a baseball bat left in the yard, bludgeoned William Petit with it, and then left him physically bound in the basement of the house. The children and their mother were also each bound and locked in their respective bedrooms.

The predators then proceeded to sack the residence for valuables. Hayes later claimed that he and Komisarjevsky decided they were not satisfied with their plunder, and that a bankbook was found which had an available balance. Hayes convinced Jennifer to withdraw $15,000 from her line of credit at the bank. A gas station's video surveillance camera captured

1 Sir Edward Coke (1552-1634) English lawyer, judge, and politician, considered to be the greatest jurist of the Elizabethan era.

Hayes purchasing $10 worth of gasoline in two cans he had stolen from the Petit home. After returning to the occupied house, and filling the car with the gas, he took Jennifer to the bank.

Bank surveillance cameras captured the transaction, which showed Jennifer Hawke-Petit slide a hand-written note across the counter informing the teller of her situation. Not sure what to do, the teller then called 911 and reported the details to police. Under duress Jennifer left the bank, was picked up by Hayes, and drove away.

The Cheshire police response to the bank tellers' "urgent bid" began with assessing the situation and setting up a perimeter. These preliminary measures employed by the police exhausted more than half an hour and provided the time used by the assailants to conclude their modified plan.

The daughters, while tied to their beds, had both been doused with gasoline; each had her head covered with a pillowcase. After igniting the fire Hayes and Komisarjevsky fled the scene. 17-year-old Hayley and 11-year-old Michaela both died.

William Petit had been able to escape his confines, crawl out the basement window, and call to a neighbor for help. According to records, the neighbor indicated that he did not physically recognize Petit, due to the severity of Mr. Petit's injuries.

Hayes and Komisarjevsky fled the scene in the Petit family car. They were immediately pursued by police who had them under surveillance and arrested them one block away from the burning family home. The entire home invasion lasted approximately seven hours.

In This Chapter You Will Be Introduced To...

...the recommended protective concepts and measures of residential security. Protecting your things is important, but they can be replaced. Protecting yourself and your family is the truly important aspect of residential security and in this chapter you will learn to do both. In this chapter you will be introduced to keeping that envelope of protection around yourself and your family in knowing how to manage and protect against the threat of a home invasion.

At A Glance

You can potentially deter a burglar with locks and alarms. Someone who invades your home may be after more than property. In a home invasion there are many different types of threats and while some protective measures may overlap to help, some do not and are specific to application—both are indispensable in providing a safe and secure environment at home.

How Do I Use This In Real Life?

Take the time to prepare your home and your protective tools so that you can truly relax. Don't try and do it all at once. Every step forward is one more productive step to encouraging an attacker to look elsewhere.

It's that simple—set up your environment to detect, deter and delay attack. This gives you an insurmountable advantage over a planned or opportunistic invasion. Knowing what to do and why can make the difference in sound residential protection and planning.

What The Pros Know

At the end of a long day at school or work or after a lengthy trip away, which one of us doesn't look forward to coming home? It's the one place where your surroundings are the most familiar; you spend the majority of your off hours, wake up in the morning after a restful sleep, and immerse yourself in the things that mean the most to you. Home is where you spend quality time with your family and ultimately it's where you kick your feet up at the end of a long day, to unwind and switch your awareness to home mode.

Home is your castle, your sanctuary, your favorite place to be; it's where you and your family are the safest and feel the most secure. It's also a primary target of the predator.

Looking at it from the predator's optic, your home is a one-stop-shop of exploitable opportunity. To the drug addict, repeat offender, and criminal opportunist your home is a treasure trove of cash, expensive jewelry, high-end electronics, weapons, tools, and precious metals. To the sexual predator, your home is a prime hunting ground where potential victims can be predictably observed and targeted, knowing that when they are asleep or otherwise occupied that they are vulnerable to attack.

Knowing that law enforcement will most likely respond, most people think; "Well, if something bad happens here at home, I'll just dial 911." In terms of any threat progression, you are far better prepared to manage a home invasion if you are armed with the full gamut of proactive, active, and reactive measures.

In taking this holistic approach, we will first analyze the anatomy of a home invasion and then use it to apply our knowledge of breaking each step of the attack cycle using appropriate proactive, active and reactive measures. Let's begin with proactive measures.

Proactive Measures

Beginning at Step 1—Look, running all the way through and including the first half of Step 3—Stalk/Verify, you have the opportunity to avoid a home invasion entirely by applying proactive measures.

You can take advantage of unlimited options and opportunity by using the likes of situational awareness and the APA process to help you eliminate soft target indicators.

Step 1 Look	Step 2 Choose	Verify	Step 3 Stalk

Unlimited Options
Maximum amount of time/ least amount of effort
Avoid
Assess, Plan, Act–*The APA Process*
Proactive Measures
Public Mode
Eliminate Soft Target Indicators

Home Invasions

A home invasion is an unauthorized and forceful entry into a dwelling. It is a crime governed by state laws, which vary by state. A home intruder is a person who enters a home without permission.[2]

Your home may be invaded by one or more home intruders wielding dangerous weapons or an object that is likely to cause death or bodily injury used as a weapon. Such is an incident that occurred in Buhl, Idaho round 6:00 AM August 7, 2012. Leo Ray was reading and snoozing in an armchair in his living room when a loud knock echoed from the front door. Employees of his company regularly start work near his home at 6:30 AM so the early knock wasn't too unusual, he said. But, as he opened the door, Leo was met with three gun barrels in his face.

After 30 dangerous seconds of thinking it was a prank, Leo said he was shoved inside the house by the three gunmen. One said, "Listen, we're here to rob you and we want your money." One of the men held a gun to Leo's left temple with a hand on his right shoulder, while another man held a gun to Leo's right temple, resting a hand on his left shoulder. Another

2 *"Without Permission" per common law means without having obtained permission to enter from the owner or lessee of the dwelling or from any other person lawfully in possession or control of the dwelling.*

person, later identified as a 16-year-old boy accused of helping the other two, stood across the room with a rope and a gun in his hands. All three wore bandanas over their faces.

One of the men asked if anyone else was home, then took Leo into the bedroom where his wife, Judy, was still in bed. "I was just waking up," Judy said. "I heard murmuring." As the quiet conversation continued, Judy said she knew something was wrong. Then, the three masked men and Leo entered the room. Almost immediately one of the men was at her side, threatening to shoot her. Soon, Judy and Leo were both tied up, facedown, on their bed. "I started praying and I told God I didn't want to die," Judy said. "I didn't want Leo to die either."[3]

Burglary Versus Invasion

There's a notable difference between a burglary and a home invasion. If you or your family is home, then it's considered a home invasion. If you're not, it's considered a burglary. Criminals don't always know what they're walking into during the day, but at night it's a different story. Most burglaries happen between roughly 10:00 AM and 3:00 PM, while most home invasions occur between 6:00 PM and 6:00 AM. In other words, during a home invasion intruders are willing and prepared to take the risk of confronting the occupant(s).

Unlike active shooter incidents in which there are no identifiable patterns of attack related behavior available for analysis, with home invasions there are common patterns available for us to analyze. Leveraging this information and using your skills in breaking the cycle at any step along the way affords a holistic approach to protecting your home and family against such a threat.

Anatomy Of A Home Invasion

Study of each of the three individual components comprising the anatomy of an attack required for a home invasion will introduce effective protective measures which can be used to manage and protect your home and your family against such attacks.

Applying the anatomy of an attack to a home invasion you end up with the usual tripod legs supporting a successful attack:

---

3 *Alison Gene Smith, "Home Invasion: 'I Told God I didn't Want to Die'" Times-news, January 16, 2013, http://magicvalley.com/news/local/home-invasion-i-told-god-i-didn-t-want-to/article_aaadf1ac-5f8e-11e2-8ff9-001ae4bcf887a.html*

1. **Predictable Target**—your home, including its occupant(s)
2. **Bad Guy**—one or more intruder(s)
3. **Process**—the attack cycle itself.

Analyzing the profile of a home intruder provides an understanding of how to prepare for and defend against a home invasion by analysis of their attack related behaviors and from the predator's optic. Let's start with the predictable target—your home.

Eliminating Indicators

The first leg of the anatomy of a home invasion is the target—your home, which is comprised of both the physical structure (house, apartment, condo), and you, your family and/or other protectee(s).

How can this predictable target be converted to a hard target? Let's take a close look at how each component may be readily hardened.

Concentric Rings Of Protection

What can be done proactively to shield your dwelling? There is a traditional protective concept called concentric rings of protection using multiple rings—circles or layers of security used to create that 360-degree envelope of protection around your dwelling and all residents.

The concentric rings—multiple circles or layers—are like an onion of security wrapped around your home. The first layer would be located at the outer boundary, with additional layers as you move inward through your home toward things you value most. Rather than placing full reliance on a single layer or ring of protection, the application of multiple layers requires an intruder to penetrate a series of protective layers to reach his goal. The more protective layers or rings that exist between the outside world and the things contained inside, the better your protection.

The *outermost* ring—the perimeter defensive layer—might include a continuous fence, locking gates, exterior motion-sensor alarms or lighting, and a dog.

The *second* ring in—the exterior defensive layer, at any area of entry to the building—might include solid hardwood or metal exterior doors, an alarm, surveillance cameras, and sturdy bolt locks.

The *third* ring in—the interior defensive layer—might include internal locking doors, additional lighting, indoor motion detectors, and so on.

The *fourth* ring in—the core interior defensive layer—could include locking cabinets, a rugged safe, a safe room, and the like.

Deter, Detect, And Delay

The concentric rings of protection serve the purpose of accomplishing the "3Ds": **D**eter, **D**etect, and **D**elay an intruder.

Deter means to cause a predator to lose interest in your home as a potential target. An example of this is an intruder who tries the front door and finds it's locked, or observes surveillance cameras or hears the family dog barking, so he moves on. Here you have hardened the target to the point of deterring the predator from continuing.

Do you hide your valuables in a dresser drawer, or in a bedroom closet or the freezer? Those are among the very first places predators look along their route to the master bedroom. They know what they're looking for and where to look for it. Don't keep anything you can't replace in any of those three locations! Find a better hiding place or even better—get a safe. If you own any weapons, when you're not home these must ABSOLUTE-LY be in a safe! No matter how heavy a safe is, it doesn't matter—they will find a way to carry it away, thus it needs to be bolted into solid concrete or the equivalent, making it a formidable deterrent. Intruders want to get in and get out again within 10-15 minutes so "ten-minute proof" your valuables—making it more difficult for them to locate and access your valuables adding unwanted time and effort to accomplishing their goal.

The goal of deterrence is to cause the predator to move along to a less-protected target.

Detection of an intruder allows you to appropriately assess and respond to a situation. The earlier you can detect an intruder the better. Remember from Chapter 7—*Situational Awareness* that assessment and response are two completely separate activities with accurate assessment leading to *appropriate* response.

Delay caused by physical protection barriers such as fences, gates, sturdy locks, and alarms placed between an intruder and the interior of your home will accomplish three objectives:

1. You force them to assess the risk of breaking their own "10-15 minute do the job and get out of there" rule.

2. You give *yourself* more assessment and response time.
3. You allow additional time for *outside help* to arrive if needed.

There are two ways help may arrive to address an actual threat: either from *inside your home,* that is you moving toward the threat to address it, or from *outside your home,* such as the police or a neighbor coming to your aid.

Visible And Invisible Barriers

Although four concentric rings of protection are desirable, a minimum of three layers of visible barriers between an intruder and the core of your house should be included as part of your residential protection planning.

With *visible* barriers or concentric rings of protection in place at your domicile, next, use common sense and good habits to create *invisible* barriers by doing such things as asking a trusted neighbor to keep watch over your house while you're away, arranging for them to pick up your mail, and making sure they have your phone number so they can call you if there are any concerns.

Depending upon where you live, some police departments will do vacation checks on homes whose owners are on vacation—they will check on your home while you're away—often at no charge.

Avoid telling people, even your relatives that you have weapons, jewelry, cash, gold, or expensive electronic equipment located in your home. Specific travel information should also be kept confidential. Use your verbal skills and avoid shouting, "Hey, I'll be out of the country for the entire month of July!" to your neighbors over the fence. The motive behind the lion's share of burglaries occurring when occupants are not present *is the result of inadvertently shared information.*

Applied verbal skills, common sense, and good habits create invisible, yet very effective, concentric rings of protection continually supporting your home's defense.

Hardening Your Dwelling

The importance of eliminating your home's soft target indicators cannot be stressed enough. The instant it presents itself as a harder target, the less interested the predator becomes.

You don't want your home to appear as a soft target. Regardless of where you live, leaving your doors and windows unlocked makes entry simple to even the least experienced predator. Obvious indicators of resident absence also give intruders confidence that they can work undisturbed and have as much time as they want. If your neighbors have a lack of interest or concern, this also helps to extend the attack cycle timeline. Making the job of breaking into your home an easy or convenient effort is a monogrammed invitation to a home invasion.

Most home intruders are deterred by alarm systems and other intrusion detection devices; it's estimated that homes without such security systems are approximately three times more likely to be broken into than those homes with security systems, dogs, and/or nosey neighbors, all of which by default increase the amount of effort required to pull off the job.

The following are some helpful tips to eliminate soft target indicators from your home:

1. Never hide a key outside the door, under the mats, flowerpot, over moldings—ANYWHERE—because if you can find it so can a predator! If you want a back-up key, then keep it with a trusted neighbor.

2. Get new locks or have tumblers rekeyed when you move into a previously occupied dwelling. You have no way of knowing who might have keys to your doors!

3. Don't leave your house keys and car keys together with attendants at public parking lots or automobile service centers. Your house keys can be quickly duplicated and your address can be easily obtained from your auto registration (which should be in your wallet, anyway) by resourceful predators.

4. Install an alarm that can be used to detect entry. Post a sign (usually supplied by the alarm company) on the doors and windows demonstrating to a predator that breaking in just became about three times more risky.

5. Don't leave ladders or tools loose outside as they serve to assist an intruder in breaking into your home. If you can't secure them safely inside, at least lock them up out of plain view.

6. Report broken street lights in your neighborhoods. Well-lit areas discourage predators by taking away their concealment (hiding places).
7. Don't follow the exact same routine week in and week out. A predator can stalk you to observe your movements and know when your home is unoccupied.
8. Keep your house number clearly visible from the street in order for law enforcement and other emergency response personnel to find you in a hurry.
9. Close garage doors whether at home or away. Open and empty usually indicates an unoccupied home, as well as possibly allowing easy ingress via an entryway unseen from the street.
10. Don't fall for the old "Does Joe live here...?" routine. Your mom was right when she told you, "Don't let strangers into your home!" Use a peephole, surveillance camera, or talk through an intercom system. Ask for identification. Legitimate callers will be more than happy to produce valid identification. Make them wait until you verify.
11. Burglars search for homes that appear to be unoccupied. A car in the driveway, motion-sensor outdoor floodlights, interior lights, and radios and TVs on timers all present the impression to an observer that someone is home.
12. Don't place your full name on the mailbox. Single women should avoid any outside indication of gender or partnership status.
13. Have good strong locks on all doors and windows. Use auxiliary deadbolts on all exterior doors and lock these doors when you go out, even if it's just around the corner for five minutes!
14. Don't lend predators a helping hand! Clear the shrubs and trees immediately adjacent to your home, which

will eliminate a potential means of upper level access as well as a place to hide.

15. Remain observant and situationally aware of unusual activities. If you see someone who appears to be suspicious around a neighbor's yard, don't be afraid to check their identity with your neighbor by phone.

16. Report to police any strangers loitering in your neighborhood or people asking strange or vague questions about your neighbors and their whereabouts.

17. Don't let your mailbox or newspapers overflow. If you are away, arrange for a neighbor or building manager to store overflow for you or have delivery temporarily interrupted.

18. Burglars want to spend no more than 60 seconds getting into a home. Protective measures that increase this timeline—deadbolt locks, bars on windows, pins in sash windows—may be just enough to change his mind.

19. Don't be a lone ranger. Develop a buddy system with your neighbors. The number of concerned neighbors remaining alert and aware of suspicious characters, noise, or activities allows a far greater opportunity for early detection.

20. Depending upon your neighborhood, you may consider using metal grillwork on glass in entrance doors and decorative side glass to prevent predators from breaking the glass and reaching inside to open the door.

21. Whenever you're working for any length of time in an attic or cellar or anyplace away from the main dwelling area it's a good idea to lock up, especially if you might not hear an exterior door opening downstairs or in another part of the house. Set your entry alarm to chime anytime a door is opened in the house when the alarm is off.

22. Don't discuss your absence in pubic or online and do not provide any information about your vacation to

anyone outside your circle of trusted neighbors and family—this is part of your invisible ring of protection.

23. Move valuables so they can't be easily observed through windows or open doors by passersby on the street.
24. Secure all entrances both at night and when leaving, including cellar doors and windows, garage doors, sun deck, patio (a dowel placed in the sliding track is additionally recommended), and porch or screen doors.
25. Dark corners and hidden cubbyholes are a friend to the intruder. Install exterior lighting that uses motion detectors or dawn/dusk detectors.
26. If you have no video surveillance or no visual capabilities whatsoever, install peep holes in solid exterior doors and man doors from the house to an attached garage.
27. If you don't have one already, consider an alarm system. Alarm systems are effective deterrents and can expedite a police response in case of home invasion.
28. Consider a dog. As a protective measure, dogs that make a lot of noise and/or have size are credible deterrents.
29. Block nuisance calls or repetitive wrong numbers. Don't give up any information to people you don't know. Even the slightest tidbit of useful information to a predator may spell the difference between moving from one step of the attack cycle to the next.
30. Prepare for recovery in the event of a burglary. There's no excuse not to take full inventory, description, serial numbers, and even multiple photos or video of your valuable personal property. An inability to describe personal property and lack of inventory and other documentation make recovery and identification difficult if not impossible for authorities, as well as making it harder to submit insurance claims for loss.

31. In case of a break-in, your neighbors should know how to reach you and should have your permission to provide this information to the authorities when reporting a suspected incident.

Home Computer Protection

Doors and windows aren't the only way for an intruder to gain access to your home and family. If you don't secure your wireless networks, everything and anything on your network including personal and confidential family information is accessible to forced system intrusions and/or unauthorized access.

The following is an excerpt from *Cyber Patrol*[4]—a resource for online safety, specifically safe internet surfing tips for parents and kids. It includes details on the ten tips for parents to share with their kids about online behavior:

1. Talk with your children to agree upon what kind of sites they are allowed to visit.
2. Keep your children out of unmonitored chat rooms and monitor where they go.
3. Place the computer in a well-trafficked area in the home where the whole family can use it.
4. Set up very specific guidelines if you are going to allow your children to have accounts on social networking sites like MySpace, Tumblr, Instagram, Facebook, and Twitter.
5. (Tell your child to) Never give out personal information online.
6. (Tell your child to) Never, for any reason, agree to meet someone in person that they met online.
7. Make sure you have access to your child's email password.
8. Did you realize that there is no way to verify anyone's age online?

4 *http://www.cyberpatrol.com/home/customer-care/online-safety-tips.aspx*

9. Make sure your kids know to tell you about anything online that makes them uncomfortable.

10. Be sure to talk to your kids about cyber bullying.

Additional recommended online safety references are supplied by Google[5] and About.com Women's Issues—12 Tips to Protect Yourself from Cyberstalking.[6]

Online Protection

1. Always password-protect your wireless connection. Don't keep those factory-set passcodes! Activate Wi-Fi Protected Access (WPA) or Wired Equivalent Privacy (WEP) options on all electronic transmitting devices such as routers, media centers, and home entertainment systems.

2. For more protection decrease the signal strength outside your intended area of coverage by locating your Wireless Access Point (WAP) away from windows, closer to the center of your home.

3. Be sure that your firewall is enabled and keep all your software current with auto-updating. Use antivirus and anti-spyware software from a trusted provider.

4. To guard against outside attack each computer and router needs a firewall. Fortunately modem routers and operating systems come with firewalls. The danger is that the firewall can be switched off or configured incorrectly by the user. The default settings are usually best left alone unless you really know what you are doing.

5. Choose passwords that are complex enough to survive guessing and brute force attacks. Use a combination of uppercase and lowercase letters, numbers, and special characters and make sure your password is at least 8 characters or longer.

---

5 *www.google.com/goodtoknow/online-safety*

6 *http://womenissues.about.com/od/violenceagainstwomen/a/cyberprevention.html*

6. Each personal computer needs an antivirus program installed. Microsoft includes built-in antivirus capability with the Windows operating system, and for previous versions of Windows you can download the "Microsoft Security Essentials" antivirus product for free. As with the firewalls mentioned above these can be switched off or configured incorrectly. The default settings are usually best left alone unless you are an expert.
7. Make sure your computer is set to automatically download and install important security updates. Not only does the operating system need to be updated but also third party programs like Adobe Reader®, Adobe Flash®, Oracle®, Java®, Mozilla Firefox® and others need to have security updates installed.
8. Don't log in as a user with administrator rights—set up non-administrator or guest user accounts for normal use and for the kids. A non-administrative user account cannot be used to change the system configuration. This will prevent most virus infections and malware. Only use an administrator account for installing software or doing system configuration changes and not for regular computer use.
9. If you have kids, set up some sort of parental control software. Microsoft has a package called family safety which is included with Windows and downloadable for prior versions of Windows. You can monitor your kids' usage of the Internet with this software and block their access to undesirable websites.

Common sense protection by the following recommended protective measures may effectively reduce human error leading to security breaches. The following is a brief list of possible errors:

- Don't open email attachments from unknown sources.
- Don't install software from unknown sources.
- Stay away from pirated software. There are pirated hacked versions of commercial software offered for

free or super low prices. You may see an internet advertisement for Microsoft Office or Adobe Photoshop (programs usually costing in the hundreds of dollars) on sale for $25. These are a great way to inadvertently download a virusor other malware, which can open up your computer to someone else taking total control.

- Virus and malware creators always sugarcoat their payload: Resist that urge to click on enticing vice-related advertisements.
- Don't believe it when browser popups claim there is something wrong with your PC and you need to buy their product to fix it. Beware of sites that claim to double your speed or optimize the registry or fix hundreds of errors that you somehow never noticed before. These programs do not work and can actually damage your PC.

The bottom line to hardening your dwelling boils down to effort. Use the predator's optic to think about your *proactive* measures in "layers." By closing a door, locking a window, changing a password, you've just made it that much more difficult for the predator. You can destroy the motivation of a predator who is trying to break into your home if it takes more effort because you have become a hard target. If you put a little effort into hardening your home, a would-be intruder will need to make at least that same amount of effort to break in.

Hardening Your Household

Having focused on how to harden your dwelling, now let's take a look at what can be done proactively to harden the members of your household—yourself, your family and/or other protectee(s).

Residential Protection Planning

The very best protection for your household against a home invasion is training and planning. Residential protection planning works by reducing any confusion and provides all household members with easy-to-follow directions should they be placed under duress.

If you are a parent, it is strongly recommended that you have periodic family meetings to discuss realistic protection concerns, such as how to answer the door or what to do in the event of an actual home invasion or if confronted by an intruder. Even if you're not a parent, it's a good idea to discuss the same with all members of your household.

The very first consideration should be the immediate safety and protection of all residents. You should introduce and explain exactly what a home invasion is and the corresponding need for protective measures. Discuss how and why these are important to their protection. Understanding how to directly apply these measures to YOUR home can make the difference between being protected or unprotected in the event of an actual home invasion.

You should first make plans based on the layout of your home, the age and physical abilities of all residents—toddlers, elderly, disabled—and the scenarios most pertinent to your dwelling. Your considerations should address the event of an actual home invasion by providing answers to such questions as the following: Should you collect the kids or should the kids come to you? Who will manage the kids, elderly, disabled, and who will dial 911? After accounting for all residents, which location in your home would you retreat to—the master bedroom, basement, upstairs bathroom? What is the most expeditious route there and why did you select that particular location or safe area?

Once you've determined what best fits your home environment, then provide specific instructions for each family member of what to do and where to go explaining *exactly* what to do and *exactly* how to do it.

Emergency Action Plan

In addition to preparing for a home invasion, any residential protection planning should also include an emergency action plan or EAP, which is a predetermined set of instructions to provide clear directions to be followed in response to a natural or manmade threat. Well-developed emergency action plans, where all household members clearly understand their roles and responsibilities, should result in fewer injuries and less damage to your home during emergencies.

Your EAP doesn't need to be anything elaborate or written down; it can be just a few simple instructions such as where to go, whom to call, and how to do it in the event of a natural disaster. For example, "If Mommy says this is an emergency and go to your room, you drop everything and

ANYTHING you're doing—do not ask questions—go immediately to your room." Your instructions should be easy to follow and there should not be more than one or two simple commands because if too complicated these plans will instantly fail under pressure. Once everyone understands the plan, it's a really good idea to run a few simple training drills to ensure that everyone knows their roles and responsibilities. You can make these entertaining enough to be relevant and attainable—especially for kids, but they should also be realistic and all family members should understand the gravity of the situation.

One example of this might be a 30-second fire drill. Make an announcement to the kids that they have 30 seconds to choose what to bring with them and what to leave behind. Tell them where the imaginary fire is and let them tell you how they would escape. Home invasions should also be drilled. Some parents may believe this type of emergency planning and education leads to paranoia, but protection professionals believe it teaches important skills that save lives.

Communication And Evacuation

The two most critical components of any residential protection plan are *communication* and *evacuation.*

As far as communication to members of the household when under duress, verbal and hand signals are great if you're in earshot or they can see you but what if they are in other rooms around the house? Do you have an intercom system? A baby monitor device? What alternative method of communication do you have available to transmit important information between residents?

For communication to emergency services, if an intruder breaches your home you may have only a matter of seconds to get to a phone and dial 911. If you dial with the speaker on, the dispatcher can listen to what's going on and the call is usually recorded.

Residential protection planning should also consider response options in the event of a natural or manmade threat disabling cell phone and landline communications. An agreed-upon plan of where and when to meet, or other arrangements, could prove lifesaving.

Evacuation is a traditional protection term meaning to get out. In the event of either a natural or manmade threat, it may be best to evacuate the premises. If need be you should designate a rally point or safe area at which all residents may assemble.

In the case of a manmade threat, if a family member can escape and call for help, an intruder will lose valuable time and any tactical advantage. An evacuation plan should include exactly where to go, who to contact, and what to say.

Proactive measures such as eliminating indicators by hardening your home and educating your family, removes the actuality and appearance of being a soft target which in turn eliminates a necessary leg in an intruder's carrying out a home invasion on your home.

Let's move forward with our capabilities in breaking each step of the home invasion attack cycle using active measures.

Active Measures

Given less time and requiring more effort, now past midway of the attack cycle you are afforded limited options and opportunity to break the cycle from the latter half of Step 3—Stalk/Plan, all the way through and including all of Step 4—Close, to mitigate the threat of a home invasion.

You can take advantage of this opportunity by using active measures such as assessment and response and situational awareness to deny a predator his or her opportunity.

Step 3 Stalk | Plan | Step 4 Close

Limited Options

Less Time/ More Effort

Mitigate

Assess & Respond

Active Measures

Alert Mode

Deny Opportunity

Deny Opportunity

A person who breaks into and enters an occupied dwelling without permission and while they are entering, present in, or exiting the dwelling commits a felony, theft, or assault is guilty of home invasion.

If no one comes to the door, would-be intruders will make their way around to the back of the house and knock again on the back door. Whichever door looks weaker tends to be the one they will use.

Criminals are generally lazy and given that predators lean more toward convenience or low hanging fruit, for the most part they avoid tasks requiring substantial effort and, as we have studied earlier, are attracted to soft targets. Searching for the easiest way in, they will make their best efforts at any unlocked entrances and storage areas.

A home intruder will typically consider the following access points:

- Back Door
- Basement Entrance—door or window
- Side Door
- Front Door
- First Floor Windows
- Garage
- Storage Areas
- Second Floor Windows—if accessible

Ever-resourceful and relying on what they may happen to find in the vicinity of your home, intruders most often gain entry using whatever they may find such as a ladder, screwdriver, baseball bat, crowbar, or a similar access tool they may use in attempting to pry or smash the door open.

Remember they will try and get in and then get out in less than 10 to 15 minutes. Typically, if only after your valuables, they prefer to hit your home during daylight hours, specifically when nobody is around to intercept their efforts.

Using active measures you can deny opportunity by accurately assessing and appropriately responding to the situation allowing you to mitigate the threat and disrupt another support leg of the anatomy of a home invasion.

Having covered active measures let's focus our remaining three options—flight, fight or freeze.

Reactive Measures

Given the least amount of time and requiring maximum effort, now at the very last step of the attack cycle you are afforded only three options and limited opportunity to break the cycle at Step 5—Attack, to defend against the threat.

You can take advantage of these three options by using reactive measures and situational awareness to either get away from, temporarily fight or surrender to your assailant(s).

Step 5 Attack
3 Options
Least Time/ Max Effort
Defend
React
Reactive Measures
Act Mode
Flight, Fight, Freeze

As discussed previously the most beneficial outcome if trapped at Step 5 is to remove yourself from the threat as quickly and efficiently as possible.

Remembering our earlier discussion of weapons and warning devices, in any potentially lethal defensive situation, a firearm operated by a qualified user is the single most effective physical protection tool available to immediately stop a physical attack by single or multiple attackers intent on taking your life, bar none.

Given the above fact, one may logically conclude that the very best defensive response against a home intruder who is motivated, capable, and has the opportunity to significantly raise the scale of injury of yourself and that of your protectee(s) is a firearm operated by a qualified individual.

If you are forced into a defensive position in your own home by home intruders, and if you do own a firearm, have access to it (and ammunition)[7], and you are qualified and willing to utilize it to defend your home and family, after you have retreated to your safest position, then it is recommended you dial 911, put the phone on speaker and provide one warning to the intruder(s). Using your verbal skills shout "get out of my house—I am in fear for my life and I have a gun. Get out." Say it only once—phone calls to 911 are in most cases recorded and this advises both incoming first responders and your assailant that you are in fact armed and prepared to utilize deadly force.

If you are considering a firearm for the protection of your home and family please refer to Chapter 10—Weapons for details applicable to ownership and usage of a firearm. Without such an optimal defensive response you are, unfortunately, relegated to less-effective measures.

It's important to be able to know and use safe areas and to consider the balance between security and convenience.

7 To meet that balance between gun safety and accessibility, an easily accessible, yet secure, gun vault is recommended. There are many quality products out on the market today and one of these can be found at http://www.titangunvault.com/gun-safe/titan-gun-vault

Safe Areas

Safe areas are designated locations either inside or outside your home where your family may safely retreat and summon help in the event of a home invasion or other threat. In reaction to a home invasion there are two types of safe areas—hard rooms and rally points.

A hard room is a designated room within the interior of your home where your family can safely and rapidly retreat in the event of a home invasion. Optimally, it should provide both cover and concealment and allow you the ability to remain for extended periods of time to include water, food, and physical protection tools.

A rally point is a predetermined area outside your home such as a neighbor's house or a nearby park. In the event family members may need to evacuate your home or end up separated, a rally point is used as a designated location where your family will regroup and further assess the situation.

Security Versus Convenience

Remember that long before it ever comes down to reactive measures—using the OODA Loop, move and communicate, moving to hard rooms, rally points, cover or concealment—there are unlimited options and opportunities to take proactive measures.

However, there is a balance between level of protection and convenience, which must be struck. The last thing you want to do when coming home at the end of your long day is to cross a moat, unlock three heavy steel gates, pass the four Dobermans, fumble with another set of keys to unlock five more deadbolts, successfully pass a retinal scan and take another ten minutes to disarm your house—all with both arms full of groceries. The same would apply to all members of your household.

On the other end of the spectrum, you don't want to leave all your doors and windows wide open 24/7 even when you're not home. The answer falls somewhere in between. You don't ever want to sacrifice convenience for security and vice versa.

Utilizing the above proactive, active and reactive measures you can now lower your scale of injury, increase your odds of prevailing, and significantly reduce your threat profile in avoiding, mitigating or defending against a home invasion.

CHAPTER 13

Protection On Foot

"The [predator] does not expect his prey to fight back...by doing what our assailant least expects us to do, we may throw him completely off."
Jeff Cooper[1]

In This Chapter You Will Be Introduced To...

...protective concepts, measures, skills and tools needed to keep that 360 degree envelope of protection when you are travelling on foot.

At A Glance

Moving to and from your car, running errands, hiking, or even just walking over to a neighbor's house, you are most vulnerable to a threat on foot when moving in between controlled areas. It's important to maintain that 360-degree envelope of protection when on foot.

Your primary objective in any physical engagement is simply to win. If you're thinking, you're not taking action. If you are not taking action, then you're immediately behind the power curve and relegated to reaction. The very best tactical advantage to disrupt the attack behavior of an assailant on foot, is by putting a stop to their attack as early as possible using whatever resources you have available.

How Do I Use This In Real Life?

Applicable to confined and/or isolated areas such as elevators, stairways and hallways, and to open areas such as parking lots and shopping malls, during the day or at night, alone or with other people, the protective concepts and measures presented in this chapter can be used against threats anytime and anywhere you may be on foot.

---

1 John Dean "Jeff" Cooper, USMC (1920-2006), "Principles of Personal Defense," "Surprise," p.41-42, 1989.

You will be able to use proactive, active and reactive measures to accomplish out-of-the-ordinary tasks such as: keep your eyes on the fight, remain cognizant of an assailant's hands—as that's what holds on to weapons, and know the hiding places where weapons may be carried and accessed by an assailant. Always assume and prepare for the very worst case in that you may be dealing with multiple attackers and an assault with a deadly weapon. Scary as it all may sound, all the information is broken down here for you in an easy-to-understand format using real-world examples.

What The Pros Know

Knowing how to manage threats and protect your home and household from a home invasion allows you to defend against one of the most common real-world threats afflicting our modern society. However, what happens when you step outside that furthest concentric ring of protection? Once you depart the bubble of residential protection and step outside your controlled areas you are most vulnerable to a threat on foot.

Most people think, "Oh, if something bad happens, I'll just dial 911 and someone will come and save me." Unfortunately, the very fact that you are on foot makes waiting for the cavalry your very least effective response option. Unlike residential protection where you may rely on the concentric rings of protection of a controlled area to buy a little time, any environment outside those rings cannot afford you such assurances.

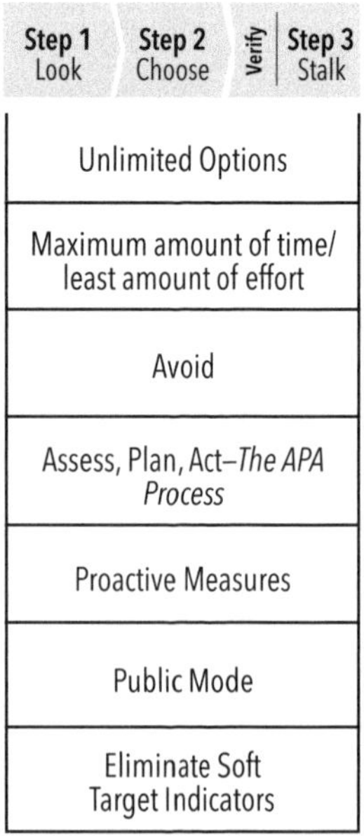

In terms of any threat progression, you are far better prepared to manage a physical threat on foot if you are armed with the full gamut of proactive, active and reactive measures.

In taking this holistic approach, we will first analyze the anatomy of a physical assault and then use it to apply our knowledge of breaking each step of the attack cycle using appropriate proactive, active and reactive measures. Let's begin with proactive measures.

Step 1 Look
Step 2 Choose
Verify
Step 3 Stalk

Unlimited Options
Maximum amount of time/ least amount of effort
Avoid
Assess, Plan, Act–*The APA Process*
Proactive Measures
Public Mode
Eliminate Soft Target Indicators

Proactive Measures

Beginning at Step 1—Look, running all the way through and including the first half of Step 3—

Stalk/Verify, you have the opportunity to avoid a physical assault entirely by applying proactive measures.

You can take advantage of unlimited options and opportunity by using the likes of situational awareness and the APA process to help you eliminate soft target indicators.

Anatomy Of A Physical Assault

Applying the anatomy of an attack to a physical assault results in the usual three legs of the tripod supporting a successful physical assault:

1. **Target**—you and/or your protectee(s)
2. **Bad Guy(s)**—one or more assailant(s)
3. **Process**—The attack cycle itself

For the beneficial outcome of defeating a physical assault, we will use PreFense® in addressing each of the three components that make up the anatomy of an attack as applied to a physical assault.

> *Subtracting any one of the tripod legs makes it impossible for a predator to carry out a successful physical assault on foot.*

Let's start with the target—possibly you or your protectee(s). What can you do to prevent yourself from being viewed as a soft target? Eliminate indicators.

Eliminate Indicators

Addressing the first tripod leg of the anatomy of a physical assault—the target—the following are recommended proactive measures designed to eliminate both primary and secondary soft target indicator (STIs).

Utilizing Your APA Process:

1. Before departing a controlled area, give yourself the "once over." Check for appropriate attire. Identify any visual STIs that may attract the attention of a predator prior to going out on foot.
2. Appear as though you know where you're going. Walk with your head and shoulders erect, eyes straight

ahead, with a look of determination on your face, arms swinging to convey pure confidence. Keep a brisk pace, appear to walk with purpose and know where you're going even though you may not.

3. Walk or run with a partner, in groups, or with a dog—a predator will observe you are not alone or a soft target.

4. Vary your exercise times and routes and location—don't be time and place predictable.

5. Stay alert and remain calm, don't wear headphones in each ear. As a compromise wear your headphones in one ear (or use a single-ear model) allowing you at least partial audio access to what's happening around you.

6. Stay off your cell phone when you should be focused on your environment. There's plenty of time when you are in a controlled area to focus your full attention on your call.

7. If wearing a hooded sweater, avoid having your hood up at or forward of your eyes as this compromises your peripheral vision.

8. Depending upon the potential threat area (e.g., rough neighborhood), do not wear jewelry, not even costume jewelry, on the street. However, consider wearing a wedding band to discourage unwanted advances.

9. Avoid street vendors and lingering in extremely large crowds as you may be perceived as a target by seasoned predators.

10. Maintain your ability to monitor visual and audio of all areas—confined areas, open areas in daylight and at night. Don't unwittingly place yourself in a blind spot as predators pick up on this.

11. Anytime you depart a controlled area make a 180 degree visual scan of your environment—ensure you remain in public mode. It takes all of 3-4 seconds to do this and immediately deters the would-be assailants.

The sooner attack-related behaviors can be observed, the sooner they can be addressed. Hence, the use of situational awareness as part of your proactive measures is strongly recommended. With that in mind—and the desired result of defeating a physical assault, let's move forward with our capabilities in breaking each step of the assault cycle using active measures.

Active Measures

Given less time and requiring more effort, now past midway of the attack cycle you are afforded limited options and opportunity to break the cycle from the latter half of Step 3—Stalk/Plan, all the way through and including all of Step 4—Close to mitigate the threat of a physical assault.

You can take advantage of this opportunity by using active measures such as assessment and response and situational awareness to deny a predator his or her opportunity.

Predators want to try to achieve their objective in as little time as possible and with little self-risk. You can use this to your advantage by denying what they seek most—an opportunity.

Think about what opportunities a predator seeks by using appropriate assessment and response:

Step 3 Stalk / Plan → Step 4 Close
Limited Options
Less Time/ More Effort
Mitigate
Assess & Respond
Active Measures
Alert Mode
Deny Opportunity

1. When walking in especially crowded areas, a common tactic among experienced thieves is to use razor blades to cut purse straps or to slit a purse open, take the valuables or the entire purse, and escape into the crowd. Remain aware of this tactic and carry bags accordingly to make them less accessible.

2. Use ATMs located in open, well lit, public areas; avoid street vendors and lingering in extremely large crowds.

3. Avoid short cuts, stay in the middle of the sidewalk or path—avoid bushes, alleys and potential choke points.

4. Do not talk to people asking for direction, change, etc. If you need to ask directions, ask families or women with children. Phrase your question along the lines of, "Excuse me! Where is [my destination], I'm meeting my husband/boyfriend there."
5. In using your observation skills look for anomalies and handle accordingly.
6. Always keep a safe distance when walking past anyone you don't know on the street, in parking lots, and especially at night in dark areas. Allow a little extra room when coming around corners or hedges where you can't see what's ahead.
7. Check the Internet, listen or watch local news, and pay attention to police reports especially in high-crime areas.
8. Remain aware of isolated and unlit areas especially at night—do not place yourself in a compromising position.
9. Use your observation skills to continually monitor your immediate environment for any threat indicators and be prepared to respond.
10. Carry bags, purses, wheeled luggage and so on, away from the street side. If you are a female walking alone, keep your purse away, from the street with your hand on it if passing by anyone who may be observing you; when walking with another keep the purse between you and that other person.
11. Maintain your situational awareness of possible assailants to include gang violence and/or other potential threats by remaining in public mode, especially in low-light situations, as most incidents occur at night and/or in low light—particularly in early morning or at the end of the daylight hours.
12. Line Of Demarcation—another useful active measure

you can add to your protection tool kit is the line of demarcation. When you walk outside your home and toward your vehicle you are between two known controlled areas—your home and the vehicle. Should you be confronted by a physical threat while walking, you must decide which controlled area are you closest to. What is the quickest route to get there?

13. Be prepared if, while you are on foot, a car starts to follow you or slow down or stop. If the driver and/or passengers make comments as they are driving next to you, immediately turn and walk in the opposite direction away from the road.
14. In preparing to call for help, plan to shout "FIRE!" rather than "HELP!" as most people don't want to get involved in other peoples' affairs, but if they believe they are at risk, then they will pay attention.
15. If you notice something about to go down pull out your cell phone—predators don't like to have their pictures taken or any recording of themselves or the event. If you don't already have a cell phone, it is well worth the investment to purchase an inexpensive one for dangerous situations and car trouble. Always take your cell phone with you!
16. As you walk, pay attention to your location and progress along your intended route. Make a mental note of potential safe areas to run to (homes of friendly neighbors, or open public businesses), in the event of a physical threat.
17. If you are already on your phone and you see someone approaching, describe the event in detail to the person on the other end—also let them know you're on your way or where you are going and what time they should expect you. Gain their assurances that they will call you and/or the authorities if you fail to be on time—especially if you are within earshot of someone approaching you.

18. Mentally prepare yourself for a potentially difficult situation where the person approaching you may gain the tactical advantage and demands your wallet or purse. Remember that everything inside can be replaced! Don't simply hand it to him—throw it in the opposite direction, away from your exit route. Odds are that he is more interested in the contents than he is in you. The instant it leaves your hand move off that X.

The following are real world examples of using active measures to mitigate an actual threat at Step 4 of the attack cycle.

Surly Grandma—Active Measure—Deny Opportunity—Distraction
In a case reported by a retired police officer (who has requested that his name and the specifics of this case be omitted), a street-savvy elderly woman was preparing to visit, after sundown, her grandchildren who lived in a nasty part of town. She ran through her APA process and followed through in her careful planning with appropriate attire, protective mindset, and a walking cane.

Walking toward her relatives' home, Grandma, using her situational awareness, kept her wits about her in public mode when her observation skills picked up a potential threat in her periphery. Snapping into alert mode, she observed two neighborhood youths looking for trouble (Step 1—Look). Spotting her walking alone, they chose her (Step 2—Choose) as their target and moved from one side of the street to the same side she was walking on (Step 3—Stalk) at which point she, fully aware of being caught in the attack cycle, instantly decided to make a plan.

As both teenage predators started to close the distance between themselves and their victim (Step 4—Close) our resourceful senior citizen turned abruptly, looked them right in the eyes and with a stern and confident voice used her verbal skills and chided them, "Hey you, don't I know your mother?"

The predators, so taken by surprise were knocked completely off balance by the actions of this surly grandmother. Completely distracted from their original plan and not knowing quite how to respond, they broke off their attack by immediately turning away without a word and scurried off into the darkness.

Powers Of Observation

In a similar incident, an attractive young woman jogging through her neighborhood noticed a man pulled over to the side of the road working on his car with the hood lifted and apparently having trouble with the car battery. He stopped the woman and asked if she would help him. Immediately snapping into alert mode her perception kicked in and she got a gut feeling that this guy wanted more than her help with his battery. She sternly declined while changing direction, increasing her speed and successfully breaking the attack cycle.

A few days later she was walking near her home with two of her friends when she observed the very same guy glancing over at her as he walked by the group. Upon realizing that she was caught right in the middle of another attack cycle she directly confronted the man with her friends saying "Hey, aren't you the guy with the jumper cables?" Outnumbered and realizing he was busted, the predator ran to his car and drove away.

Using active measures you can deny opportunity by accurately assessing and appropriately responding to the situation allowing you to mitigate the threat.

Having covered active measures let's focus our efforts on the only remaining three options—flight, fight or freeze.

Reactive Measures

Given the least amount of time and requiring maximum effort, now at the very last step of the attack cycle you are afforded only three options and limited opportunity to break the cycle at Step 5—Attack, to defend against the threat.

You can take advantage of these three options by using reactive measures and situational awareness to either get away from, temporarily fight or surrender to your assailant(s).

As discussed previously the most beneficial outcome if trapped at Step 5 is to remove yourself from the threat as quickly and efficiently as possible.

The benefits include keeping a low scale of injury and creating the safety buffer of a sub-

Step 5 Attack
3 Options
Least Time/ Max Effort
Defend
React
Reactive Measures
Act Mode
Flight, Fight, Freeze

stantial reactionary gap. However, flight is not always possible in every case. The very next best option is to put up some type of physical resistance—fight, for as short a time as possible to accomplish your best option—flight and primary objective—to win. In other words, do whatever it takes to take control of the situation enough to allow yourself the time and space to run away.

Fortunately there are additional protective measures specific to a physical assault, which can be used to help achieve your primary objective.

Make A Plan

Action is better than inaction. Doing nothing means you place yourself in the very poor tactical position of being behind the action reaction power curve. Making the wrong decision, you at least have taken action, and thus force your adversary to react, allowing you the opportunity to make a new plan the very next moment.

To make a plan in immediate response to a physical threat when on foot is nothing more than engaging your conscious mind in using the OODA Loop—as opposed to hoping the problem will solve itself and waiting to see what happens.

1. Think "What If?"
2. What is my objective (where do I move to, what can I do, etc.)?
3. What are my alternatives?

Using the OODA Loop you can quickly observe the physical threat, and orient to your position—there is a threat next to my car, or there is a threat on an intercept path directly in front of me. Gauging your distance—how far away he is, what is the reactionary gap, and other environmental factors—changing conditions—will help you decide your next objective while weighing your alternatives, and then finally acting on that decision.

Breathe, Just Breathe

To think clearly and quickly, especially under extreme duress, you need to keep cool under pressure. It is strongly recommended that you remain calm. Protection experts who must perform under extreme duress train their team members to remain calm so they can do what they're trained to do without the fear of loss, injury and pain or rationalization hampering their performance.

One easy method to remaining calm is to breathe. Just suck in a deep breath when you can, as this adjusts your physiology and is a reassuring message to your brain that you are meeting this challenge head on. Never underestimate the value of even a single deep breath to help remove anxiety. Adrenaline may still be coursing through your veins but taking that reassuring breath will help you remain calm.

Fear Factor

Fear is an unpleasant emotion caused by the belief that someone or something is dangerous, likely to cause pain, or a threat. It is an emotion like any other emotion such as happiness or sadness. In preparation to confront an actual physical threat inevitably the question of personal fear arises. What about the fear factor?

Some schools teach to change your emotion from fear to anger or from fear to some pleasant thought. The professional protection community recommends removing emotion from the process entirely. Simply detach yourself from any emotion. It is widely known that emotion takes up energy. Rather than waste one ounce of energy on how you feel about something, which will in no way contribute to a desired outcome, simply unplug. Take that same amount of energy and instead of changing it to another emotion convert it to work effort. You have a very important job—a life-saving mission. Make and follow that plan to achieve *your primary objective.* This must be your one and only priority.

Your Primary Objective

Actions speak louder than words. If you're physically assaulted by an adversary, you can bet that he's intent on raising your scale of injury. If you are engaged in a life-or-death struggle and are in fear for your life, situational awareness becomes a personal safety issue. Your objective is to win—no matter what it takes—even if you have to light his hair on fire or jam an ink pen into his eye or use your car as an impact weapon and run him over. You must do whatever it takes to win by ending aggression as quickly as possible.

In matters of physical threat management, situational awareness becomes a personal safety issue.

Although you must be cunning and tactically unconventional, it's important to find the balance between thinking on your feet and responding quickly. There's a lot going on during personal combat, and the last thing you want to do is overthink the situation, because if you're busy thinking then you're not busy winning the fight.

If you're thinking, you're not taking action. You will remain behind the power curve as long as your assailant stays in control of the fight. This is why you must take and keep the initiative, a sound tactical maxim proven effective over millennia. If you take action then he has no choice but to react to your actions—at that split second you have taken control of the action reaction power curve.

The psychological aspects of defense require no intensive training and no level of skill, only realization and the decision to be the winner and not the victim. Adopting the protective mindset in being predisposed to win is a critical step in achieving your primary objective.

Tactical Advantage

The very best strategy is to disrupt the attack behavior of an adversary by putting a stop to their onslaught as early as possible. You gain a tactical advantage in doing this earlier because of the acceleration of events that happens during the latter stages of all attack cycle timelines.

Applying the skills you have learned for residential protection planning to the times you are traveling on foot will prepare you and your protectee(s) in the event of a physical altercation. What should your spouse be doing while you're grappling with an assailant and the kids are screaming? Does someone you're with have a cell phone? A weapon or warning device? Perhaps the kids could dial 911 while mom responds with her licensed firearm? What if your spouse is out alone or the kids are alone—shouldn't they also have a plan?

To gain the tactical advantage you must also have a "Plan A." Let's say the next time you and your family are out shopping or dining, you brainstorm some scenarios in the event of a physical threat. "Honey, you grab the kids and get behind me, then move toward the car and dial 911. Kids get behind your mother and do exactly what she tells you—don't ask questions!" Your plans may include movement toward the front door of the nearest open building, your car, a rally point or some other designated location. By practicing the "what if's" during family meetings, you will develop the skills to deal with threats. Being proactive allows you to take the initiative and gain the tactical advantage.

What To Look For

In any physical altercation if you "lose sight, you lose the fight." It's best to always keep your eyes on the threat. Always face the threat, never turn away or close your eyes, NEVER shut down your awareness or turn your back toward your attacker, as doing that immediately gives him the tactical advantage.

If you ask any police officer, they will tell you that it's the hands that kill. The first thing a cop does when he pulls you over is to check your hands. He asks you to place your hands on the wheel; or, if you're out of the car, he directs you to place your hands on the hood or behind your back, or he puts your hands in handcuffs.

It's the hands that kill. When somebody is approaching you, ask yourself, what does he have in his hands? Can you see both hands? What you cannot see—especially in the hands, can kill you.

There are a number of locations on a person where a weapon may be concealed

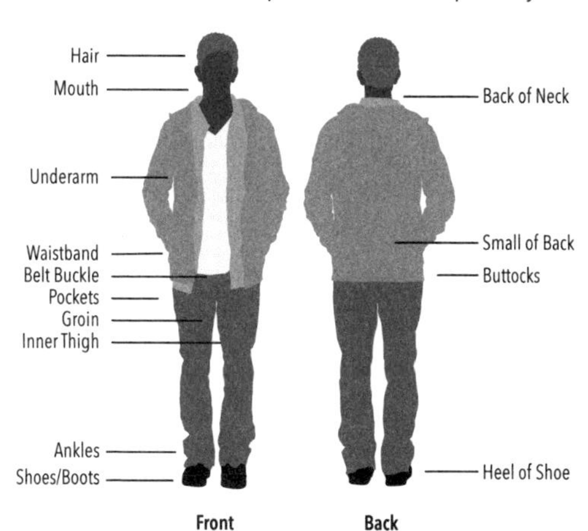

Be wary of weapons not only held in the hands of anyone who may approach you but also places on their body where they might reach for one that is hidden. The image above illustrates the most common locations on a person where a weapon may be concealed.

Way back in the days of my youth, when I was training extensively in the weapon arts using sharp and pointy objects such as knives and machetes, I observed my masters in the Philippines and in Indonesia were able to quickly see and identify threat indicators.

Even more impressively they could rapidly counter combative movements with blades literally flying around them at speeds so fast that even my trained eye could barely follow.

Eager to emulate their ability to efficiently respond my very first question was: "Master, when engaged in a physical altercation, where should I focus my attention?" The old master smiled and responded, "Stib, you must be like the bird of prey that focuses his gaze over the entire open field to search for his prey. If he focuses on a single blade of grass, then he will miss the rodent positioned only a few steps away. It is best to watch the entire field lest you miss seeing the rodent. You may choose to be like the bird of prey or like the rodent—the choice is always yours."

De-Escalate Or Defuse

Although disengaging from the threat is always your very best response option, you may not be given the luxury of a choice as the decision to move off the X or to stay and confront the threat may be made for you by environmental or situational circumstances.

If you can't immediately get off the X, then it is critical that you get yourself in a position where you can eventually get off the X—a task that may be accomplished by either defusing or at least de-escalating the situation to a point where you can move.

Fortunately, we can take advantage of some of the diversionary concepts and techniques utilized by protection experts to facilitate de-escalation or defusing two of the most common of which are distraction and deception.

Distraction And Deception

Given the choice made for us by the situation we want to distract our adversary just long enough to get off the X. Look him in the eye. When you make eye contact you are using your body language to tell your adversary, "Hey, I'm looking right at you—I see you and I know what you're up to." Remember that predators always seek the softer target. From the predator's optic, by making positive eye contact you have transformed yourself from a soft target to a hard target. Additionally, you have pulled the adversary's focus toward you and away from your spouse and/or kids, allowing them the opportunity to get away.

In an incident which occurred at the time of this writing in a suburban area, (the individual interviewed asked that they and specifics of the incident not be identified), a predator approached a person jogging in a public park on a bright and sunny afternoon. Observing the predator's approach and switching from alert mode to act mode the jogger grasped her flashlight and shined the bright light directly into the predator's eyes, asking "Can I help you?"—at which point the predator retreated.

Move toward an exit. While you are in the process of using your verbal skills to defuse or de-escalate you should also be physically moving to a position of advantage where you can eventually and in short order get yourself off the X. You can make gestures with your hands as part of your conversation which causes an additional visual distraction. Remember, when you gain distance you break the cycle by placing space between yourself and the assailant(s), thus disrupting Step 4—Close.

Use your verbal skills in an attempt to attract others. Speak loudly. Although yelling may not be appropriate in some situations, speaking excessively loudly may attract the attention of others. Keep in mind that you are utilizing these distractions and deception techniques only temporarily to defuse and de-escalate the situation long enough to get yourself off that X.

Multiple Attackers

There's a very good chance that your assailants will most likely be male, usually younger, very cunning, with a pack mentality, and they generally attack in numbers—groups of two or three. The odds are stacked against you in this scenario—again your safest bet is to get away.

Let's say that you're very well trained in self-defense, perhaps an expert Brazilian Jiu-jitsu grappler—ground fighting expert, boxer or wrestling champion, and you've been undefeated in all your tournaments and even a couple of scuffles in the street.

Failing to leverage The 90% Advantage, fists soon fly and you take him down to the ground where you are the superior fighter. Suddenly his gang buddies appear. While you're grappling and even on top of your assailant, his buddies are kicking the stuffing out of you with their steel -toe work boots. This would be a less-than-optimum solution to your original problem.

It is commonly known throughout the professional community that most physical altercations end up on the ground. There is about the same chance that you will be dealing with multiple attackers.

It's OK if there really is only one opponent and you're both in a controlled environment with a referee. But ask any police officer who has gotten into an altercation on the street—it's hardly ever one on one. Still other statistics have shown that most altercations occur at night and also with multiple attackers. You must keep in mind the ever-present danger of multiple attackers.

Ducks In A Row

The very best solution to multiple attackers is to not fight a two-front war. Never find yourself directly in between them with one on either side of you—best is to keep them both (or more) in front of you. The ultimate solution—although not the easiest to achieve is keep them aligned in such a manner as one would need to get over or around another one of his fellow attackers to reach you.

Exit Or Equalize

If you are unarmed and your assailant has a weapon (handgun, knife, etc.), the optimal solution is to:

1. Immediately break away
2. Place either distance or an object between yourself and that weapon
3. Do what it takes to move off the X

If the predator has a weapon you are by no means under his control—even if he has a gun. Move off the X. The fact of the matter is predators are not trained marksmen.

Even if he has a gun and it's functional and it is loaded, he's probably very reluctant to call further attention to himself in firing the weapon since in addition to surveillance cameras, everyone and their grandmother now has a camera in their cell phone.

Our absolute worst-case scenario would be he takes a shot at you while you're running away in a zigzag pattern. Moving targets are EXTREMELY difficult to hit and the odds of him actually hitting you are quite low.

Most people think "Well, if he's moving at me with a knife or something in his hand, then I'll just blast him with MY gun, pepper spray, stun gun." However, if you recall the reactionary gap, the problem is that at conversational ranges the assailant's weapon is already engaged in the assault before you even start to reach for your own firearm or pepper spray or even to use your feet to get off the X.

Reaction is always slower than action. If you cannot use your feet to get away it becomes necessary to assist your footwork with a counterattack.

Violence Of Action

We've all heard the phrase "fight fire with fire." In the world of protection it translates to "violence of action may only be met with violence of action." Any reactive response less than violence of action will result in victimization and/or raised scale of injury. Most of us are peace-loving individuals with little or no desire for mortal physical combat. Violence of action is not part of our usual daily schedule.

However it must be acknowledged and embraced to be effective. Having a gun in your face or a knife at your throat is not an everyday occurrence for most of us.

If you ever need it, when the time comes simply give yourself mental permission to do what it takes to solve the problem.

Think of these additional reactive measures as they apply to physical assault as a buffet of available information—take what you believe is useful and what fits you, what is directly applicable to you and your family, what matches your physical attributes, your mindset, and the environment in which you find yourself. Even if you walk away with just one concept or measure covered in this section, it makes you a harder target than when you started.

Do the unexpected. Take the perspective of the entire threat progression. Think outside the box and be like that razor sharp grandmother who followed her APA process, accurately assessed and appropriately responded to a physical threat as a result of her raised awareness, switched to alert mode, turned around, looked her would-be assailants right in the eye and proceeded to break the cycle.

CHAPTER 14

Ground Transportation

"One is not exposed to danger who, even when in safety is always on their guard."
Publilius Syrus[1]

In This Chapter You Will Be Introduced To...

...ground transportation protection, threats and risk management techniques. Walking, driving, or taking the bus exposes you to a number of threats unique to ground transportation—and opportunities to make yourself an unattractive target. Discover common tactics used by predators, and learn how to prevent them from being effective.

This chapter covers arrivals and departures, parking lot safety, approaching your vehicle, escape routes, how to disrupt common vehicular attacks, how to manage a disabled vehicle, what to do if you're followed, selection and usage of taxis, rental cars, threat management in public transportation (subway systems, buses, and trains), and what to do if you encounter an active shooter while mobile.

At A Glance

Ground transportation is a crucial part of our daily lives. Most of us spend a significant part of our day moving between the events that make up our lives. The risk of abduction is highest when moving from place to place. As we move we are choosing to expose ourselves to an uncontrolled and potentially risky environment. Taking a few precautions makes you unattractive to predators and will cause them to go after more attractive targets in the environment.

---

1 Publilius Syrus—a Roman first century BC writer of maxims contemporary, with Cicero, noted for his collection of versified aphorisms.

How Do I Use This In Real Life?

Read the chapter in its entirety. Then pick one skill each week to incorporate into your daily routine and make it a habit. Doing it sporadically is better than not at all, but if you can develop both your awareness of the problem and the protective habits recommended in this chapter, you will lower your threat profile and take the initiative in keeping your family and yourself safe when on the road.

What The Pros Know

The one key thing to remember is that you are better off fighting it out on scene then leaving with an attacker—under any circumstances. Regardless of how you find yourself in a bad situation, the only way an attacker should get you in their vehicle or to depart with them is if you are unconscious or already dead.

Compliance at the point of abduction is a near certain death sentence. The ensuing hour between abduction and death are typically unspeakable. If you cannot avoid being attacked near a vehicle, fight it out on scene.

Whether driving your own vehicle, taking a train, riding in a taxi, or renting a car domestically or abroad, ground transportation is an integral aspect of our daily lives. The least secure of controlled areas, ground transportation invites a number of predatory opportunities.

Arrivals And Departures

Always on the prowl for soft targets, predators can either be on foot, behind cover and concealment, or in a vehicle themselves. Depending upon your area of travel, especially in high-threat areas, when in public mode and using ground transportation your situational awareness should extend beyond not only those who may be staring at you from curbside but also to drivers and passengers of other vehicles.

In a parking lot or at street-side parking, you are most vulnerable when exiting and entering your vehicle. Caution should be used especially upon the junctures of arrival and departure.

When it comes to threat management and protection in and around your car, the manner in which you arrive and depart, to include how you manage a parking space can either work to your advantage or against you depending upon how you use it in a life-threatening situation.

You are exposed in the open space between your last controlled area and the inside of your locked and moving vehicle—which is also considered a controlled area. The less time you spend getting to and from the safety of a controlled area, the less time a predator has to plan for and execute a successful attack. The trick to maintaining that 360-degree envelope of protection is in reducing the amount of space and time you spend between your destination on foot and your vehicle.

Bad things can happen during an arrival or a departure, when approaching your vehicle, in a parking lot, or at any time while you are driving. Such an incident may include you and/or any passengers during daytime or at night, and is commonly referred to as a vehicular assault. Using proactive, active and reactive measures can limit your vulnerability and exposure to vehicular-based threats.

In taking this holistic approach, we will first analyze the anatomy of a physical assault and then use it to apply our knowledge of breaking each step of the attack cycle using appropriate proactive, active and reactive measures. Let's begin with proactive measures.

Proactive Measures

Beginning at Step 1—Look, running all the way through and including the first half of Step 3—Stalk/Verify, and in public mode you have the opportunity to avoid a vehicular assault entirely by applying proactive measures to vehicular assault.

You can take advantage of unlimited options and opportunity by using the likes of situational awareness and the APA process to help you eliminate soft target indicators.

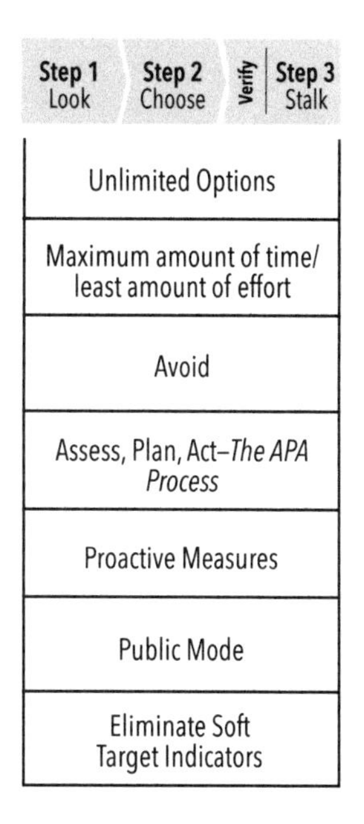

Anatomy Of A Vehicular Assault

Applying the anatomy of an attack to a vehicular attack you end up with the same three legs of the tripod supporting a successful attack.

1. **Target**—you and/or your protectee(s)
2. **Bad Guy(s)**—one or more assailant(s)
3. **Process**—the attack cycle itself

Using PreFense® to achieve the desired outcome of disrupting a vehicular assault, we will address the tripod components that make up the anatomy of a vehicular assault.

By subtracting even one of the tripod legs, it is not possible for a predator to carry out a successful vehicular assault.

Let's start with the target—you and/or your protectee(s). What can you do to prevent yourselves from being perceived as a soft target? Eliminate indicators.

Eliminate Indicators

Addressing the first tripod leg of the anatomy of a vehicular assault—target—the following recommended proactive measures are provided to eliminate both primary and secondary soft target indicators. Utilizing your APA process.

1. Inspect your vehicle as you would inspect yourself before going out into public. Check to see if there any bumper stickers, flags, magnetic signs, or other visual indicators of the contents or the passengers of the vehicle that might attract the attention of a predator. Such a visual indicator may be a sticker that reads, "Hey, we just won the state lottery!"

2. When driving, always plan far enough ahead of time to allow yourself plenty of travel time so that you're not rushed, frazzled, confused, or distracted by your environment. Predators are ready to assess your state of being as an STI upon stepping out the door of your vehicle.

3. Make a mental note of exactly where you parked. Be absolutely sure of this and even write it down if you have to.

4. Before walking out to your car, consider what you would look like from the predators optic if they saw you confused, lost or disoriented outside the building,

panicked and/or looking for your car. Would they leave you alone and seek a softer target or would you be at the top of their selection list?

5. Regarding any valuables you have three options: take them with you, lock them in the trunk, or hide them from plain view such as under garments or under the seat. In addition to rolling up all the windows and locking all the doors, take a quick second to flip your passenger seat forward to allow a clear view of the back area and move your driver's seat all the way forward. Well-seasoned predators recognize this measure and will figure that you're most likely a hard target.

6. If your vehicle is disabled and you feel you may be in an unsafe area, do not exit the vehicle, raise the hood, or open the trunk, as this is a clear indicator to predators that you are immobile and in distress. You may certainly use your cell phone, but do it in the safety of your vehicle with windows up and doors locked.

7. Always book your rental car in advance allowing you sufficient time to call and reconfirm at least two days prior to ensure availability and confirm pick-up location. Have your reservation number and rental agency contact information with you. Airports and rental car agencies are favored predatory hunting grounds.

8. Avoid renting a flashy car as this sends a loud and clear message to any predator that the driver of this vehicle is affluent and therefore a desirable target.

9. Upon arrival, it's a good idea to drive past or around your destination to get a good look at the area to confirm that you have arrived at the correct address, to obtain immediate area familiarization, and to scan for any potential threats. Having visual confirmation and knowing exactly where you need to go after parking your vehicle eliminates any appearances of confusion or indecision.

10. When walking back to your car recall exactly where you parked, and if needed, pull out that piece of paper where you wrote down what parking space floor, number or section. Quickly, in your mind, determine how you will get to that exact location. Movement with confidence to a specific location is something that usually doesn't make it through the selection filter of the predator's optic.
11. Upon arrival, maintain situational awareness; stay in public mode and utilize your observation skills to remain observant of any anomalies or irregular activity.
12. When travelling abroad, especially in certain high-threat areas such as war zones or areas of political upheaval or social unrest, you should be aware of anti-foreigner sentiments and that improvised explosive devices planted in, on, or near vehicles known to be operated by foreigners are often used to express such sentiment. Exercise caution when approaching your vehicle and look for any objects which may seem out of place, such as a child's toy[2] or similar object attached to or in proximity of your vehicle.

Eliminating indicators by hardening yourself and your protectee(s) in and around your vehicle eliminates the appearance of a soft target, thus eliminating a tripod leg resulting in the disruption of carrying out a successful vehicular assault.

The sooner attack-related behaviors can be observed, the sooner they can be addressed. Hence, the use of situational awareness as part of your proactive measures is strongly recommended. With that in mind—and the desired result of defeating a vehicular assault, let's move forward with our capabilities in breaking each step of the cycle using active measures.

Active Measures

Given less time and requiring more effort, now past midway of the attack cycle you are afforded limited options and opportunity to break the cycle from the latter half of Step 3—Stalk/Plan, all the way through and includ-

2 In certain high-threat areas around the world, an improvised explosive device (IED) may be fashioned from a child's toy such as a miniature stuffed animal and the like.

Step 3 Stalk | Plan | Step 4 Close

Limited Options

Less Time/ More Effort

Mitigate

Assess & Respond

Active Measures

Alert Mode

Deny Opportunity

ing all of Step 4—Close, to mitigate the threat of a vehicular assault.

You can take advantage of this opportunity by using active measures such as assessment and response and situational awareness to deny a predator his or her opportunity.

Deny Opportunity

Again, any predator, motivated and capable, seeks opportunity. Think ahead about what opportunities a predator seeks by using your appropriate assessment and response.

Parking close to a parking attendant station, elevators, or a stairwell nearest the building entrance and on the ground level reduces the amount of time you are alone outside your vehicle and walking toward your next controlled area.

If you know you'll be returning to your vehicle after sundown, park your car in a well-lit area under or near bright lights nearest to the building and closer to the exit.

1. Avoid parking next to vans as these are a primary tool of the predator seeking to abduct unsuspecting victims.

2. If possible, when walking to or from your vehicle try to travel with other people, as there is safety in numbers and this will deny a predator the opportunity to single you out, especially important in the latter steps of an attack cycle.

3. If you are carrying packages, don't fumble with them at the car door, and be sure that you have one hand free to operate the key. Have your keys in hand before you leave the building, so you do not need to stand by the car searching for them. If your key chain has a panic button take a second and quickly look at it so you know where it is if you may need to press it. If you have kids with you, once the door is open keep them between you and the car and in your field of vision at all times while loading them into the vehicle.

4. Even when in motion it is important to keep all doors locked and windows rolled all the way up. If it's too hot and the vehicle is not equipped with air conditioning then roll windows down far enough to allow airflow, but not far enough for a predator's hand or the barrel of a gun to reach in.

5. People have a tendency to get into their car after shopping, eating, or working, and sit there on a phone call, making a list, or going through a bag. Keep in mind that a predator may be watching. If he observes you switching from Public Mode to Home Mode in your car he knows you have provided him the opportunity to get in, stick a weapon in your face, and tell you where to go. As soon as you get in your car, lock the doors, roll up the widows and depart the area denying opportunity to the predator.

   In an unfortunate incident in Upper Darby, Pennsylvania, three young males on the prowl to rob someone Christmas night terrorized, kidnapped and sexually assaulted a Newtown Square woman. The victim, 22, was carjacked at gunpoint, raped and forced to perform oral sex while being driven around the city of Philadelphia and Upper Darby for five hours, according to police.

   She came out to have a cigarette and was sitting in the car looking at pictures in her cellphone in the parking lot, waiting for her boyfriend to come out of the bar. Three guys came up and pushed her aside and carjacked the car. Over the next five hours, they drove all through Philadelphia, raping her.[3]

6. If your vehicle becomes disabled and comes to a stop, try to slowly pull off the road safely out of the flow of traffic. Remain in your vehicle with the doors locked and the windows rolled up and utilize your cell phone to contact police or roadside assistance depending upon your situation.

3 *Linda Reilly, "Three teens charged in horrific Christmas night carjacking, sex assault on woman, 22," Main Line Media News, December 28, 2012. http://www.mainlinemedianews.com/articles/2012/12/28/region/doc50dd971d-71bc8731672534.txt*

7. Predators will reach in directly through open windows of cars even while the car is in motion. Therefore renting a car with functional air conditioning, especially abroad, is an essential car rental safety feature because it allows you to drive with closed windows.

8. Try to avoid any personal distractions; don't be preoccupied with texting on your cell phone or reading your email, or looking at other electronic devices. Instead, maintain situational awareness as you move toward your vehicle and get in.

9. After scanning your immediate environment, quickly depart the building and walk briskly, with determination. Remember the idea is to spend as little time as possible en route to your vehicle.

10. In the event of a flat tire, if you think you're in an unsafe area, drive very slowly to a service, police, or fire station.

11. It is not advisable to rent vehicles abroad unless you are very familiar with the area. An experienced predator can identify foreign drivers by their driving patterns and sometimes by the car that you rented.

12. When driving through what you perceive to be a high-threat area, always scan ahead and continually check your side and rear-view mirrors for any anomalies or irregular activities, i.e. potential threats.

13. When driving behind another vehicle and slowing down or stopping, be sure that you stop far enough back so that you can see where their car's back tires touch the road surface. This allows you sufficient space in case you need to pull out or around them quickly, without having to back up first or getting boxed in.

14. Stay in the left lane when approaching an intersection will allow you to be furthest from any predators approaching from either side of the street and with optimal escape routes.

15. When driving overseas a common ruse used by carjackers is to place large objects and even disabled children in front of your car at an intersection and then attack your vehicle when you are forced to stop to avoid hitting the object. If you observe such tactics or suspicious bystanders with broken glass at an intersection it's a good idea to avoid stopping if this may be done safely.
16. When exiting your car the last thing you want to do is switch from public mode to home mode, focus all of your attention on an important phone call, leave your car door wide open and invite opportunity for a determined predator.
17. When travelling abroad, if you don't have a choice and must rent a car, be intimately familiar with both the vehicle and rules of the road. In certain countries the driver's wheel and stick-shift may be different than what you're accustomed or the side of the road you drive on may have changed. Keep in mind that predators are trained to observe foreigners who may be unfamiliar, disoriented, under the influence of a controlled substance or confused.

Using active measures you can deny opportunity by accurately assessing and appropriately responding to the situation allowing you to mitigate the threat.

Having covered active measures let's focus our efforts on the only remaining three options—flight, fight or freeze.

Step 5 Attack
3 Options
Least Time/ Max Effort
Defend
React
Reactive Measures
Act Mode
Flight, Fight, Freeze

Reactive Measures

Given the least amount of time and requiring maximum effort, now at the very last step of the attack cycle you are afforded only three options and limited opportunity to break the cycle at Step 5—Attack, to defend against the threat.

You can take advantage of these three options by using reactive measures and situational awareness to either get away from, temporarily fight or surrender to your assailant(s).

As discussed previously the most beneficial outcome if trapped at Step 5 is to remove yourself from the threat as quickly and efficiently as possible.

Fortunately there are additional protective measures specific to a vehicular assault, which can be used to help achieve your primary objective.

When you know you will be using ground transportation it's far better to plan ahead and consider your options when you're calm, rested, and have plenty of time to do so as opposed to painting yourself into a corner later by trying to come up with a reactive response in a matter of seconds while in the middle of an assault and under duress.

1. Be wary of who is asking for your help. Some people can be very sympathetic to other drivers who appear to be in distress. Ted Bundy, the serial killer, was a relatively attractive, well-educated male who continually played on the sympathies of unsuspecting women. He would often walk with a cane or a fake limp and ask for help either to get into his vehicle or with his vehicle, and then would abduct his next victim when she was distracted by whatever he had asked for help with. If someone approaches you for help, especially in unusual circumstances, you cannot discount the possibility that it may be a predatory tactic to draw you deeper into the attack cycle.

2. If you walk back to your car and notice that a van is parked on your driver's side enter your car from the passenger door. A common tactic of predators is to attack their targets by pulling them into their vans while the soon-to-be-victims are attempting to get into their cars.

3. If you are a female, look at the car parked on the driver's side of your vehicle and in the passenger side of that car. If a male is sitting alone in the seat nearest your car, you may want to walk back into the mall, or your workplace, and ask a guard or employee to walk you back out.

4. If you failed to check the interior of your car and find that someone is in the car threatening you, put on your seatbelt and pretend to follow instructions. Consider your previous learning points—once you leave with the attacker, your chances of survival are minimal. Place the car in reverse or drive as appropriate. Place the accelerator on the floor and slam the car into the nearest larger object that is more then 30-50 feet away (You want to be able to accelerate to 30MPH or more if possible. Odds are that you will be saved by the seatbelt and/or airbag while your assailant (most likely in the back seat) will be on the receiving end of the impact. The instant the vehicle stops, get out and move away from the vehicle.

5. Whenever possible, back into a parking space as this will allow rapid departure and decrease the chances of someone trapping you.

6. Maintain situational awareness and use your observation skills to determine if anyone may be observing you or your vehicle, quickly scanning your environment just before leaving the building for any potential threats. Should you have ANY concerns whatsoever, you MUST have someone accompany you all the way to and until you are safely inside your vehicle with the doors locked. Remember to trust your gut feelings.

7. If in low or no light, keep a flashlight switched on and ready to use as both a deterrent and a weapon IN YOUR HAND before you walk out to your car.

8. As you get closer, look around your vehicle for anyone who may be behind it, under it or nearby in any bushes or behind a tree. Look around you, look into your car, and look at the passenger side floor and in the back seat.

9. If the perimeter of your vehicle is clear then just before you open the door, take a quick glance inside front and back to see if there is anyone inside the car.

10. Given the high risk of carjacking domestically and especially abroad, there is the need for defensive techniques as both a driver and a passenger. One such technique if you are drawn into a physical altercation and are thrown into the trunk of a car, use your flashlight or feel with your feet and hands in the dark to find where the back tail lights are located. Once you have identified them, position your body so that your feet have access to kick the lights, breaking them out of the car. Stick your hand or arm or whatever will fit outside that hole and wave it around non-stop. The driver won't see you but everyone else with a cellphone behind the car will see you. As reported by Consumer Reports, "(As required by law) Beginning in the 2002 model year, all cars began coming with a glow-in-the-dark release handle inside the trunk that allows people to escape from locked trunks. But many cars manufactured before that year still represent a risk."[4] There are, however, retrofit kits available for most models.

11. Some women prefer to use the "pretend you're on the cell phone so you won't be harassed" method when walking to and from their vehicle which is perfectly acceptable as long as you remain in public mode and are using your observation skills to scan for threat indicators. Recall your training from the previous chapter in protection on foot; looking him in the eye lets him know "Hey, I see you and I'm onto you."

12. Check to see if the car seats have been moved from the exact position you left them on arrival. If so then calmly go back to the building and immediately notify police or security.

13. Using your situational awareness, if you observe that you may be pulling up to a threatening situation at an intersection simply slow it down and try to time the light to avoid stopping if you can do it safely.

4 http://www.consumerreports.org/cro/2012/02/a-kit-makes-trunks-in-older-cars-safer/index.html

14. If you are stopped and someone approaches your vehicle do not roll down the window or unlock the doors. Look directly at them and shake your head and say "no". Remember your best option is to move off that X and keep moving.

    If you are unable to move and they remain persistent, your cell phone is your best friend. Depending upon the situation your cell phone response can range from calling the authorities to taking their picture—neither of which a predator wants.

15. If you suspect that you are being followed call a friend or relative and give them the plate number and description of vehicle and driver(s). A street-savvy predator will pick up on this and break off the attack.

16. If you suspect you are being followed you may utilize timing the lights, stop signs, on and off ramps and the like while connecting to 911 explaining your situation.

17. In the event that you are being harassed by another driver, such as flashing lights, tailgating, gestures or honking, don't let it bother you. Simply keep moving. If they persist and appear to be following you, drive toward the nearest public place—preferably a police or fire station—and park right in front of the building.

18. If you recall at the end of Chapter 12—Residential Protection, the entire Petit family incident began as a result of Mrs. Petit not noticing that she was being followed home. If you think you are being followed, make several consecutive right turns when it is safe to do so. If the vehicle in suspicion is still behind you, there is a very high likelihood that you are in the middle of Step 3—Stalk of an attack cycle.

19. If you are being followed, use your cell phone to call authorities and don't be shy about allowing the predator(s) to see you do it. Don't drive home. Instead drive to a police station or other well-lit, high-visibility safe public location.

20. A very common carjacking method is for predators to pull up behind you as an unsuspecting driver and bump your car expecting you to get out and assess the damage. If you feel as though you've been intentionally bumped DO NOT exit the vehicle. You'll be a lot less vulnerable if you drive to a safe public place close by to check the damage.

21. In the event you are physically attacked near or around your or another vehicle there exists the very strong potential for abduction especially if in the vicinity of an SUV or a van. Remember violence of action—its far better to fight it out right then and there than to face the consequences of being taken away to a remote area.

    To maintain anonymity for the victims of the following real-world incident, certain details of this event have been omitted:

    In the middle of a sunny afternoon in a rural area, a single female in her mid-thirties pulled into a gas station with her disabled mother. Upon arrival the mother hobbled with her cane toward the building to use the restroom while her daughter refueled the vehicle. An unmarked white van pulled up next to the woman pumping the gas on the opposite side of the island. Taking note of the van, as soon as she was done and replaced the nozzle she moved toward the driver's side door of her car at which time the sliding can door opened and a large aggressive male burst out, grabbed her and tried to pull her into the van. Knowing that verbal skills can be the bridge between escalation and de-escalation in any survival situation, in a load voice she commanded him to back away which would have drawn attention of onlookers had there been any—but there were not—she was alone

    Cognizant that her chances of survival were zero if she were abducted she realized that she had to fight for her life right then and there. Immediately making a plan she proceeded to use everything and anything at her disposal to counterattack the assailant. During the struggle she pressed 911 on her cell phone just in time before her attacker knocked it out of her hands. Although the phone was knocked out of her hands, it bounced off the back seat and landed on the passenger-side back floorboard with the dispatcher able to record most of the incident.

The assailant produced a gun and unwilling to fire it, he struck her in the head several times with it, the steel breaking her nose and causing deep lacerations. Resolute in her protective mindset and fighting through what seemed like an eternity to her, disregarding her injuries she continued to punch, kick, fingernail eye gouge and use her knees, elbows and everything else she could think of until finally he had had enough and withdrew. He put away his gun, slipped back into the van and drove away—but not before she got the license plate and reported it to the dispatcher who was still on the line. Although badly bruised, suffering a broken nose and other injuries on the lower end of the Scale of Injury, she had saved both her life and that of her mother.

It was discovered later, after her assailant was apprehended by authorities, that he was an escaped convicted felon who had committed multiple counts of rape and murder and was driving a stolen vehicle.

22. If you're being shot at on a highway, remain calm, immediately move away from the threat area. You may not be able to determine where the shots are coming from so don't slow down or stop in trying to find out! If you notice an active shooter firing from a vehicle it's best to place as much distance as possible between yourself and that vehicle as quickly as possible.

    On a Highway—Wixom, Michigan—Between October 16-November 6, 2012, Raulie Wayne Casteel repeatedly opened fire on drivers and pedestrians on different stretches of a highway in Michigan. The attacks occurred over the course of three weeks. Reports state that Casteel often fired from his car.

23. If you are being shot at in a vehicle and you are immobile or unable to drive, keep your head down and drop to the floorboard as quickly as possible.

When you're not the one at the wheel—especially with a hired driver there are additional considerations referencing personal security worth mentioning.

Taxis

Preparing for travel in a taxi requires the same area familiarization and pre-travel planning as with your own vehicle. Gaining a general familiarity with your destination is a matter of threat management. For example, if you're trying to get to the north side of town and the driver is continually moving south, this should alert you to a potential problem.

When travelling abroad it's best to travel with friends, family, and/or co-workers whom you know in the area. If this is not possible, and you need a taxi from your hotel, especially when abroad, the best option is to have the concierge call one for you. In the event of an actual incident, the investigating authorities would at least have a solid start point affording greater probability of your safe recovery. Seasoned predators are equally aware of this and tend to shy away accordingly.

If you are unable to utilize vetted transportation or the hotel concierge, there are a few protective measures to help keep you out of trouble.

1. When looking for a taxi, also look for similarities. If all the taxis in the area are yellow then it's a good bet you can safely take a yellow cab.

2. Look for phone numbers and advertisements on the vehicle as any cab driver would want to advertise their services. After checking similarities and before getting in look for a meter, radio, ID badge, or that he's in communication with a dispatcher on his cellphone. Do not use completely unmarked taxis.

3. Use your observation skills. Although they may not use a meter, all taxis use radios or cellphones to communicate with their dispatchers. If you don't see a phone number, a radio and a door handle for passengers or anything else identifying this vehicle and the driver as a legitimate taxi service then you're taking a big risk. Get out and find another one.

4. After you're in the cab, keep your personal property nearby and know exactly where that door handle is in case you need to exit the taxi in the event of an emergency.
5. In the event you do need to exit the cab in a hurry, try to do so in a crowded public area or near local authorities.
6. Predators can and may reach into a taxi directly through open windows, and they may do so even while the cab is in motion. You can break the cycle by rolling up your windows when someone approaches.
7. Pay a taxi driver while still in the car to ensure the proper change. Completing your payment transaction while still inside the vehicle will prevent the exposure of your wallet, its contents and other STIs in public and to the watchful eye of experienced predators.
8. When possible, avoid putting luggage in the trunk of a taxi to facilitate a rapid exit if necessary.
9. Be wary when exiting a bus, train, escalators, and especially taxis, as pickpockets tend to strike at these times.
10. Once registered at a hotel, keep a hotel business card to show taxi drivers where to go, should you not be able to communicate well with your driver.

Public Transportation

Seasoned travelers know that predators who stalk public transportation systems continually search for their next victim. Some protective measures to foil these predators include the following:

Eliminate Indicators

1. Know where you are going. Even if you don't, at least LOOK like you know where you're going.
2. Street-hardened predators are adept at picking out the tourist in a crowd. Wear your carry bag or purse over

your shoulder with the zippers or opening flaps turned toward you and not against fellow passengers.

3. Avoid continual referral to your public transportation map while on or waiting for the train, as this only advertises the stark soft target indicator that you're not sure of where you're going. Instead, stand near the route map posted in the car.

Deny Opportunity

1. While waiting for the train or bus, stand back away from the tracks and try to position yourself near the largest group you can find.
2. Predators are enticed by fanny packs on subways and trains as in crowded cars these can be easily sliced open with a razor blade and may include you. A good rule of thumb is to leave your expensive backpacks at the hotel and carry your camera, maps, and valuables in a shopping bag from a local grocery store or in something equally as inconspicuous.
3. Remember that there's greater safety in numbers—avoid sitting in an empty car. If you find yourself alone, exit the empty car and enter another one at the first possible stop. The center cars on the train are generally the most crowded.
4. Beware of loud arguments or noisy incidents. Distance yourself without attracting attention as these could be staged to distract you as part of an attack cycle.

Utilizing the previous proactive, active and reactive measures you can lower your scale of injury, increase your odds of prevailing, and significantly reduce your risk of being involved in a vehicular assault.

CHAPTER 15

Hotels And Dormitories

"Everywhere you hang your hat is home. Home is the bright cave under the hat."
Lance Morrow[1]

In This Chapter You Will Be Introduced To...

...the specific security threats that are resident in hotel, motel, dormitory and temporary lodging. Learn the difference in risk profiles for the variety of choices on the lodging market both domestically and abroad, and how to minimize the risks of your selected choice!

At A Glance

Every location I have ever stayed at has had a mix of desirable security features, and undesirable ones. Learning to recognize and capitalize on the desirable features puts you a step ahead of your fellow lodgers. Taking a step further and planning to capitalize on those desirable features, and or taking steps to minimize the risk from undesirable features is what will keep you safe!

How Do I Use This In Real Life?

If you know that a hotel provides controlled access, then you can focus on escape planning in case of a fire, as that is a more likely threat. In a motel which provides easy access to the parking lot, a fire is not such a large issue, but someone entering the room is made easier. Use this chapter like a checklist to acquaint yourself to a variety of threats and mitigation strategies associated with temporary lodging!

---

1 Lance Morrow (b1939) a popular essayist and award-winning writer, chiefly for Time Magazine, also an author of several books.

What The Pros Know

Short duration stays are challenging. You don't have time to get to know the environment, your knowledge of the local area is limited and you typically have things you want or need to accomplish while you are there. Developing the habit of quickly identifying and planning to utilize desirable security features is the key component of staying safe in temporary lodging facilities—and you start your practice immediately!

Fertile Hunting Grounds

For purposes of discussion, a hotel is any commercial short-term lodging establishment providing accommodations and services for travelers. Some hotels offer amenities such as shopping and restaurants located on site, and these are often high foot-traffic environments, which tend to attract the attention of predators.

Motels differ from hotels in that they are structurally designed to provide immediate access to the parking lot. While this design is convenient for vehicle access, ironically it allows just as easy access to your room by predators, without the added physical control of a secure lobby or security personnel.

Dormitories, or dorms, are for the most part university or collegiate living quarters. Providing open bay, semi-private or private rooms for residents, most dorms contain common bathroom facilities and recreation areas. More along the lines of "affordable living" for college students, dorms afford the benefit of proximity to study and lecture halls. Dorms are considered fertile hunting grounds for the predator preying upon the naivety and inexperience of college students, many of whom are away from home for the first time.

A homestay is an affordable type of lodging arrangement utilized in business, tourism and/or study-abroad programs where you may rent a room in a home owned by a local family or business. Available in most destinations worldwide, homestays are often used as an alternative to the more expensive commercial lodging.

Popular for language and cross-cultural exchange, the most frequent users of homestays are usually college and exchange students or other young travelers. As a result of marketing, patrons may be lulled into a sense that they're in the protective arms of a casual and pleasant environment. However such facilities generally lack any form of controlled security other than what may be established by the property owner, such as exterior lights and the like.

Another prevalent method of lodging away from home is what is commonly referred to as couch surfing. Hugely popular with younger people who generally run on strict budgetary constraints and either have very limited experience or no idea whatsoever about security concerns, it lends itself to a higher risk profile.

One of the more popular couch surfing sites, Air BNB[2] does verify the hosts as far as identification. They also cover any property loss up to $1M. They also have lots of user reviews. You may also take advantage of online hotel reviews such as www.tripadvisor.com and others as another way of vetting the place you will be staying ahead of time.

Looking at these from a threat management perspective, hotels, motels, dorms, couch surfing and homestays—collectively "lodging," all share the common denominator of being away from a safe and familiar environment, and a woeful lack of concentric rings of protection. As such, they offer a target-rich environment to both the seasoned and opportunistic predator. In terms of any threat progression, you are far better prepared to manage a physical threat while lodging if you are armed with the full gamut of proactive, active and reactive measures.

In taking this holistic approach, we will first analyze the anatomy of a physical assault while lodging and then use it to apply our knowledge of breaking each step of the attack cycle using appropriate proactive, active and reactive measures. Let's begin with proactive measures.

Step 1 Look	Step 2 Choose	Verify	Step 3 Stalk

Unlimited Options
Maximum amount of time/ least amount of effort
Avoid
Assess, Plan, Act–*The APA Process*
Proactive Measures
Public Mode
Eliminate Soft Target Indicators

Proactive Measures

Beginning at Step 1—Look, running all the way through and including the first half of Step 3—Stalk/Verify, and in public mode you have the opportunity to avoid a lodging attack entirely by applying proactive measures.

You can take advantage of unlimited options and opportunity by using the likes of situational awareness and the APA Process to help you eliminate soft target indicators.

2 *https://www.airbnb.com*

Anatomy Of A Lodging Attack

Applying the anatomy of an attack to a lodging attack—an assault on your person, property and/or protectee(s) in and around your lodging—you end up with the usual three tripod legs supporting any successful attack:

1. **Target**—you and/or your protectee(s)
2. **Bad Guy(s)**—one or more assailant(s)
3. **Process**—The attack cycle itself

Eliminate Indicators

Addressing the first leg of the anatomy of lodging attack—the target—the following are recommended proactive measures designed to eliminate both primary and secondary soft target indicators. Utilizing your APA Process:

1. Select the most suitable lodging based on location and itinerary. Selecting lodging on the way is the least sound risk management option, with a high probability of you appearing out of place. Selection with adequate time prior to departure is substantially more secure.

2. Your lodging choice should include a cursory investigation into the specific area that you are planning to travel, ensuring that it is a relatively low crime area where there has been minimal violence, little or no robbery, no or low terrorist activities or previous attacks.

   Search the Internet, check with the US Consulate if travelling abroad, and add to your confidence by paying close attention to any news bulletins or information from friends, colleagues, or co-workers who may be currently or recently in that same area.

3. Walking into a known high-threat area, especially following a high-profile incident, presents an indicator. Call the manager at your lodging choice and ask them about any recent incidents.

   You have the right to ask if there were any violent incidents in the past few weeks. If so, what type of violence? If overseas, did it reflect any anti-foreigner sentiment or was it limited to local crime? What is the likelihood of continued violence throughout your stay? Should you consider a more secure lodging alternative? Will your ground transportation to and from be in any way affected?

4. In some cases your lodging selection may be made for you. However, if you have any say in the matter, request to stay someplace that has a recognized name and reputation, preferably with modem electronic key-card access. Keep in mind that certain lodging located very near to government offices, embassies, consulates, and recognized religious communities are considered favored anti-foreigner terrorist targets.

5. Predators start the attack cycle by immediately scanning the vicinity looking for soft targets. By eavesdropping on your conversation with the front desk they search for such useful information, such as your room number or exploitable personal information such as a credit card number, address, or phone number (you can write these down for the desk if needed), and determine by how you conduct your business whether or not to choose you as their next target.

6. Use your verbal skills to avoid divulging to an observant predator any of your travel details such as "I'll be gone from 6 PM until 10 PM," or any personal information such as address, phone number, credit card and the like. You can eliminate yourself as a soft target by focusing your attention on your surroundings and not divulging any useful information.

7. Whether you are on a temporary or extended stay abroad, once you reach your hotel, motel, or homestay, it is critical to determine a hard room and a rally point. The hard room will afford you the ability to lock yourself inside a safe and secure environment (get in) in the event of an imminent threat if you cannot leave the building. Having preplanned emergency egress

to allow you to reach a rally point at a more distant location will be advantageous if you are able to leave the building (get out). Plan to either get in or get out; running around in circles under duress not knowing what to do can mark you as a soft target.

Find a hard room in your lodging with as few entry doors as possible (one door would be ideal), so that you can easily see anyone coming in or going out. Remember that it should optimally provide you cover and concealment with few if any windows to help reduce the likelihood of your presence becoming known to others.

Bathrooms are a good example of a hard room in a hotel, motel, or homestay. They are found in most temporary lodging, are generally relatively small, and yes, those old-fashioned cast iron bathtubs make for great cover. Plan to take your cell phone and your go-bag with you, as you never know how long you might need to stay in your hard room. Being a hard target especially under stress pushes you further down on the predator's target list.

8. Know exactly who to contact and how to reach them, should you find yourself in an emergency situation. Ensure that you have a valid number and that your cell service does in fact have a strong enough signal and can connect while in your room. Have your ICE number(s) preset. Make alternate plans for communication such as access to a hardline if the signal is spotty or unavailable.

9. Upon arrival notify the front desk if you or any members of your group may require special evacuation assistance in the event of an emergency.

Eliminating indicators by hardening yourself and your protectee(s) in and around your lodging eradicates the appearance of a soft target significantly lowering your threat profile and the likelihood of a predator carrying out a successful lodging attack.

The sooner attack-related behaviors can be observed, the sooner they can be addressed. Hence, the use of situational awareness as part of your proactive measures is strongly recommended. With that in mind—and the desired result of defeating a lodging attack, let's move forward with our capabilities in breaking each step of the assault cycle using active measures.

Step 3 Stalk | Plan | Step 4 Close

Limited Options

Less Time/
More Effort

Mitigate

Assess & Respond

Active Measures

Alert Mode

Deny Opportunity

Active Measures

Given less time and requiring more effort, now past midway of the attack cycle you are afforded limited options and opportunity to break the cycle from the latter half of Step 3—Stalk/ Plan, all the way through and including all of Step 4—Close, to mitigate the threat.

You can take advantage of this opportunity by using active measures such as assessment and response, situational awareness and denying a predator the opportunity.

Deny Opportunity

Again, any predator, motivated and capable, seeks opportunity. Think ahead about what opportunities a predator seeks by using your appropriate assessment and response:

1. After making your selection and confirming your reservation(s), ensure that at least one person at home or at the office has your exact itinerary and specific hotel information such as physical address, phone number, and the names of other folks you will be with. It's a good idea to call them after you're checked in and ensconced in your room, to place their mind at ease that you have arrived safe and sound.

2. Optimally you want your room above the first floor to avoid easy predator access. Try to reserve a room on a floor that is high enough to deter unwanted access but within reach of most first-responder rescue ladders; a recommended selection is from the second to the fourth floors.

3. Additional precautionary considerations to assist in your lodging selection should include: Are there any notable upcoming events occurring at the hotel or nearby during your stay, which will increase traffic? Are you travelling during a holiday or at a time where getting to and from the hotel will pose more of a challenge? Will you be able to check in upon arrival or will you need to store your luggage for a period of time with the hotel? Try to have this all worked out before your arrival so you don't present the appearance of confusion or exhibit other soft target indicators.

4. Upon arrival use your situational awareness, stay locked into public mode, and utilize your protective skills to navigate through the lobby and at the front desk.

5. Use your observation skills to perform a cursory perimeter inspection by visually scanning the surrounding streets, sidewalks, pedestrians, and parked vehicles for anyone who may be observing you, your protectee(s), personal property, or the front door of the hotel.

6. Don't have all your attention focused on your ceil phone upon arrival. Instead, keep a close eye on your luggage and others with whom you may be travelling, as predators are known to engage unsuspecting otherwise-occupied hotel patrons immediately upon arrival.

7. At the front desk, use your verbal skills and do not shout your room number across the lobby to other members in your group. If you feel that in any way your room number has been compromised it is perfectly acceptable to request an alternate room. You may ask the clerk to not verbalize any personal information as most are trained to write it on your room key card sleeve.

8. Before you leave the lobby, take a few seconds to identify stairways, elevators, and entrances and exits in case you have to get out in a hurry. Look for areas where crowds might be expected to form (near doors and restaurants, storefront or bar entrances) to assist in your evacuation plan.

9. Except when not accessible, take the elevator instead of the stairs, which are generally isolated. Finding yourself alone in an empty stairwell, especially late at night, opens up tremendous opportunities for the predator. Find elevator access not only to your room but to other parts of the hotel.

10. Determine where and how you can contact hotel employees other than at the front desk if needed especially during less busy hours.

11. When you enter the elevator, take a quick glance over at the number of floors to determine your physical position relative to roof, stairways, lobby, parking lot, and/or basement access.

12. When first entering your room, switch to alert mode and perform a thorough "room clearing" to affirm that the room is currently unoccupied. Check to see if there is any objects remaining there from a previous occupant.

13. After the door is closed ensure that you have a fully functional door lock. If the lock doesn't work, immediately request another room.

14. Use your observation skills and remain in public mode at all times especially upon exit and entry into the hotel and your room.

15. When in your room, it is advisable to keep your hotel door locked and dead-bolted at all times. Remember to never open your door until you can positively identify who is on the other side asking you for access.

16. Establish your concentric rings of protection to include various warning devices such as a lightweight portable door stop alarm and the like.

17. Always arrange to meet any visitors in the lobby with other people around—never disclose your room number or invite someone you don't know into your room under ANY circumstances.

Does the hotel or homestay offer a safe for storing valuables in the lobby or executive offices? Although not the case with most five-star accommodations, it is not advisable to use a room safe in certain hotels that may use standard access codes which are known by a majority of staff. It's best to utilize the hotel's lobby or executive office safe to secure any valuables —and be sure to request an itemized receipt, which allows an added ring of protection.

Using active measures in a lodging attack stops a predator in moving from pre-attack behavior to attack behavior and thus eliminates his carrying out that attack.

Having covered active measures let's focus our efforts on the only remaining three options—flight, fight or freeze.

Reactive Measures

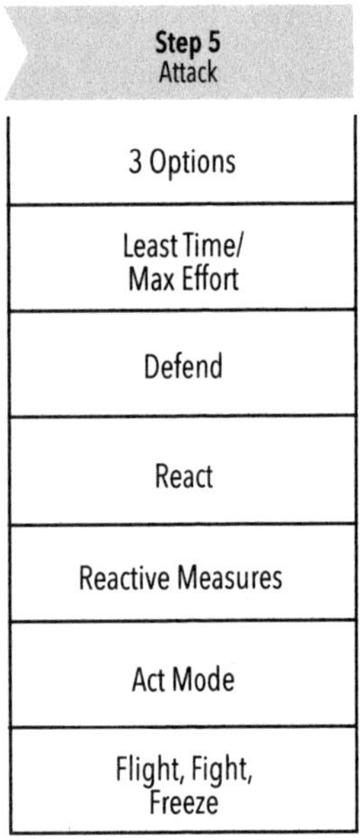

Step 5
Attack

3 Options
Least Time/ Max Effort
Defend
React
Reactive Measures
Act Mode
Flight, Fight, Freeze

Given the least amount of time and requiring maximum effort, now at the very last step of the cycle you are afforded only three options and limited opportunity to break the cycle at Step 5—Attack to defend against the threat.

You can take advantage of these three options by using reactive measures, situational awareness, and defensive principles to either get away from, temporarily fight or surrender to your assailant(s).

Fortunately there are additional protective reactive measures specific to a lodging attack which can be used to help achieve your primary objective:

1. If someone calls telling you that they need to come into your room for services and it doesn't seem right, verify it with the front desk and ask if someone from their staff is supposed to have access to your room, as predators have been known to pose as hotel staff so as to gain access.

2. When returning to your hotel late at night, use the main entrance. Be observant and remember to look around before entering parking lots.

3. When you leave your room, leave the "DO NOT DISTURB" sign on your door. It acts as a decoy in giving the appearance that you may still be inside. If you need room service, call housekeeping but leave the sign on the door. Another option to give the impression that you may still be in your room is to leave the TV, iPod, or radio turned on with raised volume.

4. Close the door securely whenever you are in your room and use all the locking devices provided.

5. Don't needlessly display guest room keys in public or carelessly leave them on restaurant tables, at the swimming pool, or other places where they can be easily stolen.

6. In matters of threat management and protection, hotel management, security, and even local law enforcement may be viable options. However, given the urgency of an immediate attack, none of these options may be viable. In exigent circumstances you may need to exit the building (get out) to a pre-determined rally point or move to a hard room (get in). If there is not enough time or if the incident (for example a riot or aggressive civil protest) will not allow you to exit the building and seek assistance, there may be no other option but to retreat to a hard room.

7. Take your go-bag with you and/or keep one in your hard room, as it is the safest and most secure location available allowing you the option to retreat and lock down in times of dire emergency. Optimally your hard room should have minimal physical protection tools such as multiple light sources and means of communication such as a backup or local cell phone and/or outside hardline with which you may be able to signal for help.

Protection In Elevators

1. When getting on an elevator, it's best to allow other passengers in front of you. Being the last person on board positions you to be the first out in an emergency.
2. If the doors open and you notice someone suspicious or it just doesn't look or feel right, wait for the next car. If you don't have that option, let other passengers select their floors first as it's common for predators to tell you, "What a coincidence that's my floor too!" so they can follow you out.
3. It's best to be the last person on and closest to the control panel while keeping your back to the wall and maintaining situational awareness. Should you be challenged you're only an arms-length from the alarm which you can hit in an emergency, as well as any other floor buttons you need to hit allowing you rapid departure.
4. When managing a threat in an elevator, do not press the emergency stop button as this could significantly decrease your options as far as moving off the X quickly, if the elevator stops in a place that the doors cannot open.

Utilizing the above proactive, active and reactive measures you can now lower your threat profile, decrease your scale of injury, increase your odds of prevailing, and significantly reduce your risk of being involved in a lodging attack.

CHAPTER 16

Travel Protection

"Traveling...forces you to trust strangers and to lose sight of all that familiar comfort of home and friends. You are constantly off balance."
Cesare Pavese[1]

In This Chapter You Will Be Introduced To...

...travel specific risks and nuances. Travel security is just like security at home, but there are additional factors to consider. After reviewing the travel specific risk parameters and threat indicators, we will cover travel specific mitigation techniques. Learn to plan, pack and act more confidently and appear more like a bad choice to a predator.

At A Glance

When traveling, especially overseas, you are a target. You are less familiar with the environment, you typically have a large concentration of valuables in your possession, and you may have a language barrier—all of which make you an attractive target to a predator. As with everything in preventative defense, much of this is under your control. Wearing an American Flag may show national pride, but in Ankara[2], it will most likely get you targeted. Planning your transportation to your hotel at the airport is one technique, but you are much more likely to be successful if you have researched your options and chosen the lowest risk prior to getting on the plane.

How Do I Use This In Real Life?

Many of us have to travel for work. Use these mitigation techniques like a checklist when you are packing and planning for your trip. You can say that you just want to get away, and don't want to adhere to a scripted plan.

1 *Cesare Pavese (1908-1950) Italian poet, novelist, and literary critic.*

2 *Capital city of Turkey.*

You are going on vacation and don't want to worry about anything. That works out great until you are huddled up at a bus stop trying to get to your hotel, and the next bus is at 7:00 AM. Planning does not limit your ability to have fun. In fact, it ensures you are in position to take maximum advantage or every opportunity to enjoy yourself!

What The Pros Know

There is nothing secret or sexy about travel preparation. Professionals do not have any tools or tricks at their disposal that you have not been introduced to in this book. What they know is fortune favors the prepared. Taking the time to plan, pack and prepare for a trip is what separates the pros from the rest of the pack!

When traveling abroad, your threat profile is raised by the time you leave national airspace. How can you avoid becoming the victim of a travel threat and increase your ability to be more comfortable in unfamiliar or even threatening environments? How can you decrease your travel risk and protect yourself should you end up in the wrong place at the wrong time?

Threat Profile

Lowering your threat profile—a protection term applied to potential threats, the likelihood of them occurring, and their associated impact— is critical to your threat management and protection during travel.

As a US citizen traveling abroad, your threat profile is significantly raised, in that anti-American sentiment is prevalent especially throughout emerging nations. You're already viewed as a potential target because of your nationality and perceived religious affiliation. Often characterized as "ugly Americans," we are perceived as affluent by almost all other countries and therefore listed as high-value targets. To make matters worse, a vast majority of Americans speak only English—which places you at a tremendous disadvantage in non-English speaking countries.

While travelling abroad you are continually off balance in unfamiliar environments, disoriented, suffering from jet lag, and usually carrying all of your valuables including a significant amount of cash—all of which make you an attractive target. Whether on business or on vacation, from the instant you present your passport to foreign officials, you are continually distracted with searching for appropriate contacts, securing reliable transportation and lodging, dealing with foreign currency exchange, hurdling language barriers and navigating unfamiliar destinations.

In the words of a travel journalist, "It's hard to imagine a more tempting target than a group of people uprooted from their familiar surroundings, trying to relax or distracted by travel hassles, many of them carrying valuables."[3] Highly experienced adversaries are more than aware of this as you groggily step off that airplane. From the perspective of these seasoned predators you cannot possibly be more of a soft target.

If you are a female travelling overseas—outside the US, Canada, the EU, Australia, and a handful of other countries—you are NOT considered equal to males. Consequently, your gender burdens you with a raised threat profile and in most cases from the predator's optic you are considered a desirable soft target.

Such was the case on February 7, 2013. In a zinc-plated coffin, Sarai Sierra's body was flown back from Turkey, a belated tragic return that brought a wife and mother home to Staten Island for burial, but left many unanswered questions about her death.

She was killed in Istanbul while travelling alone. It was her first trip abroad, and until recently, there was little in her life that would suggest that she would undertake such an adventurous endeavor or meet such a violent end. For Ms. Sierra, 33, the trip had seemed so easy, booked on her iPad and previewed in gauzy digital photos by virtual friends: a room was reserved in Istanbul and a side trip was arranged to meet a man in Amsterdam whom she had met online.

Even after a friend she was to travel with backed out, Ms. Sierra pressed on, departing on Jan. 7. She met digital friends for the first time on gritty Istanbul streets and in Amsterdam cafes, posting delicately crafted images taken with her phone to a cheerful band of social-media followers and she stayed in constant contact with friends and relatives at home through Skype and instant messages. Friends said it was as if she had never left.

For her husband, the grim discovery of his wife's body left open the mystery of her death. How did a tech-savvy young mother, whose growing passion for photography drew her overseas, end up dead by the ruins of Istanbul's old city walls?

Such connectedness quite likely helped her feel secure in strange new surroundings, said Kathleen Cumiskey, a professor of psychology, gender and sexuality at the College of Staten Island, where Ms. Sierra was a part-time student. "What it does is generate this sense that you're not alone,

---

3 *Barbara S. Peterson, "Crime in the Suites," Entrepreneur Magazine, September 4, 2008; http://www.entrepreneur.com/article/197034#ixzz2VYO13hk8*

which can really mess with your perception of risk," she said, adding that social media "lulls you into this sense of security because it is a world of your own creation."[4]

Seasoned foreign adversaries are cunning, intimately familiar with the area, highly experienced, well-rested, switched to alert mode, and have anticipated targeting you.[5]

All of these factors place you at a disadvantage before you even leave the airport. Knowing this should provide the motivation to maintain that protection envelope and the willingness to apply your situational awareness, be prepared with your protective measures and use your protection skills.

Mitigating Travel Risk

The international airport is your best and last controlled area and you are the most vulnerable when you move away from it. Departing the airport, your taxi, limo, or hotel shuttle bus is the next controlled area and eventually your hotel, motel, or homestay is your next controlled area. The further you move away from a controlled area the greater your travel risk, which in turn raises your threat profile.

Many people who travel extensively roll their eyes at such admonition, as they feel they are highly experienced and have thus gained a strong sense of comfort and familiarity based on previous experiences.

However, familiarity breeds complacency. Even the most seasoned traveler knows that such familiarity has a tendency to erode situational awareness and attenuate protective skills.

OK, this may all be true, but you still need to travel. So, how can you lower your threat profile? How can you avoid becoming the victim of a threat and increase your ability to be more comfortable in potentially threatening environments? How can you decrease travel risk and protect yourself and your protectee(s) when on the road? We make the personal choice when travelling to be prepared or remain unprepared. Those who choose to adopt the protective mindset and make threat management and protection a priority throughout their itinerary have made the conscious decision to remain prepared—a paramount step in mitigating travel risk.

4 *J. David Goodman, "Mystery Deepens as Staten Island Woman's Body Is Returned From Turkey," The New York Times, February 7, 2013, http://www.nytimes.com/2013/02/08/nyregion/sarai-sierras-body-is-returned-from-turkey-but-mystery-remains.html*

5 *To find updated information on tourist attacks see http://touristkilled.com*

In terms of any threat progression, you are far better prepared to manage travel risk if you are armed with the full gamut of proactive, active and reactive measures.

In taking this holistic approach, we will first analyze the anatomy of a travel attack and then use it to apply our knowledge of breaking each step of the attack cycle using appropriate proactive, active and reactive measures. Let's begin with proactive measures.

Proactive Measures

Beginning at Step 1—Look, running all the way through and including the first half of Step 3—Stalk/Verify, and in public mode you have the opportunity to avoid a travel attack entirely by applying proactive measures.

You can take advantage of unlimited options and opportunity by using the likes of situational awareness and the APA Process to help you eliminate soft target indicators.

Step 1 Look	Step 2 Choose	Verify	Step 3 Stalk
Unlimited Options			
Maximum amount of time/ least amount of effort			
Avoid			
Assess, Plan, Act–*The APA Process*			
Proactive Measures			
Public Mode			
Eliminate Soft Target Indicators			

Anatomy Of A Travel Attack

Applying the anatomy of an attack specifically to a travel attack— an assault on your person, property and/or protectee(s) while you are travelling—we end up with the same three legs of the tripod supporting any successful attack.

1. **Target**—you and/ or your protectee(s)
2. **Bad Guy(s)**—one or more assailant(s)
3. **Process**—the attack cycle itself

Let's start with the target—you or your protectee(s). What can you do to prevent a predator from viewing you as a soft target?

Eliminate Indicators

In addressing the first leg of the anatomy of a travel attack—the target—we know that a critical component of avoiding travel risk is preparation. What can you do to ensure that envelope of protection before you depart the comfort of your own home? By running your APA Process you can:

1. Take the time to research beforehand to gain a pre-deployment collection of information to include identification of embassy/ consulate location and contact information and familiarization with the area where you will be travelling so you won't appear lost or disoriented. Consult the Internet, a travel bureau, or your destination hotel for any maps and other important air travel, ground transportation, and/or pedestrian routes relevant to your physical movement.
2. Don't overpack. Pack as lightly as possible taking only what you will need for the trip. Being hampered with overweight or oversized luggage is not only cumbersome in the event you need to move rapidly, but it is a predatory beacon.
3. Establish a travel support net. Be sure someone at home or work has your detailed travel itinerary, with airport and hotel information. In the event of a travel glitch or unexpected event having a travel support net that includes local contacts will also prove beneficial.
4. Place identification both inside and on the outside of your suitcase.
5. "If you look like food, you will be eaten."[6] Avoid loud unconventional clothing, and especially items that may identify your nationality or religious affiliation. Refrain from wearing hometown ball caps, sweatshirts, or even sneakers as these items may be considered indicators to a predator that you are a foreigner. Try to fit in with the locals as best you can as standing out in a crowd acts as a beacon.
6. Avoid behaviors such as appearing lost, confused, disoriented, intoxicated, rude, disorderly, loud, obnoxious, careless, and so on, all of which are viewed as STIs from the predator's optic and will draw unwanted attention.

6 Quote attributed to Clint Smith, proprietor of Thunder Ranch; a respected tactical firearms instructor.

7. Depending upon your destination, you may want to remove any jewelry, not carry it at all, or if you cannot remove a ring at least turn the stone around to the inside of your hand.
8. Keep your cash, passport, legal docs, ID, and valuables concealed. Avoid fanny packs and thin-strap carry bags. Any strap too thick to be easily cut will work.
9. When in public, avoid looking up at tall buildings, it is a dead giveaway that you are not a local.
10. Be wary of flaunting cash or other valuables.
11. Avoid folding or unfolding a map in plain view. If you must consult a map or use your GPS, do so in private and away from plain view of passersby.
12. Mind your own business, keep to yourself, and don't offer your assistance to locals, as it's a very common ploy among predators and their accomplices employed in their pickpocketing, harassment, or abduction skills to draw you into the attack cycle.
13. Don't leave your bags unattended even for one minute. It takes only a matter of seconds for a trained adversary to slip an explosive or other devices or drugs into your luggage without your knowing.

On April 25 and 26, Turk and Caicos Royal Police charged Texas businesswoman Cathy Sulledge-Davis, 60, and retired neurosurgeon Horace Norrell, 80, of Sarasota, with carrying ammunition as they were departing the country at the Providenciales International Airport. There was no gun found in either case. The two were arrested and eventually allowed to return home after paying $4,000 in cash bail. [Authorities] called the circumstances surrounding the arrests "unusual" and "mysterious" and said he hopes Americans are not being preyed upon in a nefarious scheme.[7]

14. Using a case specifically designed for laptops or iPads only serves to alert predators. Use a nondescript carrying case such as a well-padded briefcase or similarly

7 *http://www.miamiherald.com/2013/05/10/3391660/arrests-of-vacationing-americans.html*

ubiquitous carry case. Sporting style backpacks are common among young travelers— and young travelers generally have little in the way of valuables to offer.

15. Know the local laws regarding computer usage. In some countries, visitors must purchase a license to use the Internet, or even email. In almost all countries when sending and receiving email at a cybercafe know that your communications are probably being monitored.
16. Never place your laptop—or any other electronic equipment in checked baggage—keep it with you on the flight.
17. Keep your laptop with you when riding in a taxi—do not place it in the trunk.
18. Be wary of tag teams. Groups of predators often use distraction techniques when targeting victims in public areas such as restaurants, waiting rooms, airports, or metro trains. One common technique involves staging an incident such as dropping coins in front of the victim while the others lift your targeted personal property from behind. Another technique is distracting the victim by spilling coffee, ketchup, or mustard where the culprit feigns assistance to the victim, while a cohort makes off with your gear.
19. Never accept drinks from anyone you don't know. If a bartender is preparing a drink, watch closely. Do not leave any drinks out of your view.
20. Women travelling overseas—especially to emerging nations— should consider using inconspicuous luggage that does not denote affluence or femininity.
21. Shield from view documents or logos that denote citizenship. For example, hold a US passport with the national emblem facing inward or under other papers while standing in long lines. Citizens of Israel and the US should be especially careful.

22. Mace, pepper spray, and even Swiss army knives may be considered weapons and as such are illegal in many countries.

    Be sure to sterilize your bags of any firearms, ammunition, impact, edged or other weapons before travel—or know for certain they are legal in the country you are travelling to prior to departure.

23. Separate your home currency from local currency so that home currency—an indicator to a predator - is out of view during transactions. When possible, carry traveler's checks instead of cash and never carry more than two credit cards.

24. Be advised that in some countries wearing camouflage clothing is legal or at least frowned upon. Regardless, even if it is legal, it is not recommended.

25. Use your verbal skills to avoid giving up any personal information, avoid open discussion of local politics or religion, and avoid using profanity.

Eliminating indicators by hardening yourself and your protectee(s) during travel eliminates the appearance of a soft target resulting in the disruption of one of the tripod legs of carrying out a successful attack.

The sooner attack-related behaviors can be observed, the sooner they can be addressed. Hence, the use of situational awareness as part of your proactive measures is strongly recommended. With that in mind— and the desired result of defeating a physical assault, let's move forward with our capabilities in breaking each step of the assault cycle using active measures.

Step 3 Stalk | Plan | Step 4 Close

Limited Options

Less Time/ More Effort

Mitigate

Assess & Respond

Active Measures

Alert Mode

Deny Opportunity

Active Measures

Given less time and requiring more effort, now past midway of the attack cycle you are afforded limited options and opportunity to break the cycle from the latter half of Step 3—Stalk/Plan, all the way through and including all of Step 4—Close, to mitigate the threat.

You can take advantage of this opportunity by using active measures such as assessment and response, situational awareness and denying a predator the opportunity.

Any predator who is motivated and capable seeks opportunity. Especially in a foreign country, where poverty is the largest driver of violent crime such individuals will lean more toward convenience and avoid taking risks that would require substantial effort or possibly cause bodily harm.

Predators want to try to achieve their objective in as little time as possible and with little self-risk. You can use this to your advantage by denying what they seek most—an opportunity.

Deny Opportunity

Any predator who is motivated and capable seeks opportunity. Think ahead about what opportunities a predator might seek from you, by using your appropriate Assessment and Response:

1. Depending upon your destination(s), verify that your cell phone will work during every leg of travel. Check with your carrier to ensure connectivity as well as consider purchasing local short-term cell phone service. You do not want to be left without communication.

2. Renew your passport at least six months in advance of expiration. Bring extra passport photos along with photocopies of your passport's front two pages in case your passport is lost or stolen.

3. Find out how to report the loss or theft of your credit card(s) overseas: 1-800 numbers do not work abroad.

4. Pack, carry, and utilize a quality go-bag. In the event of an emergency incident abroad the contents of this strongly recommended physical protection tool will be more than worth the effort of packing it for your trip.

5. Verify the identity of airport transportation services, vehicles, and drivers. Positively identify staff members.

Check to see if they are wearing the same logo, uniform, or colors of the appropriate service provider.

6. Monitor local incidents by checking the newspaper at your hotel, or check local news stations for any reports of violence at or near any of the destinations of your itinerary. If there have been reports of violence, what type of activity was it? Did it involve anti-foreigner resentment or was it limited to local activities? What is the likelihood of additional violence occurring throughout your remaining travel itinerary? Will ground transportation or pedestrian travel routes to and from your destinations in between controlled areas be affected?
7. Keep cash in a different location on your body, separate from your passport and wallet. Determine the credit limit on each credit card and avoid charging over that limit.
8. Immediately prior to any movement, briefly check your cell phone, check with the hotel desk, or the Internet for any air or ground transportation warnings.
9. Avoid foreign street vendors and lingering in extremely large crowds.

Using active measures you can deny opportunity by accurately assessing and appropriately responding to the situation allowing you to mitigate the threat.

Having covered active measures let's focus our efforts on the only remaining three options—flight, fight or freeze.

Reactive Measures

Given the least amount of time and requiring maximum effort, now at the very last step of the cycle you are afforded only three options and limited opportunity to break the cycle at Step 5—Attack, to defend against the threat.

Step 5 Attack
3 Options
Least Time/ Max Effort
Defend
React
Reactive Measures
Act Mode
Flight, Fight, Freeze

You can take advantage of these three options by using reactive measures, situational awareness, and defensive principles to either get away from, temporarily fight or surrender to your assailant(s). As discussed previously the most beneficial outcome if trapped at Step 5 is to remove yourself from the threat as quickly and efficiently as possible.

Fortunately there are additional protective measures specific to a travel attack which can be used to help achieve your primary objective:

1. If you feel stressed or uncomfortable in any situation, maintain your situational awareness. Remain calm, and be conscious of how your body language might be displaying your discomfort, anxiety or fear, especially if you are in an unfamiliar environment and don't understand the language.

2. In the event of an actual threat, remember there may be many predators and very few of you, so apply all of what you now know. Make a plan, move off the X, or use whatever reactive measures are required to disengage from the threat as quickly as possible. Utilize your extensive repository of thought, action, skills, and tools to move yourself and your protectee(s) away from the threat and to safety.

3. If you think you may be in the attack cycle of abduction and are in a public area make as much noise and commotion as possible to draw attention to your situation. The same holds true if abduction takes place in your hotel room, motel, or homestay—make lots of noise and attempt to arouse the suspicion or concerns of hotel employees and neighboring patrons. At the very least, the fact that an abduction has taken place will be brought to the attention of local law enforcement in a timely manner and the investigation process can begin. Otherwise, it could be hours or even days before your absence is reported.

Predictable Patterns

Kidnapping is VERY big business overseas and as a result, one of the most dangerous behavior characteristics you can exhibit abroad is predictability. Customarily beginning their attack cycle at the airport, kidnappers will run surveillance outside your hotel, motel, or homestay and along your ground transportation routes.

Although such predators remain a prominent threat to all travelers, most people are blissfully ignorant of the very real and growing threat of kidnapping, child abductions, and sexual assault. The most common statement after the fact is always, "I thought it would never happen to me or to our children."

Such was the case of an American businessman who was working as an expatriate for a large US corporation residing in Asia. To preserve anonymity we will refer to him as Mr. Smith.

Having worked in the same area overseas for several months, Smith was viewed by adversarial foreign nationals as an affluent American because he chose to be very well-dressed, drive to work in a large vehicle, and reside in a high-profile neighborhood.

Every morning Mr. Smith got up at exactly 6:15 AM, made coffee, got dressed, finished putting on his tie, and walked out the door by 7:00 AM. At that same time every day he would press the button which opened the driveway gate and back out, turn left on to the same street, and take the same route to work. In later interviews his neighbors said "you could set your watch by this guy's routine." Such clockwork routine is known in the protection world as predictable patterns.

Note a few of the soft target indicators from the predator's optic:

1. **American**
2. **Affluent**
3. **Predictable Patterns**

Following the attack cycle, predators observed Mr. Smith and his clockwork routine and given such predictable patterns, they were easily able to map out specific timing and locations of where he was the most vulnerable. Unaware of eliminating his soft target indicators, Mr. Smith failed to break the attack cycle at Step 1 and again at Step 2.

He had been advised and encouraged by his co-workers beforehand to vary his times and routes to and from work, but as his friends later told investigators, when asked about his predictability Mr. Smith said, "Abduction? That will never happen to me."

Within less than three days of his declaration, Mr. Smith had failed at Step 3—Stalk of the attack cycle at which time his kidnappers had planned their attack, moved in on their target Step 4—Close and finally at Step 5 he was brutally attacked, after which he was never seen or heard from again.

It's important to take every precaution to not present yourself as a soft target. Vary your arrival and departure times and common travel routes—don't be time and place predictable. Avoid predictable patterns.

Overseas Emergency Action Plan (EAP)

All protection professionals, no matter where they work in the world, use EAPs to get their protectee(s) off that X and away from the threat, especially in evacuating a foreign country.

An overseas EAP is like your EAP at home but on steroids, since you may need to factor in transportation to the nearest airport and abandonment of personal belongings and/or sensitive materials.

Planning for an emergency evacuation is a way to prepare for potential emergencies, accidents, area-wide disasters, power outages, hazardous material spills, fires, bomb threats, civil disturbance, earthquake or other natural or manmade threats. Your advance planning will help to reduce the risk and loss of life. It is important that everyone in your immediate family or group is familiar with the EAP throughout their travel itinerary.

In the event of an emergency such as national disaster, or political or civil unrest, do you have a plan to get back to the hotel? What transportation is available to expedite getting you and your family safely to the airport? To whom do you plan to make that first phone call if your environment went from bad to worse and you need to get out of the area in a hurry?

Any overseas EAP—just like the one you prepared at home—should be comprised of the three general components referred to as the three W's—Who, What, and Where.

When we ask "who", we are asking, in the event of an emergency who should be contacted? Should you dial 911, should you call the US embassy, should you call your boss, should you call your best friend? Should you call your spouse?

The person you contact is completely dependent upon your situation. If you are at the hotel, and it's a medical or police emergency, then of course you may rely on first responders, but after that who would you contact? Do you have that number on speed dial?

If you can't connect with that person is there an alternate number? If so, is that also on your speed dial?

The next part of your emergency action plan is the "what"—when faced with an actual threat what should you do? Do you call someone? Do you press a red button? Do you send someone an email? Especially when travelling overseas, what would you do if you needed to immediately get out of the country?

Lastly you should consider "where"—where should you go in the event of an emergency. Would you run and knock on the neighbor's door? If you are in a hotel during a hostage situation, do you run into the street? Where would you go in the event of a bomb threat or an active shooter at the hotel? Where is the nearest hospital, airport, or urgent-care center?

Having an emergency action plan is critical to your protection and that of your protectee(s). Either have it written down on an easy-to-read card in your wallet or commit it to memory.

Emergency action plans must be specific to each lodging, work, or travel area. If you are in charge of a group, EAPs can be additionally used to outline various emergency responsibilities of staff, evacuation routes and evacuation assembly areas, emergency supplies, and emergency notification plans.

If an incident occurs or you are directed to evacuate the facility, your emergency action plan (either written or at least carefully thought out beforehand) will be ready to help you. An example of an overseas emergency action plan follows:

1. Take a deep breath, remain calm, and follow instructions if issued.
2. Assist children and disabled persons.
3. Leave the area in an orderly fashion and close the doors behind you but don't lock them (emergency response personnel may need access).
4. Follow established evacuation routes (an evacuation route/location map is in each room of the building.)
5. Do not block the street or driveway.

6. Once out of the building, move away from the structure and directly to the designated rally point.
7. Make sure everyone you expect is accounted for with a head count.
8. Stay at the rally point until everyone expected has arrived.
9. Once everyone is accounted for, move toward the airport in the rental car.

Given the specifics of your exigent circumstances, evacuation may not always be the very best option. If you notice that there is no immediate threat in your exact location, consider that it may be more dangerous to jump into a crowd of panicking people potentially trampling each other in the middle of a violent civil protest.

In certain instances, your best option might be to remain in place and ride out the storm waiting for the incident to subside—especially if you're in your hard room with illumination and communication tools and possibly water and other basic necessities.

It's ultimately up to you to make such decisions based on your situational awareness and observation skills.

Layered Complexity

In consideration of exigent circumstances leading you to evacuation there may be added layers of complexity which must be factored into your EAP:

1. **Night Time**—low, ambient-only or no light.
2. **Inclement Weather**—rain, snow, heavy winds, sleet, hail, sand storm.
3. **Noise** - explosions, gunfire, aircraft, people shouting.
4. **Visual Impairment**—smoke, dust, fog or haze.
5. **HAZMAT Environment**—chemical or biological agents.
6. **Violent Attack**—bad guy(s) present and active - firearms, explosives.

7. **Significant Injury Or Injuries**—raised scale of injury.
8. **No Communications**—lost your phone, signal down.
9. **No Support Or Backup**—you are completely alone.
10. **No Personnel Accountability Or Travel Net.**

You should at least be mentally prepared to appropriately respond, regardless of the layers of complexity, as far as what actions are necessary for you to safely move off the X and towards safety.

Although your situational awareness and protection skills will determine your course of action, having a plan is critical. Even a makeshift or last-minute plan is better than not having one at all.

Failure to plan for adequate travel protection can cause serious ramifications such as property loss, physical injury, or much worse.

Mitigating your travel risks, establishing that envelope of protection upon arrival, with a well thought out plan for each aspect of your trip, will lower your threat profile and allow you to set an appropriate level of situational awareness in support of your travel protection.

EPILOGUE

"If by insight alone you cause another to take even one stop away from ignorance you have succeeded in raising awareness."
Buddhist Adage

Dear Reader,

It's my most sincere hope that by taking the time and effort to read through this work you have gained a change in perspective about your own personal security and will adopt, into your own life, the principles of preventative defense.

Throughout my entire career, I have witnessed the terrible effects of bad things that have happened to good people. As a consequence I have devoted my life to raising the awareness of as many good people as I can reach so that potential tragedy can be avoided.

Empowering others with useful knowledge, lifesaving skills and reducing the number of victims in our society remains my life's passion. As such, I hope you will take this valuable information to heart, apply it and help us make a safer and less violent world.

Very respectfully,

Steve Tarani

Please visit the PreFense® website for continuing information or if you would like to share your story of how preventative defense made a difference in your life.

http://preventativedefense.com

http://myPreFense.com

PREFENSE® CODEX

		Potential Threat	Actual Threat	Step 1 Look	Step 2 Choose	Verify / Step 3 Stalk / Plan	Step 4 Close	Step 5 Attack
Threat Management	Unlimited Options						Limited Options	3 Options
Threat Management	Maximum amount of time/ least amount of effort						Less Time/ More Effort	Least Time/ Max Effort
Threat Management	Avoid						Mitigate	Defend
Threat Management	Assess, Plan, Act–*The APA Process*						Assess & Respond	React
Protection	Proactive Measures						Active Measures	Reactive Measures
Protection	Home Mode			Public Mode			Alert Mode	Act Mode
Protection	Eliminate Soft Target Indicators						Deny Opportunity	Flight, Fight, Freeze

Anatomy Of Attack	***Characteristics Or Attributes***	***Functionality—What Makes It Work***	***Disruption— What Stops It From Working***
Target	Exposed Vulnerable.	Person, Place or Thing perceived by a predator as a soft target.	**Eliminate Indicators**
Bad Guy	Motivated Capable.	Given the Opportunity.	**Deny Opportunity**
Process	Steps of the Attack Cycle.	The only means of carrying out a successful attack.	**Break the Cycle** at any step as early as possible.

PreFense®		
Preventing Bad Things From Happening To Good People		

Protective Concepts		
OODA Loop	Threat Progression	Avoid, Mitigate, Defend
Protection Envelope	Behavioral Management	Hard And Soft Targets
Predator's Optic	Soft Target Indicators	Anatomy Of An Attack
Attack Cycle	Breaking The Attack Cycle	Event Indicators
Threat Indicators	Protective Mindset	Awareness Modes
Scale of Injury	Reactionary Gap	Two-Second Rule
Changing Conditions	Cover And Concealment	Concentric Rings
Deter, Detect, Delay	Flight, Fight Or Freeze	Violence Of Action

Protective Measures		
Proactive Measures	**Active Measures**	**Reactive Measures**
Common Sense	Break the Cycle	Make A Plan
Good Habits	Deny Opportunity	Move Off The X
Situational Awareness	Assess and Respond	Move And Communicate
APA Process		Get In Or Get Out
Eliminate Indicators		Counterattack

Protective Skills		
Mode Skills	Observation Skills	Verbal Skills

Physical Protection Tools		
Cell Phone	Go Bag	Daily Carry Tools
Detection Devices	Deterrance Devices	Weapons

GLOSSARY

Action Reaction Power Curve Reaction—Always follows action and this is the reason why you need to reduce your reaction time as much as possible.

Active Shooter—An armed person who has used deadly physical force on other persons and continues to do so while having unrestricted access to additional victims.

Actual Threat—Reference to a natural threat or manmade threat. May also refer to a specific subject such as an event (hurricane, blizzard) or a human adversary who has motivation, capability, and opportunity.

Anatomy Of An Attack—The component parts of a successful attack and how they work together minimally requiring three items: 1. a bad guy, 2. a target and 3. a means or process of attacking that target—aka the attack cycle. Break any one of the legs of this tripod and all chance of a successful attack is equally destroyed.

Anatomy Of A Lodging Attack—The study or analysis of each of the tripod legs supporting a successful physical attack in, near or around your lodging.

Anatomy Of A Travel Attack—The study or analysis of each of the tripod legs supporting a successful physical attack during travel.

Anatomy Of Vehicular Assault—The study or analysis of each of the tripod legs supporting a successful physical attack in, near our around your vehicle.

APA Process—An anticipatory threat management tool to help you collect and evaluate relevant information, make educated decisions and act accordingly. APA is an acronym for Assess, Plan and Act, an easy-to-follow three-step process:

1. Assess—evaluate any potential or actual threats you may encounter.

2. Plan—prepare to avoid, mitigate or defend against them.
3. Act—if necessary, take commensurate action.

Assessment And Response—A proactive measure describing rapid and accurate evaluation of observed threat indicators resulting in an appropriate course of action.

Attack Behaviors—The activity of stalking, moving in on, and attacking a target.

Attack Cycle—A universal five-step process comprised of defined steps which must be followed by any predator to complete a successful attack.

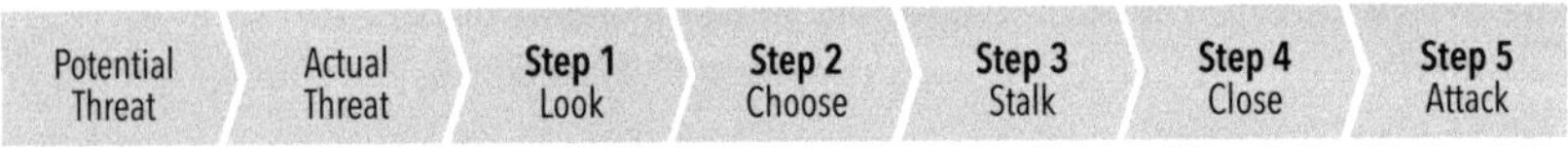

Potential Threat	Actual Threat	**Step 1** Look	**Step 2** Choose	**Step 3** Stalk	**Step 4** Close	**Step 5** Attack

Attack Cycle Timeline—Measurement of the amount or length of time from the very beginning step of an attack cycle to the end of the very last step. All attack cycles accelerate in the latter stages placing the demand of greater effort applied in less time.

Attack Related Behaviors—The combination of pre-attack behavior and attack behavior.

Awareness Modes—There are four states of awareness ranging from very relaxed to hyperaware.

Awareness Mode	***Application Of Your Attention***	***Radar Setting***
Home	On an activity—TV, phone, cooking.	Radar Off
Public	On your environment.	Radar On
Alert	On a specific subject (potential threat).	Blip on the radar
Act	On your immediate physical actions.	Blinking lights and buzzers blaring

Awareness Response Relationship—The functioning aspect of situational awareness describing: "If you are aware you can act, if you are unaware you can only react." The greater your awareness, the greater the effectiveness of your response.

Bad Things Happen—You can decide to ignore these facts and equally ignore the consequences or you can decide to increase your awareness and be prepared to do something about affecting those consequences.

Behavioral Assessment—A support element of behavioral management addressing a predator's motives and the mechanics of attack related behavior.

Behavioral Control—A support element of behavioral management addressing how you may impose your will upon or influence attack related behavior.

Behavioral Management—A protective concept describing the assessment and control of attack related behaviors resulting in the influence and disruption of a predator's plans and ability to carry out a successful attack.

Breaking The Attack Cycle—It is possible to defeat the attack cycle at any stage—especially Steps 1, 2, and at the onset of Step 3. The earlier you break it, the better. Similar to putting out a kitchen fire, things get more difficult to handle the longer you let it burn. By the time you allow it to progress to Step 4 or 5, your timing and options and opportunities to break the attack cycle are significantly reduced.

Carry Tools—Protective equipment that can assist you and your protectee(s) in moving off that X. These can include a pocket knife, multi-tool, carry pack, go-bag and a sturdy ink pen.

Changing Conditions—In any real-world threat scenario there are always three conditions that change continuously: the condition of your environment, the condition of your threat and the condition of yourself and those who may be with you.

Common Sense—Sound or prudent judgment based on initial perception of the situation or facts in practical matters.

Communication Tools—Communication is paramount in an emergency response. The most common method of communication is our cell phones. Provided that your battery is charged and you have a signal, your cell or satellite phone is critical for sending and receiving important information.

Concealment—A protection term meaning a place to hide. Not all hiding places will provide you cover.

Concentric Rings Of Protection—The greater the number of layers the greater the level of protection. The purpose of each layer is to Deter, Detect and Delay a predator.

Controlled Area—A secure location such as an airport, bank, corporate or federal building and the like, where there are plenty of security doors, locks, secured elevators, security guards and surveillance cameras to help keep certain threats at bay.

Conversational Range—The distance between you and another person or persons at which you are able to hold a normal conversation. It's generally measured as an arm's length and is at that exact distance or contact range where the potential for personal injury begins.

Counterattack—A reactive measure meaning to fight back using force against force in a last ditch effort to dominate a very nasty situation.

Cover—A protection term meaning something you can hide behind, in or under that will literally stop bullets such as an iron bathtub, solid brick fireplace or engine block. Some cover can also be used as concealment.

Daily Carry Tools—Those tools strongly recommended by the professionals that you should carry with you every day.

De-Escalate And Defuse—Protective concepts utilized to help break the attack cycle at the later steps.

Detection Devices—Designed to warn you of an imminent threat in or near your immediate environment.

Deter, Detect, And Delay—Aka the 3D's—a recommended method of residential protection affording you the critical opportunity of assessment and response.

Deterrence Devices—Designed to conspicuously gain or capture the attention of others.

Distance-Injury Relationship—The closer a physical threat is to you the greater your potential of incurring physical injury.

Distraction And Deception—Protective concepts used in influencing attack-related behaviors to achieve the desired effects of defusing and de-escalation.

Edged Weapons—Includes the likes of steak or kitchen knives, razor blades, broken glass, improvised edged weapons fashioned from common objects such as coat hangers or soup cans, used in such a manner as to de-escalate, defuse, and otherwise deter a physical attack.

Emergency Action Plan (EAP)—A pre-determined set of instructions to provide clear and simple directions to be followed in response to an emergency.

Event Indicator—An observable pre-event activity preceding every action. Examples of this include someone taking a breath before they speak, or moving a foot over the brake pedal before braking.

Fight—When engaging a physical threat, counterattack; do whatever it takes using anything at your disposal to put yourself in a condition where you can eventually move off the X.

Firearm—The most efficient weapon for stopping a lethal human threat.

Flexible Weapons—Includes the likes of purse straps, computer cables, your T-shirt, lengths of rope, and so on.

Fight—When engaging a physical threat move off the X. Increase the reactionary gap by placing distance and/or objects between yourself and the threat.

Fight, Fight, Or Freeze—A protective concept describing the three immediate reactions we as humans may have in response to a life-threatening challenge.

Freeze—Although not recommended as a viable response option, it's possible to freeze when engaging a physical threat.

Friendly Five©—Those daily carry tools recommended for protection professionals and other legal firearm owners.

Friendly Four©—Those daily carry tools recommended for non-gun owners.

Fundamental Of Protection—A comprehensive repository of thought, actions, skills and tools employed by protection professionals that you can use for your own protection and that of your loved ones.

Get In Or Get Out—A reactive measure describing when moving off the X there are only two locations to which you can move and that is into a high-threat area—get in—or away from one—get out. The safer of the two is to get out.

Go Bag—The go bag is designed to get you off the X and assist with protective movement. Your go bag is a kit that you can hold in your hand.

Good Habits—Consistent practice of common sense thoughts and actions leading to a beneficial change in lifestyle.

Hard Room—A designated room within the interior of your home or office where occupants may safety and rapidly retreat in the event of a physical attack.

Hardening Your Home—Predators stay clear of controlled areas. If your home appears to be a difficult target, then they will move on to less-protected targets.

Hard Targets—Those who are aware of their environment know that bad things happen and such threats can be addressed with threat management and protection.

Have A Plan—To help defeat the attack cycle in the later steps it's important to be able to make an immediate-response plan. Having a split-second plan by making one up on the fly allows you the advantage of being prepared to deal with an immediate physical threat.

Home Intruder—A predator who breaks and enters into your home without permission and with intent to commit a felony larceny or assault in the dwelling.

Home Invasion—An unauthorized and forceful entry into a dwelling. It is a crime governed by state laws.

Illumination Tools—Illumination or artificial light source tools include everything from keychain lights to glow-sticks to flashlights.

Immediate Response Action Plan—A plan made on the fly as a direct result of a split-second decision, under duress, and in support of your OODA Loop.

Impact Weapons—May include any ridged object that can withstand substantial impact or shatter bone.

Improvised Weapons—Anything you can hold in your hands under duress and in threatening circumstances that could be used to defend yourself against a physical assault. Also known as weapons of opportunity.

Line Of Demarcation—A reactive measure used to determine both direction and physical location from movement. In other words, if when you perceive a threat you're closer to your car, then get to the car. Conversely, if you're closer to the front door then get inside that building.

Lodging Attack—Any physical attack in, near or around your lodging and/or that of your protectee(s).

Man-made Threats—Transnational in origin, they are further classified by type into seven general categories: political, organizational, criminal, national, commercial, individual, and circumstantial.

Mechanical Compliance—The opposite of pain compliance, this can be usage of a weapon or your environment to impose your will upon an assailant in stopping a physical attack.

Mode Skills—A protective measure that enables us to appropriately power our radar up or down based on the circumstances of our environment.

Move And Communicate—A reactive measure which combines both movement from one position—physical location, to another position while either signaling with hands, verbal skills or other communication tool(s).

Move Off The X—Using this reactive measure as an immediate response option, you may quickly remove yourself from harm's way and get to safety.

Natural Threats—Those threats manifested as natural disasters such as earthquakes, tsunamis, landslides, and so on.

Navigation Tools—Include but are not limited to maps, compasses and GPS.

Observation Skills—The professionals accurately assess their surroundings, taking mental note of both the usual and unusual, of people and of activities. Some techniques to gain these skills include observing body language, maintaining a panoramic view, orienting to your position and distance, and noting changes in or absence of normal activity.

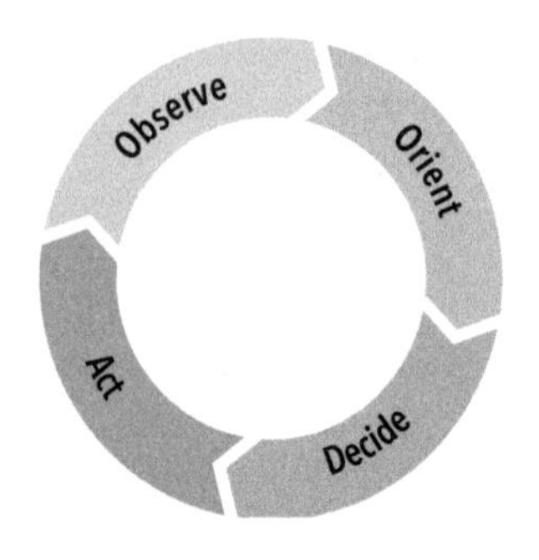

OODA Loop—An acronym derived from a combination of four dynamic decision-making steps: Observe, Orient, Decide, and Act. A reactive measure designed to help you stay ahead of the action-reaction power curve and make rapid, compressed, definitive and appropriate decisions more quickly than your adversary.

Options And Opportunity—It is possible to break the attack cycle along every step of the way, however, breaking it as early as possible affords you the most time and least amount of effort. The attack cycle timeline in all attack cycles accelerates in the latter stages relegating you to less response time requiring greater effort.

Personal Weapons—Includes your closed fists, open palms, knees, used in such a manner as to de-escalate, defuse, and otherwise deter a physical attack.

Potential Threat—An environment, situation, area, activity, or person(s) perceived as possibly dangerous or harmful.

Pre-Attack Behaviors—Activities a predator engages in to prepare for an attack, such as searching for, choosing, and beginning to stalk a target.

Predator's Optic—Predators see the world as made up of either soft targets or hard targets. Whenever possible, a predator will shy away from hard targets and focus his/her attention on less protected targets.

Predictable Patterns—a protective concept describing the same routine day in and day out—a prominent soft target indicator to a kidnapper.

PreFense©—A holistic approach to threat management and protection preventing bad things from happening to good people.

PreFense© 90% Advantage—The beneficial time, options and opportunities presented at the preamble of a threat progression during which a threat may be appropriately managed as opposed to the tail-end ten percent of the same threat progression.

Physical Protection Tools—Communication tools, illumination tools, navigation tools, and defensive tools as part of your daily carry tools.

Primary Soft Target Indicators (PSTI)—Those awareness-based soft target indicators that gain the attention at first glance of the predator.

Proactive Measures—Protective measures which are utilized in threat management and protection to avoid mitigate or defend against a threat before it turns into an attack.

Protection—A concept, method or practice which prevents someone or something from suffering injury, damage, violence, disruption or loss in the event of an attack.

Protection Envelope—An invisible 360 degree envelope of protection wrapped like a bubble around yourself, your protectee(s) and your assets regardless of environment.

Protection Solution(s)—Any PreFense©-based thought, action, skill, or tool, (or combination thereof), that you can use to safeguard yourself, your family and your assets against damage, violence, disruption, or loss.

Protective Concepts—A functional idea which, when applied, achieves a specific protection objective—e.g. the idea of securing your home when you're not there—accomplished by locking your doors and windows prior to your departure.

Protective Measures—Recommended established protection methods and practices incorporating protective concepts and used by protection professionals to manage bad things before they happen (proactively), as they are happening (actively) and to respond (reactively) to an attack.

Protective Mindset—Situational awareness can be optimized by anyone willing to adopt the core components of the protective mindset which include:

1. Motivation—Be predisposed to win.
2. Responsibility—"Protection is my responsibility"
3. Reality—"Hey, threats are real!"
4. Acknowledgement—"Uhhh, I have this gut feeling..."

Protective Skills—Trained expertise gained over time relevant to keeping yourself and your protectee(s) safe, including skills such as how to carefully observe the environment and how to move a protectee safely from one place to another.

Protective Intelligence—The art and science of collecting and assessing relevant information about adversaries who may have the interest, motive, intention, opportunity, and capability of mounting attacks against you and the things you care about.

Rally Point—A designated safe area outside your home or office such as a specified neighbor's house or a nearby park.

Reactionary Cap—A protective concept defining the relationship between distance and time. The shorter distance between you and the threat, the less time you have to respond; conversely the greater the distance, the greater the amount of time.

Reactive Measures—Those protective measures which may be employed in response to an attack.

Real-World Incidents—Brief reporting of an actual event that is made available for your review and consideration to further illustrate a protective concept, method, or practice.

Residential Protection—Your home as a controlled area—the result of hardening both your dwelling (the physical building) and all residents.

Residential Protection Planning—The very best defense against home invasion is education and planning. Parents should hold family meetings and run drills to ensure that everyone knows their roles and responsibilities.

Safe Areas—Any physical locations considered a hard room and/or a rally point.

Scale Of Injury—There are five levels of physical injury, with the lowest being no injury at all—the very best possible outcome and exactly how we'd like to walk away from any physical threat engagement.

Secondary Soft Target Indicators (SSTI)—Those preparedness-based soft target indicators noticed by the predator which firmly place a soft target on the selection list and cause the predator to move from Step 1—Look of the attack cycle to Step 2—Choose.

Situational Awareness—Maintaining a relaxed observance of any threat indicators and being prepared to appropriately respond.

Soft Targets—Those who are unaware, disregard or don't care that bad things happen and/or are unaware of their environment, and/or unaware of threat management and protection and/or unprepared to protect themselves.

Soft Target Indicators (STIs)—Any appearance or activity outwardly exhibited indicator that screams "Hey look over here, I'm an easy target, pick me!" to a predator. These can also be further classified into primary (awareness based) and secondary—(preparedness based) soft target indicators.

Threat Avoidance—Very simply put: don't be there in the first place—do not intentionally place yourself in harm's way.

Threat Categories—Risk managers have classified them into two categories: natural threats and man-made threats.

Threat Indicators—Anything you observe about your environment that triggers a concern that conditions have changed from non-threatening to threatening and indicates a need for your attention.

Threat Management—Avoiding, mitigating, or defending against a threat before it turns into an attack.

Threat Progression—A step process ranging from a potential threat to an actual threat to pre-attack behaviors to attack behaviors that demonstrates the transition of threat through recognizable stages.

Potential Threat → Actual Threat → Pre-Attack Behavior → Attack Behavior

Travel Attack—An assault on your person, property and/or protectee(s) while you are travelling.

Travel Risk—A protective concept describing danger or harm that you and/or your protectee(s) may be exposed to during travel.

Travel Support Net—Any person or persons at your home, work, or travel location that have your detailed travel itinerary, including airport and hotel information, who are ready and available to support your travel needs.

Two-Second Rule—A recommended reaction time of less than two seconds as part of any effective physical response.

Vehicular Assault—Any physical attack in, near, or around a vehicle utilized in ground transportation.

Verbal Skills—Vocal ability to assist in completing an objective. These can be used to tactfully defuse a heated argument, to succinctly communicate information or to avoid giving up sensitive or too much information.

Visible And Invisible Rings—Multiple rings of protection, both visible and invisible, significantly increases your protection against intruders trying to access your home.

Violence Of Action—A protective concept describing a mindset ancillary to the protective mindset whereas under certain physical threat conditions it may be necessary to meet fire with fire in attempting to break the cycle.

Warning Devices—Recommended physical protection tools to detect and deter a threat from escalating to a physical attack.

Weapons—A means of gaining an advantage or defending oneself in conflict. A physical protection tool utilized to help stop a physical attack.

Weapon Categories—There are seven general categories of traditional weapons which can be utilized as tools to help you stop a physical attack:

Category 1. Firearms
Category 2. Stun Guns
Category 3. Pepper Spray
Category 4. Impact Weapons
Category 5. Edged Weapons
Category 6. Improvised Weapons
Category 7. Personal Weapons

Weapons Of Opportunity—Improvised weapons.